Daughters, Fathers, and the Novel

Daughters, Fathers, and the Novel

The Sentimental Romance of Heterosexuality

Lynda Zwinger

The University of Wisconsin Press

The University of Wisconsin Press
114 North Murray Street
Madison, Wisconsin 53715

3 Henrietta Street
London WC2E 8LU, England

5   4   3   2   1

Printed in the United States of America

Library of Congress Cataloging-in-Publication Data
Zwinger, Lynda Marie.
    Daughters, fathers, and the novel: the sentimental romance of
  heterosexuality / Lynda Zwinger.
    184 pp.   cm.
    Includes index.
    1. English fiction—History and criticism.   2. American fiction—
History and criticism.   3. Fathers and daughters in literature.
4. Sex (Psychology) in literature.   5. Sentimentalism in literature.
6. Women in literature.   I. Title.
PR830.F36Z9   1991
823.009'3520441—dc20
ISBN 0-299-12850-4   90-50656
ISBN 0-299-12854-7 (pbk.)   CIP

For Thomas F. and Ruth McDonnell Zwinger

Contents

Acknowledgments

I want to thank my teachers Marcus Klein, Leslie Fiedler, Joe Fradin, Bill Warner, and Duncan Kennedy. Amy A. Doerr read, critiqued, and encouraged this project from its inchoate beginnings. I want also to thank teachers whose forums were journals not classrooms: Annette Kolodny, Jane Gallop, Shoshana Felman, Nancy K. Miller, Nina Auerbach, Jacqueline Rose.

Colleagues at the University of Arizona have helped me with support, encouragement, and perceptive and useful readings of endless versions of chapters: Susan Hardy Aiken, Tenney Nathanson, Patrick O'Donnell, Barbara Babcock, Edgar Dryden, Herb Schneidau, and Susan White. Chapters 3 and 6 in particular benefitted by the critical acumen of Susan Hardy Aiken, Tenney Nathanson, and Patrick O'Donnell. William Veeder, Richard Poirier, Betsy Draine, and Richard Pearce have each helped to make this book better than it would have been.

Finally, I thank Jesse Rounds who helped me learn to take myself seriously as a working scholar, and Tom and Ruth Zwinger, who taught me intellectual curiosity, tenacity, and hopefulness.

Versions of Chapters 2 and 4 appeared in *Nineteenth Century Fiction* (1985) and *Raritan* (1987), respectively; permission to reprint this material is gratefully acknowledged.

Daughters, Fathers, and the Novel

Introduction

This watching of the birds we are accustomed to call the "science of
augury"; we shall presently see that in its origin it is pure magic, "pure
doing"; the magical birds *make* the weather before they portend it.
———Jane Harrison, *Themis*

"There's no explaining a good woman," he said to himself.
———Lester, *Jennie Gerhardt*

Beauty, who goes to live with a Beast at her father's behest, spends much of
her time responding to a question which turns out to be something like, Will
you love the Beast for (in) me? It is after all, her father's narrative claims,
Beauty's demand (for a rose) that called forth the Beast to begin with. Her
story is over—her status as daughter disappears—when her answer is yes.
Dora, on the other hand, answered "No" with such perseverance that her
father of the moment, Sigmund Freud, found himself ever after unable to
write a satisfying resolution. The story that he did manage to write, as Claire
Kahane points out, represents itself as a "narrative of Dora's desire," but is
nonetheless (I would argue, is *therefore*) essentially a representation of his
own desire (Kahane 20). The father, in these and other versions of Western,
middle-class family stories, always has a question he will neither articulate
nor take responsibility for. The daughter strives to discover and then answer
satisfactorily (or not) the form the paternal question seems to take in her
particular relation to her father. Whether she answers yes or no, the daughter
is positioned as the one who provokes the question, who *makes* the unspoken
story happen.

   If, as Jane Harrison maintains, a credible myth is one shaped by our apprehension of and response to the known, then it is through the stories we tell
about our world that we learn to know what we know—or what we think we
know. Lester's baffled response to the good woman can be found in many of
our stories, and the explanatory myths engendered therein often enough turn

to something like magic: the good woman is her own maker; she is the natural origin of that which she comes to represent. In the five novels which I examine in this study, the good woman of each novel is a father's daughter, constructed not by nature nor yet by a neutral or neuter system of cultural and narrative precepts, but constructed, rather, to the very particular specifications of an omnipresent and unvoiced paternal desire.

The fictional daughter and her father are, in fact, two of the most compelling and problematic figures in the history of heterosexuality and its attendant/engendering stories. While most Western fictional versions of the feminine are split into explicit or implicit polarities (mirroring the perceived split that is sexual difference)—goddess/demon, virgin/whore, saint/sinner, hearth angel/fallen woman, nurturing/devouring mother—when she is a daughter, as defined by the significant presence of her father in the text, she is not split. If she is to retain her value for him, her father must leave her whole, which means that he is unable to take advantage of this most common, perhaps most effective, technique of managing the fear and anxiety provoked by sexual difference. As Jane Gallop puts it, in *The Daughter's Seduction,* "Difference produces great anxiety. Polarization, which is a theatrical representation of difference, tames and binds that anxiety. The classic example is sexual difference which is represented as a polar opposition (active-passive, energy-matter—all polar oppositions share the trait of taming the anxiety that specific differences provoke)" (93).

So desire for the daughter cannot be managed by the logic of oppositional splits, the way desire for the mother, for example, can; it is simply epistemologically impossible to transfer something like the nurturing/devouring mother split onto the figure of the daughter. (A daughter gone wrong is a daughter no longer: when Little Em'ly says yes to the wrong man she forfeits her right to the affectionate diminutive that names her as daughter.) But are there other, less obvious, ways to manage sexual difference? In particular, have we ways of managing the daughter's difference from her mother (who can be sexually possessed by her father) while still retaining the excitement potential derived from her (sexual) difference from her father (who possesses her too—but with a difference)? In this study, I will explore an alternative "binding and taming" gesture, the particular representation of woman that I have named the daughter of sentiment.

The daughter of sentiment was created in—and perhaps helped to create— the novel. She begins, with Clarissa Harlowe, to live a life of duress, distress, and strangely belied adoration. She continues her travail through the nineteenth century in British and American novels that tell stories centered in the family, and she lives still, ever acquiescent, ever hopeful, in such modern versions of the family true romance story as *Story of O.* The daughter of senti-

ment is here defined by and in relation to her fictional father, and, by extension, her literary fathers as well—the definitions and relations encoded in
patriarchal readings of her. As Annette Kolodny points out in her analysis of
"The Panther Captivity," a culture's defining fantasies represent *choices*. I
envision my project as Kolodny envisions hers: to add to past readings a particular attention to the place of the fictional daughter as that place has been
imagined in our literature. In the course of my readings, I want to reveal *as
choices* fictional constructs that present themselves to nonfeminist criticism
as inevitable and inevitably incidental to the more serious business of the plot.
Finally, it is my intention to point out the extent to which those fictional
choices—the sentimentalized representation of woman as desiring daughter
and of the father as innocent of any but culturally sanctioned designs upon
her—ground the system of cultural constructs and prescriptions that we have
learned to think of as heterosexual desire.

Although it has its beginnings in drama's "man of feeling," sentimentality
in the novel is largely a woman's affair.[1] Ian Watt tells us in *The Rise of the
Novel* that eighteenth-century sentimentalism "denoted an un-Hobbesian belief in the innate benevolence of man, a credo which had the literary corollary
that the depiction of such benevolence engaged in philanthropic action or
generous tears was a laudable aim" (174). Sentimentalism expresses a hopeful
view of the perfectibility of the individual,[2] the kind of spiritual quid pro
quo—be good and reap your reward (generally in the coin of adoration by
those influenced for their good)—personified in the sentimental daughter, the
virgin in True Womanhood training.[3] The sentimental daughter is a dutiful
acolyte to her father, with a loving heart, an innocent mind, and a positive lust
for self-abnegation. Dickens' daughters probably represent the type in its pur-
est, most notorious form: nearly all of them spring fully fledged, young, beautiful, and good, into his novels.

The daughter of sentiment has suffered critical scorn and popular approval
precisely for her (admittedly daunting) collection of virtues. When the narrative functions of those qualities have been recognized (as, for example, in
Brissenden's study, *Virtue in Distress*), they have been deplored by the more
harsh, apologized for by the more lenient, traditional critic. But even where
this figure can be fully assimilated to a type of fiction which is finally ephem-
eral (modern romance novels, for example), and even when the reader is
moved to deplore her, there is more to see. For the appeal of the sentimental
has always what Jean Hagstrum has called an "erotic coloration," and insofar
as the daughters discussed in this study are tinted by the problematic of desire,
they are worth another reading. These fictional father-daughter paradigms of
desire and resistance are, as I point out in the course of the readings which
follow, also locatable in the perspectives and problematics of the dominant

critical discourse and feminist responses, deviations, and subversions. The desirable daughter and her fictional father structure even (especially) the most sophisticated readings of cultural reality, interpretative possibilities, and our fictional versions of each.

The oedipal myth we accept as a given of Western culture suggests that the son grows into desire through his frustrated longing for his mother, his father's woman. The family romance of the novel, however, often tells a different story to those who would hear it. This same son learns to be a man from this same father, and the son is much more likely in these stories to observe his patriarchal nemesis and model in the throes of desire for an altogether different woman—a daughter, his daughter.

In *Clarissa Harlowe,* for example, it is his precociously paternal position that motivates the young James Harlowe's frenetically vengeful attitude toward his younger sister. The father's desire is ventriloquized through him, cloaked in rage and hostility, and performed with the unseasoned passion of youth. He and his father construct a common cause of their intuition that the dutiful daughter cannot remain obedient once she is nubile. Clarissa insists on being active in the struggle over how she is defined, and her very activity is taken as evidence that she is no better than she should be—even her literary progenitor, Samuel Richardson, felt the force of this interpretation to such a degree that he found it necessary to direct his reader, at crucial points throughout the narrative, toward the sentimental reading he increasingly insisted upon for his heroine. But the debate over Clarissa's status and stake in what happens to her that rages in the novel and in the history of readers' responses to her suggests that this is no easy task. If *Clarissa* is about submission, what is the status of the submissive daughter who must refuse to submit? Something in the very nature of the father-daughter relationship seems to precipitate the transgression of Clarissa.

In Dickens' *Dombey and Son,* the innocent daughter must woo her unmoved, hard businessman father throughout the course of the novel. Dombey is presented as a man with a need he will neither admit nor submit to. He insists upon exaggerated homage from those around him, yet rejects the one character who consistently and genuinely offers it to him—his own daughter, who ought to be a comfort and solace to him, but instead embodies for him a persistent and mysterious dread. Florence is presented as the obvious answer, the only one who can love him properly. But her father refuses to ask the appropriate question. Florence Dombey's father resists his daughter mightily, and his obsessive rejection of his daughter is first presented in the context of the Paul Senior/Florence/Paul Junior triangle, and is continued through the Dombey/Florence/Walter triangle. What is Dombey afraid of? How does his final adoption of the sentimental view of his dutiful daughter affect that fear?

What fear does the final domestication of this familial struggle provoke in the novel's readers?

Louisa May Alcott produced, in *Little Women*, a daughter story of uncommon tenacity and power. Her focus on the awkward daughter, Jo March, sentimentalizes the paternally directed composition process that produces the father's daughter. In the course of this novel the oedipal configuration recurs: Jo rejects the young, handsome, rich Laurie; he is too like a brother for her. Her desire is finally activated by one who could be her father's brother. At the end of her painful struggle to become her father's little woman, Jo (and her adolescent female reader) is presented with the most appropriate reward for being good imagined anywhere in this tradition: Jo March marries Papa Bhaer and, not incidentally, cheerfully gives up her budding career as a writer to become nurturing mother to a house full of sons.

Daughters who write have a formidable and forbidding set of fictional pre-scriptions and pre-figurations to contend with when they choose to write the father-daughter relation, and Alcott wrote in painful awareness that she herself had not successfully completed her own daughter training; her sensation fiction and her adult novels illuminate the extent to which her presentation of the father-daughter relation in *Little Women* was consciously sentimental-ized. In *Little Women* we read the fictional sentimental daughter as written by an aspiring real-life sentimental daughter, one who in the very act of writing culturally sanctioned domestic romance must struggle against the patriarchal construction of familial desire. Actively pursuing both fatherly approval and a mastery of language—which is to say, an unmediated relation to both the Father and the Word—she is finally unable to manage either position to her own satisfaction.

The Golden Bowl offers a father-daughter relation so intense, and so long-lived, as to be perverse in its very sentimentality. The relationship of Maggie and Adam Verver plays upon a fantasy of maintaining the paternal-filial love story far beyond the bounds of ordinary propriety—the marriage of the daughter, the marriage of the father (to Maggie's friend and contemporary), the birth of the Principino, the adultery of the nonrelated spouses, none of these magically dissolves (as it is supposed to, in fiction at least) the father-daughter bond. Adam Verver's "son" is defeated hands down: both daughters belong to the little patriarch, and an ocean intervening is no obstacle. The crack in the family bowl caused by desire and proximity is smoothed away and gilded by the shining alibis of sentiment and distance. My reading of this novel examines the extent to which the ambiguity and perversity of the Verver passion derives from the very sentimentalization thus far traced through the preceding novels. James's story of filial passion basically in-scribes, behind the cover story of the daughter of sentiment, the oedipal story written in the feminine and founded on the figure of the daughter who couldn't say yes, but didn't say no.

The daughter of sentiment is, in short, enlisted by stories that narrate the son's defeat. James Harlowe, Jr.'s, victory is only physical, as Clarissa's loss of virtue is only technical: the sentimental Clarissa, the one who stops writing and starts praying, is virtually canonized by the novel's end—she is embraced at last by the Father of all. Walter Gay marries Dombey's cast-away daughter but placidly hands her back to him when she has produced her father's name-sake. Laurie cheerfully quits his claim on Jo in favor of Papa Bhaer. Prince Amerigo pays his duty to his father-in-law first in the marriage that does not disrupt the father-daughter intimacy, then in the loss of his lover, and finally and forever in the unspoken and unarticulable desire of the woman who will always be Maggie Verver.

The passivity and submission that characterize a dutiful daughter also define a desirable woman. A daughter is an apprentice; how she treats her father is how she'll treat her man. *Story of O* presents yet another sentimental daughter, granddaughter of James Harlowe, of Paul Dombey. The daughter of senti-ment is a heterosexual, patriarchal alibi: what do we really want with a sub-missive, sweet, self-abnegating, vulnerable, loving daughter? To have our way with her, of course, and *Story of O* inherits the patrimony this daughter's father has willed to us. In this story—another one in which the daughter serves for love, the son gives her up to the patriarch, and the father's fiction prevails—the implicitly erotic (the sentimental) becomes the explicitly eroticized (the pornographic). The father-daughter dance of asking the un-speakable and hearing the unsayable is disguised by our apparent modern freedom to print whatever fits.

As the earlier heroines were motivated by a touching faith in their cultures' fictions of domestic love, O is motivated by an equally touching faith in the fiction of romantic love. O is given to a new lover/master, the patriarchal Sir Stephen, by the young man with whom she is in love, who in his turn feels what René Girard has called mimetic desire for the older, more powerful man.[4] She learns that her new lover is not so easy to please as her previous lovers (mere boys all) have been, that he demands something of her that no one else has ever demanded. We learn that that desideratum turns out to be identical to what is demanded of the other sentimental daughters examined in this study: utter self-abnegation and blind complicity. It is not enough to say yes repeatedly, unendingly: the sentimental daughter must say it sincerely and as though she has posed the question herself. The irony of O's story is perhaps the lesson of this investigation: having learned to embody his demand, she becomes all women, any woman, the feminine—and therefore by definition incapable of satisfying his desire.

It may very well be true that the mother is the first woman the son loses (has always already lost) to his father. Our strongest taboo, we say, the one upon which civilization is founded, is the incest prohibition directed at the son's desire for the mother, and the stories we center on this prohibition are, often enough, written as high tragedy. But the daughter, who is in theory equally covered by the taboo against incest, who is supposed to ensure a smoothly flowing system of exchange among men—the daughter figures in stories of an altogether different kind. If the specter of father-daughter incest, as a literal rendering of desire, is the cornerstone of anything, it is not civilization so much as heterosexual desire. The stylized flirtation with transgression, the mock violations, the elaborate fictions of complicity and mutuality, the creed that a woman cannot be violated against her will (if she gets it, she asked for it)—these are elements of the father-daughter romance; a romance predicated upon the figure of the sentimentalized, desirable daughter and shadowed by the figure of the defeated son.

Stories of heterosexual desire are always about power. When father-daughter "seduction" is in question, however, the coercion is veiled; the daughter's need for love and approval is glossed as complicity or even mutuality, while her vulnerability increases the titillation always encoded by virtue in distress. The father-daughter story lays the foundation of culturally sanctioned heterosexual desire—the one in the father's place looking to defeat death, love, sexual relation; the one in the daughter's place looking to him for love, attention, approval. The desirable daughter's appeal inheres mainly in her value as an always potential site of transgression. Insofar as sentimentalizing her masks that value, it serves to protect her desiring father from himself, as desiring what he should not take; from her, as presumptively desiring what he can not or will not provide; and from desire itself, as an amorphously threatening and finally mortal condition.

Given the compelling nature of such fictions—and the father-daughter romance confirms Michel Foucault's remark that "power is strong . . . because, as we are beginning to realise, it produces effects at the level of desire" (*Power/Knowledge* 59)—what difference does it, can it, make when a daughter writes the novel? What happens to the sentimental family romance when a daughter *constructs* the novel? Can the daughter-writer do more than merely illustrate paternal desire? Any appropriate investigation of these questions requires a study of its own. But Chapter 6 begins to explore the kinds of questions precipitated by reading the three major women novelists of the nineteenth century through the father-daughter story as outlined in the first five chapters, and, I hope, begins to lay the groundwork for an ongoing discussion about the possibilities/plausibilities of constructing a feminist heterosexual erotic narrative that would not be grounded in a daughter's need for approval from a paternal, or even a paternalized, source of unspoken desire.

"My father has, you know, a terrible voice": The Curse of the Fictional Father

And I will say nothing but No, as long as I shall be able to speak.

—Clarissa

Whose daughter is she? And is she not a *daughter?*

—Lovelace

Samuel Richardson's *Clarissa* queries the intersections of family, class, sexuality, and gender, sometimes affirming, sometimes subverting the accepted pieties. Its critical history raises many crucial questions, perhaps the most immediate of which is the question of the relationship of the writer and his text. That Samuel Richardson was a rather ordinary member of the middle class of his time has been something of a problem, if not an embarrassment, for the literary critical establishment. T. C. Duncan Eaves and Ben D. Kimpel, authors of the standard critical biography of Richardson, assert disarmingly that "it is rather disappointing that so little of the Richardson that went into Clarissa and Lovelace shows in his life" (618). For Eaves and Kimpel, the way to explain this perceived discrepancy between the lived life and the written text is to activate the age-old difference between the "imaginative and the speculative mind." In their view, Richardson was an exemplary member of his class:

> Few writers have led less interesting lives and had less interesting "ideas." His life and his ideas have historical interest as revealing the best side of an impor-

tant and often maligned class, because he sincerely tried to live up to what that class was supposed to stand for. Richardson was narrow, but he was not hypocritical. He was a businessman, but he was not ruthless or exclusively selfish. In the descent of the "protestant ethic," which has been blamed indiscriminately for all the ills of western society, from Milton to Samuel Smiles, he was below the former but above the latter. Quite aside, however, from his historical position is his position as a writer of fiction. In *Clarissa* he realized a Christianity older and more internal than that which supported business ethics. He also dramatized aspects of his mind which he was unable to describe in terms of non-fiction, or rather which he would never have thought of trying to describe. For anyone interested in literature, the apparently complete divorce between the author of *Clarissa* and the kindly but slightly ridiculous printer who collected the *Moral and Instructive Sentiments* makes Richardson an especially good example of the creative mind at work, unsupported by learning, analytic intelligence, or even much experience, and thus thrown back on its own native strength. (618)

This defense of the too-ordinary Richardson, sympathetic and valiant as it is, doubles as an implicit reading of middle-class family life as ordinary and unsensational. And it is clear, particularly in the critical armature Richardson appends to his text in its second and third editions, that Richardson as a reader buys into the orthodox familial ideology of his time.[1] He wants his Clarissa to be read as an exceptionally successful product of that ideology, and her persecutors as familial heretics in various degrees. But it is precisely in his writerly devotion to minutiae, to "writing to the moment" (Eaves and Kimpel 100), that Richardson subverts his own preferred reading; it is precisely in his attention to detailed representation that Richardson captures the subtext of his own novel and of his (and our) culture's familial fictions. For the family is the primary locus of the contradictory play of solicitation and denial that constructs and represses (constructs, it might be said, *by* repressing) heterosexual desire.

In her provocative study *The Daughter's Seduction*, Jane Gallop announces as one of her projects an effort to help feminism avoid the "pitfall of familial thinking in order to have greater effect upon the much more complex power relations that structure our world" (xv). It is her hope that she will be able to "seduce" the father (psychoanalysis) and the daughter (feminism) out of their respective resistances; this seduction, Gallop speculates, may consist in "the introduction of heterogeneity (sexuality, violence, economic class conflict) into the closed circle of the family" (xv). The readings presented in this study probe the same modern, Western middle-class category—"the family"—that Gallop uses as a straw-man power paradigm. But the family herein located is not the uncomplex, closed, feudally hierarchical nuclear state that Gallop posits as the "other" to her notion of "heterogeneity." On the contrary, families—biological or fictional, psychoanalytic or metaphoric—need not be "introduced" to sexuality, violence, and economic class conflict. The "familial thinking" Gallop wishes to trouble and disrupt consists of a set of alibis our fictions of family enable us to mobilize in the face of any suspicion that nuclear, father-headed families are the breeding grounds both for such heterogeneity and for the cover stories that enable us not to see it.

That familial power relations in the abstract present themselves, even to psychoanalytically oriented readers, as relatively uncomplex and straightforward testifies to an enormous cultural investment in the seductively sentimental gloss we prefer to read our familial pieties through. This study takes as its object one of the most important familial stories of all: the sentimental story that Freud told himself and that his adherents and nonadherents alike are still rehearsing, the story that protects us from the unsavory knowledge accounted for by the seduction theory, the story that exempts the father from any suspicion of active endogamous desire. The seduction theory was simply too disruptive for even this piety-flouting patriarch, and he was impelled to abandon it.[2] The usual Freudian/psychoanalytic scenario flatly denies the possibility of literal "seduction"; the solicitations, the "seductions," the transgressions incited by the familial structure are preferentially located by Freudian theory (and other patriarchal discourses) in the daughter, in the mother, perhaps as a last resort in brothers, uncles, aunts, cousins—anywhere but in the head of the family.[3]

Richardson suggests, in his "Author's Preface" to *Clarissa, Or, The History of a Young Lady,* that "every private family, more or less, may find itself concern'd" in the subjects of the correspondences contained in the work (xiii). The first sentence of the novel, addressed to Miss Clarissa Harlowe from Miss Anna Howe, who write "familiar letters" to one another, announces the familial theme: "I am extremely concerned, my dearest friend, for the disturbances that have happened in your family" (I 1). The Harlowes are, manifestly, far from immune to "sexuality, violence, economic class conflict"; they engender such heterogeneity within the familial circle whence it radiates into the larger social exchange system as gossip, news, and grist for various moral mills. The disturbances of the Harlowe family center, sensationally so for the community of spectators in which they move and the readers whom Clarissa's dilemma has also titillated for a couple of hundred years, upon the "young lady, whose distinguished merits have made her the public care" (I 1), who is noted for "excelling all [her] sex" (I 2)—the beautiful, pious, intelligent, witty, obedient, youngest daughter of the Harlowes.

It is my thesis that Richardson's advertisement was well aimed, that the Harlowe family tells itself a story in which "every private family" continues to be implicated. We are still telling both familial and sexual stories similar to certain of the stories inscribed in _Clarissa_. (Other stories, as we shall see, are adumbrated but finally repressed by the novel and its readers alike.) That we are still telling ourselves a sentimentalized family story implicates us, as Sue Warrick Doederlein has pointed out, in the very discourse Richardson helped to invent. Beginning from Foucault's premise that "sexuality is an elaborate system of power and knowledge developing in the eighteenth century," Doederlein points to the compelling challenge posed by any reading of Clarissa which proposes to elucidate the role of sexuality and desire: "To subject to analysis the imaginative discourse which gives voice to changes that have become an organic part of all those who would undertake the project seems an impossible task" (404).[4]

Feminist readers have often noted the absence of a specific gender analysis in Foucault's otherwise brilliant analysis of Western sexuality and power; perhaps the impossible task becomes slightly more possible when we remember to read a gendered sexuality. And because the discourse of sexuality figured in this novel begins in the family, _Clarissa_ must be read with special attention to the dynamics between Clarissa and the Harlowes. It is important, that is to say, to resist focusing more or less exclusively on the Clarissa-Lovelace relationship, thereby relegating the familial dynamics to the status of mere preliminaries. On the other hand, a family-based hermeneutic strategy will not in itself suffice. John Allen Stevenson, for example, reads the family-Clarissa dynamics in his insightful Lévi-Straussian analysis of the "family disturbances" as masking an incestuous impulse toward endogamy. Stevenson's essay devotes needed attention to the Harlowes' place in Clarissa's situation, but does not clearly distinguish the father and the mother (reading them as "parents") or the brother and the sister (reading them as siblings). Consequently, he is unable to see the extent to which the sexuality of the family and its members is being _produced_ by rather than reflected in the very discourse he is reading. And that blind spot results in his having to locate Clarissa's resistance to the family's projects in a fear of sex and sexuality, a reading which convertly reinvokes Freud's daughter: Clarissa is, in spite of the admittedly mitigating unreasonableness of her family, reinstated by this reading as provocateuse of her own violation.

When attention is given not only to gender, not only to family, but to inscriptions of gendered familial positions and their implication in the sentimentalized erotics of fictional father-daughter relations, then we can begin to read Clarissa's sexuality as in process, as being created in and by the shrill exercise of the Harlowe patriarchal voice. My reading of this germinal story which essentially established the novel as a culturally intertwined and implicated discourse and spawned a whole genealogy of greater and lesser "Clarissa" stories, aims particularly at locating its inscriptions of the father's daughter, the daugher who is continually reinscribed and reinforced in our gendered, familial, sentimental stories of desire.

John Butt in his introduction to the Everyman's edition sees the plot of the novel as presenting "an individual" who is "brought into conflict with the social code" (vii), this particular social code being the one that legislates the father's right to dictate the marriages of his children. But James Harlowe, Senior, has two other children: his first-born son and heir, James Harlowe, Junior, and his second child, Arabella. Clarissa is the only Harlowe child who runs afoul of his patriarchal code; her father shows no inclination to intervene in the marital preferences of his two older children. The place Clarissa occupies in the Harlowe family, then, must lie at the intersection of the father's authority and the concept of filial piety she is supposed to embody. Clarissa is a dutiful daughter, the most dutiful daughter anyone in her world has ever known. Why is it that she seems to provoke impossible tests of her duty?

"Who Loves Not Power?"

The sentimental daughter, in order to win that title and the love and approval which are its wages, must conduct herself according to certain rules of behavior. Clarissa accords her parents absolute and cheerful obedience, practices her religion carefully, dispenses charity to the deserving poor, runs the household for her mother, admonishes her friends and acquaintances when they need moral assistance, and strives constantly for a dutiful perfection.[5] She is, in fact, a legendary daughterly success who seems to have managed her achievement without so much as slightly alienating those in her set to whom she is offered as an exemplar.

And then, suddenly, the family disturbances begin: "Our family has indeed been strangely discomposed" (I 3), Clarissa says, and the "tumults" that have begun the unraveling process have all centered upon her. She has, she says, "borne all the blame" to such an extent that

> I have sometimes wished that it had pleased God to have taken me in my last fever, when I had everybody's love and good opinion; but oftener that I had never been distinguished by my grandfather as I was: since that distinction has estranged from me my brother's and sister's affections; at least, has raised a jealousy with regard to the apprehended favour of my two uncles, that now and then overshadows their love. (I 4)

Clarissa thus begins her story of the family troubles at a point anterior to the beginning Anna designates in her request that Clarissa "write to me therefore, my dear, the whole of your story from the time that Mr. Lovelace was first introduced into your family . . ." (I 2). In her assumption that Clarissa's story begins with Lovelace, Anna has been, naturally enough, intrigued by the rumor mill's repetition of stories that "the younger sister has stolen a lover from the elder" (I 2). And Anna's information is, in fact, correct: Robert Lovelace is first (and mistakenly) introduced into the household as Arabella's suitor, and he has, as he says, "much difficulty . . . so fond and so forward my lady! to get off without forfeiting all with a family that I intended should give me a goddess" (I 145). But the cracks in the fiction of the homogeneous family interest have begun to appear before he shows up. Long before Lovelace takes away James's sword, his grandfather's will, in Clarissa's words, "lopped off one branch of my brother's expectation," resulting in his becoming "extremely dissatisfied with me." Clarissa continues:

> Nobody indeed was pleased; for although every one loved me, yet being the youngest child, father, uncles, brother, sister, all thought themselves postponed, as to matter of right and power (who loves not power?); and my father himself could not bear that I should be made sole, as I may call it, and independent, for such the will, as to that estate and the powers it gave (unaccountably as they all said), made me. (I 54)

Clarissa's revision of the story's point of origin reminds us that the patriarchal family is not simply an affectional unit, that power is measured by the ability to direct the circulation of property and people, and that power is at least as important within the family as it is in the rest of the world. Clarissa's voluntarily giving the management of her estate into her father's hands pleases him, but does not rectify the anomaly of a dutiful daughter with real power of her own. Real estate owned by a marriageable daughter is real estate that is in danger of escaping the patriarchal family altogether. Conversely, a daughter who owns real property is a daughter who can, from a practical viewpoint at least, dispense with any filial piety that does not agree with her. The estate may be in Mr. Harlowe's hands, but it nevertheless entitles Clarissa to an independence of her father's will that he finds distressing to both his family and personal pride.

Clarissa has already demonstrated a taste for the kind of power proper to a dutiful daughter. She is undisguisedly pleased with and careful of her reputation as a paragon of piety. It is not surprising that her brother and sister would like to see her humbled. Long before the family tumults begin, James and Arabella chafe under Clarissa's reputation, as indicated by this piece of a quarrel between the two sisters:

You are *indeed* a very artful one for that matter, interrupted she in a passion: one of the artfullest I ever knew! And then followed an accusation so low! so unsisterly! That I half-bewitched people by my insinuating address: that nobody could be valued or respected, but must stand like cyphers wherever I came. How often, said she, have I and my brother been talking upon a subject, and had everbody's attention till *you* came in with your bewitching *meek* pride, and *humble* significance; and then have we either been stopped by references to Miss Clary's opinion, for sooth; or been forced to stop ourselves, or must have talked on unattended to by everybody.

Did you not bewitch my grandfather? . . . Why, truly, his last will showed what effect your *smooth* obligingness had upon him! . . . an estate in possession, and left you with such distinctions, as gave you a reputation of greater value than the estate itself?

Were I a man, she should suppose I was aiming to carry the county—popularity! A crowd to follow me with their blessings as I went to and from church, and nobody else to be regarded, were agreeable things, house-top proclamations! I *hid not my light under a bushel,* she would say that for me. (I 215–18)

Arabella, clearly, has been out-daughtered by her younger sister and does not like it; her stake in the anti-Clary cabal is clear enough. As for James, who aspires to the peerage and is used to being deferred to as heir apparent, he has had to live with a younger sibling of the inferior sex who consistently gets the better of him in verbal exchanges. She knows how best to have her brother at his weakest point, as when she "gently" taunts him about his intellectual prowess—which is manifestly inferior to hers:

Let me take the liberty further to observe, that the principal end of a young man's education at the university is to learn him to reason justly, and to subdue the violence of his passions. I hope, brother, that you will not give room for anybody who knows us both, to conclude that the toilette has taught the *one* more of the latter doctrine, than the university has taught the *other.* I am truly sorry to have cause to say that I have heard it often remarked, that your uncontrolled passions are not a credit to your liberal education. (I 138)

The nettled James takes the position, in his response, that he will not stoop to argue with "such a conceited and pert preacher and questioner," adding that he doesn't know "what wit in a woman is good for, but to make her overvalue herself, and despise every other person" (I 138).

The Gages of Duty

The sibling quarrels and jealousies are evident enough, and Clarissa gives them prominent place in her analysis of her predicament. What she cannot see, however, plays an even more prominent part: even though they have, in a sense, produced her, they do not believe in her. The daughter of sentiment is, after all, a creature of fantasy—who would be willing to do such work for such wages? Clarissa's lust for the intangible rewards of love and approval runs counter to the largely material understanding of the rewards of duty held in common by the rest of her family.[6] Her grandfather's estate was awarded, as the preamble to his will states, "because my dearest and beloved grand-daughter Clarissa has been from her infancy a matchless young creature in her duty to me . . ." (I 21). The Uncles Harlowe appear to be inclined to follow suit. Approving at first of Mr. Lovelace's addressing Clarissa, they mention in James's and Arabella's presence their intentions to augment the honor Clarissa's marriage to Lovelace will do the family with bequests of their own. " 'See, Sister Bella,' " cries James, " 'This little siren is in a fair way to *out-uncle*, as she has already *out-grandfathered* us both!' " (I 58). In addition to the material envy she can see, Clarissa has to contend with her family's genuine inability to credit her protestations that she doesn't care as much about money as she does about their love.

Clarissa is also completely, perhaps stubbornly, blind to the genuine alliance of interest between her father and her brother. Until her brother's return from Scotland, Mr. Harlowe encourages Lovelace's visits to the family and consents to Clarissa's correspondence with him. She reads his letters describing his European travels to the family circle as winter evening entertainment; Mr. Harlowe says they show Lovelace to be "a person of reading, judgment, and taste" (I 12). He does assert what turns out to be a crucial reservation with respect to the courtship—"that he would determine nothing without his son" (I 11)—and he also keeps "in readiness the reports he had heard in his disfavour, to charge them upon him then, as so many objections to his address" (I 13). Upon Junior's return, the patriarchal interest locates itself elsewhere, and the anti-Lovelace campaign begins, turning quickly enough into an anti-Clarissa, pro-Solmes campaign.

The prolonged reverse seduction of Clarissa by her family is a sexual struggle: obsessed as they seem to be with Clarissa's status as object of exchange, their strenuous solicitation on Solmes's behalf is provoked and exacerbated by their conviction that Clarissa has always already been had by Lovelace (and that, therefore, so have they all). They use specious and circular arguments to prove their point, as, if you don't love Lovelace, you will accept

Solmes; if you refuse Solmes it proves you want Lovelace. Her protestations
that she would rather live single than marry either one are dismissed as mere
maneuvering (a single Clarissa, be it noted, would not expand the family
holdings). When Clarissa attempts a stratagem, admitting to a prepossession
in Lovelace's favor (though she has assigned an equivocating meaning to the
term in order to say so) so as to make her aversion to Solmes credible in her
family's terms, they pounce upon the "admission" as all the more reason why
she should be married to Solmes immediately—to protect her from herself,
and the rest of them from the "man of violence." Clarissa's major mistake is
to assume the issue is susceptible to rational argument, to try to persuade her
family that her brother is wrong about her intentions.

For ambiguous states of desire, such as Clarissa seems to be trapped in—
attracted to a man she knows very well would be an unsuitable and unhappy
match for her—can be neither articulated nor acknowledged at Harlowe
Place. No one, including Anna Howe, is able to believe that Clarissa does not
want to marry Lovelace, or to run away with him if marriage is refused her. (It
was in the face of the persistence of this kind of reading that Richardson
himself tried to repress the more ambiguous Clarissa, as William Beatty
Warner has pointed out.) More important, what Clarissa wants to call
James's plan for the advancement of the family is indeed her father's plan.
Committed to paper, predicated upon Solmes's offers, the plan is the law of
the father, embodying his name (whether Junior or Senior), speaking the letter
of that law and name univocally, patriarchally. But Clarissa continues to address her adversaries as though they each—father, brother, sister, paternal
uncles—had individual voices. When Clarissa attacks the plan in a letter to
Antony Harlowe (". . . shall the remote and uncertain view of family-
aggrandizement, and that in the person of my *brother* and his *descendants*, be
thought sufficient to influence me?" [I 157]), his response is spoken in the
paternal register:

> Your brother, madam, is your brother; a third older than yourself: and a *man*:
> and pray be so good as not to forget what is due to a brother, who (next to us
> three brothers) is the head of the family; and on whom the name depends—as
> upon your dutiful compliance depends the success of the noblest plan that ever
> was laid down for the honour of the family you are come of. And pray now let
> me ask you, if the honour of that will not be an honour to you? If you don't think
> so, the more unworthy of you. (I 164)

The Solmes offers have become inseparable from the family pride. But Clarissa adamantly declares her aversion to him as a husband. They do not want
to appear to themselves or to their community to be eager to sacrifice a daugh-

ter's happiness to their own greed. Ascribing Clarissa's dislike of Solmes to a prior, and unworthy, prepossession for Lovelace offers them a perfect way out: they can justify their own prepossession in favor of Solmes as not only material but moral—marriage to him will save their daughter from the "vile rake." Upon the disposal of Clarissa's person depends not only "family aggrandizement," but the family "honour" of producing a daughter capable of the ultimate in "dutiful compliance."

Distinguished Duty

In analyzing her preposterously sudden fall from favor, Clarissa locates three relevant issues:

> Hatred to Lovelace, family aggrandisement, and this great motive, *paternal authority!* What a force *united* must they be supposed to have, when *singly* each consideration is sufficient to carry all before it! (I 61)

Her offer to live single endangers the family aggrandizement element; her prepossession (interpreted as an intention to be his) for Lovelace exacerbates the hatred to Lovelace element (which he is also aggravating at every opportunity); her refusal of Solmes offends the paternal authority element. So if Clarissa makes some small progress—for example, in temporarily persuading her Uncle John that she is sincere in her distress and in her offer to live single and make James and Arabella her heirs (I 303–7)—such progress is nullified in a full family conference by one or both of the other elements. Paternal authority, while it resides ultimately in Mr. Harlowe, is accepted by the rest of the family as existing by proxy—by his father's explicit authorization—in James's person as well. And it is precisely in her failure to accept James as her father's representative that Clarissa's failure to understand her own place lies. When James declares "that he shall never be easy or satisfied till" Clarissa is married (I 24), he speaks, as becomes increasingly evident, for her father as well.

When Clarissa returns from her two-week visit to Anna, she is greeted coldly and harshly by a family that has determined, in her absence, to accept Solmes's suit. They demand an explanation from her of the visits she is reported to have received at the Howes' from Lovelace, and she complies. James then speaks:

> I was no sooner silent than my *brother* swore, although in my father's presence (swore, unchecked either by eye or countenance), that for his part he would

never be reconciled to that libertine; and that he would renounce me for a sister
if I encouraged the address of a man so obnoxious to them all. (I 30)

Her father confirms that James's position is his own:

My father, with vehemence both of action and voice (my father has, you know, a
terrible voice when he is angry!), told me, that I had met with too much indul-
gence in being allowed to refuse *this* gentleman, and the *other* gentleman; and it
was now *his* turn to be obeyed. (I 30)

In spite of his vehemence, his terrible voice, and his unequivocal demand for
"*his* turn," Clarissa clings to the delusion that her father is being influenced
against his own inclination. A few days later, left alone with her father (for the
last time as it turns out), Clarissa begs "that I may have only yours and my
mamma's will, and not my brother's, to obey." Her father storms out of the
room, "saying that he would not hear me thus, by subtlety and cunning, aiming to distinguish away my duty, repeating that he would be obeyed" (I 37).
Clarissa's subsequent banishment from her father's presence will be lifted
only on condition that she be found "*worthy of the name of daughter*" (I 91).
    Clarissa, still unconvinced, keeps trying. She writes her father a letter in
which, as she reports to Anna, she begs that she not be sacrificed to "projects
and remote contingencies," promises "implicit duty and resignation to his
will" in anything "but this *one* point," and concludes with the hope "that my
brother's instigations may not rob an unhappy child of her father" (I 120).
She receives a short reply signed "A Justly Incensed Father" in which he emphasizes her brother's function as his spokesman: "It is *my* authority you
defy. Your reflections upon a brother, that is an honour to us all, deserve my
utmost resentment" (I 20). A month later, Clarissa has held out stoutly
enough to be addressed by her father (in another letter) as "Undutiful and
Perverse Clarissa"; he will not listen to her, nor will she hear any more from
him "till you have changed your name to my liking" (I 211). The day she
receives this missive, Clarissa refuses to see Mr. Solmes, provoking them all to
"tumults" again. Her brother and sister ask that she be "consigned over entirely to their management," and her father immediately agrees (I 212).
    This contest of wills is ultimately a sexual one, and is begun within the
family, *before* Lovelace takes her away from her father's house. James's language and behavior begin, with her father's blessing, as a courtship by proxy:
"Hitherto, I seem to be delivered over to my brother, who pretends as great
love to me as ever" (I 33). James speaks of and to his sister in the ambivalent
language of seduction: he calls her such names as "little siren" (I 58), "fallen
angel" (I 169), "pretty miss" (I 263), and, more sarcastically, "Delicacy,"

"Purity," and "Virgin modesty" (I 263); refers to her "shameful forward-ness" and to himself as one upon whom she is "continually emptying [her] *whole female quiver*" (I 222); and promotes a scheme whereby she will be confined to her Uncle Antony's house, furnished complete with a moat and chapel, during which time her uncle "won't promise, that he will not, *at proper times*, draw up the bridge" (I 256).

James's behavior as his father's proxy mimes the drama of seduction—particularly as presented in this novel—and curiously foreshadows the behav-ior to which Lovelace himself will subject Clarissa. For the paternal ventrilo-quy being still in force when Lovelace finally rapes the Harlowes' exemplary daughter, this family romance culminates in violation by proxy too.

Decent Indecency

Intervening in an interview between Solmes and Clarissa, James Junior rushes in from the next room where the whole family has been monitoring the conversation:

> He took my hand, and grasped it with violence. Return, pretty miss, said he; return, if you please. . . . O thou fallen angel, said he, peering up to my down-cast face—such a sweetness *here!*—and such an obstinacy *there!* tapping my neck. . . . But you shall not have your rake: remember that; in a loud whisper, as if he would be decently indecent before the man. (I 381)

James then hands the struggling Clarissa over to Solmes. Later in the same interview, he begs Solmes to help her family save her from ruin:

> "Look at her person! (and he gazed at me, from head to foot, pointing at me, as he referred to Mr. Solmes) think of her fine qualities! . . . She is worth saving, and, after two or three more struggles, she will be yours, and, take my word for it, will reward your patience. . . . depend upon it, you will be as happy a man in a fortnight, as a married man *can* be." (I 382)

This is innuendo worthy of a Lovelace, as is James's recommendation of re-venge, "I know of no other method of being even with her, than, after she is yours, to make her as sensible of your power as she now makes you of her insolence" (I 396). And, in what turns out to be Clarissa's final interview with Solmes, who is trying to warn her of Lovelace's designs on her honor, James's position moves from that of proxy to perpetrator:

Base accuser! said I, in a passion, snatching my hand from my brother, who
was insolently motioning to give it to Mr. Solmes; he has not! he dares not! But
you have, if endeavouring to force a free mind be to dishonour it!

O thou violent creature! said my brother. But not gone yet—for I was rushing
away.

What mean you, sir (struggling vehemently to get away), to detain me thus
against my will?

You shall not go, Violence; clasping his unbrotherly arms about me. . . .

And I struggled so vehemently to get from him, that he was forced to quit my
hand; which he did with these words: Begone then, Fury! How strong is will!
There is no holding her. (I 406)

Thus the paradigmatic, melodramatic, virtue-in-distress scene is played
first at home, by the father's namesake and heir, with the father's connivance
and authority (and sometimes his explicit direction—James Junior being
reeled back into the other room for instructions and debriefing [e.g., I 397]).
Clarissa's attempts to separate her father's will from her brother's are
doomed to failure because the distinction is only semantic; their interests—of
patriarch and junior, father and heir—are identical. Hers have nothing to do
with it, a fictional daughter's interests in her marriage rarely being consonant
with her father's. (Shakespeare's last play invented a story where the father
and the daughter's interests in her marriage are identical—but even Prospero
takes his pleasure in acting the part of the forbidding father.) Clarissa's job is
to be dutiful; paternal love and approval are contingent upon her obedience,
and no other merit. She is not, as she mistakenly thinks, entitled to esteem for
her past behavior. She has to keep re-earning it by renewed submission. And
when she reaches nubility, the required submission comes to center on her
body—no credence is given to any profession of obedience that is not backed
up by a surrender of her person—as the only credible figure of the surrender
of her will to the patriarchal desire. (This is a configuration we will see again
when Sir Stephen—another representative of the English patriarchy—
demands of O an identical submission.)

Any response to the desire of the father is doomed by definition because
response itself is doomed. The Harlowes prepare for resistance in advance of
proposing Solmes to Clarissa: but why should they expect disobedience from
a hitherto model daughter? Because nubility is the true test, as Clarissa's
mother points out:

Parents . . . when children are young, are pleased with everything they do. You
have been a good child upon the whole; but we have hitherto rather complied
with you than you with us. Now that you are grown up to marriageable years is
the test. . . . (I 79)

In Clarissa's case, saying No to her previous suitors has been tolerated, even applauded (on the score of her youth and her wisdom in seeing flaws in the applicants). Implicitly, she is saying she hasn't seen anybody good enough to tempt her out of her father's house. But when her father decides he has an interest in a candidate (an interest both generational and economic—Solmes is not a young man), her refusal of his chosen successor then becomes a No to her father's continuing control of her person, as Clarissa would delicately put it. Which is to say, that when push comes to shove, she says No to her father's desire.

Topping the Brother's Part

Lovelace is a more sophisticated rake than his companions in debauchery. It is the pursuit itself which piques his interest: "More truly delightful to me the seduction progress than the crowning act: for that's a vapour, a bubble!" (II 337). Clarissa as quarry prolongs the contest because, being the most vigilant of her sex, she guards against the small intimacies that Lovelace has always depended on as preliminaries to the final attack. Although he replicates and parodies the family setting she has left behind—isolating her from contact with anyone but those of his choosing, requiring as often as he can her company at meals, even introducing her in the first stages of their adventure as his sister—he cannot surprise her into accepting or offering familiarity of any kind:

> . . . could I but have gained access to her in her hours of heedlessness and dishabille [for full dress creates dignity, augments consciousness, and compels distance]; we had been familiarized to each other long ago. But keep her up ever so late; meet her ever so early; by breakfasttime she is dressed for the day; and at her *earliest hour,* as nice as others dressed. All her forms thus kept up, wonder not that I have made so little progress in the proposed trial. But how must all this distance stimulate! (II 341)

Like Clarissa's father, Lovelace resents the impenetrability of a will which he regards as only professedly founded upon duty.[7] The question he sets himself to answer is whether Clarissa's much-vaunted virtue is not "founded rather in *pride* than in *principle*" (II 35). Lovelace distinguishes "manly" from "womanly" virtue: "By virtue in this place I mean chastity, and to be superior to temptation . . ." (II 39). He reasons against his reverence for Clarissa (a reverence which persists in dialectical relation to his desire to transgress it):

> The pride of setting an example to her sex has run away with her hitherto, and
> may have made her till *now* invincible. But is not that pride abated? What may
> not both *men* and *women* be brought to do in a *mortified state?* What mind is
> superior to calamity? Pride is perhaps the principal bulwark of female virtue.
> Humble a woman, and may she not be *effectually* humbled? (II 36)

The virtue Lovelace decides to put to the test is not strictly, then, a question of
virginity: virginity is merely the final bulwark of the feminine pride Clarissa,
and the sex for which she is an examplar, takes in virtue.

Lovelace is possessed by the deeply compelling desire that can be provoked
only by the forbidden; his obsession with Clarissa is exacerbated by the paradox of a woman both dutiful and "impenetrable," both "angel" and daughter
(I 148). The first kiss he coerces from her—while playing her brother at St.
Albans—he says, "delighted me more than ever I was delighted by the *ultima-
tum* with any other woman. So precious does awe, reverence, and appre-
hended prohibition make a favour" (II 16).

Clarissa's long courtship/violation by a man who has her under his "protection," upon whom she is utterly dependent, and who will not accept any
version of Clarissa but the one he himself reads, resembles nothing so much as
a continuation of the treatment she has undergone at her father's behest.
When Anna predicts the method Lovelace will choose to subdue her, she
might be describing the Harlowes' chosen methods of persuasion—indeed,
the specific reference to the good Mrs. Harlowe's "progression" emphasizes
the familial parallels:

> and so he will have nothing to do, but this hour to accustom you to insult; the
> next, to bring you to forgive him, upon his submission: the consequence must
> be, that he will by this teasing break your resentment all to pieces: and then, a
> little *more* of the insult, and a little *less* of the submission, on his part, will go
> down, till nothing else but the *first* will be seen, and not a bit of the *second:* you
> will then be afraid to provoke so offensive a spirit; and at last will be brought so
> *prettily* and so *audibly,* to pronounce the little reptile word OBEY, that it will do
> one's heart good to hear you. The *Muscovite* wife then takes place of the *man-
> aged* mistress. And if you doubt the progression, be pleased, my dear, to take
> your mother's judgment upon it. (I 342)

This is the process begun by her father through his namesake, not instituted
but continued by their successor Lovelace. Much as he likes to boast that the
Harlowes have been unwittingly working for him all along (he depends, he
tells Belford, "upon the cunning family's doing my work for me, equally
against their knowledge or their wills" [II 17]), Lovelace is himself a blind
representative, in his turn, of Clarissa's frustrated father's will.

Leslie Fiedler describes Lovelace as a Don Juan "transformed into the monogamous seducer" with a "life's work in a single woman" (66). But the only
male who can have a life's interest in a single woman is her father; a seducer
tied for life to one object of desire enacts the dark side of paternal desire. Once
she leaves her father's house, Lovelace, in his attempt to wear Clarissa's will
down to a surrender of her body, takes the place James Junior has occupied—
both are proxies for the man for whom the daughter is a life's work. When
Clarissa and Lovelace arrive at Mrs. Sorlings' in St. Albans, Lovelace introduces himself as Clarissa's brother, explaining that he has carried his "sister"
away from the danger she was in of marrying a "confounded rake" against
the wishes of her "father and mother, her elder sister, and all her loving uncles,
aunts, and cousins" (II 13). Lovelace thus inserts himself—more ironically
than he knows—into the configurations of Clarissa's actual family at the
point James occupies, prompting this Shakespearean boast to Belford: "I
topped the brother's part on Monday night . . ." (II 16).

Throughout the rest of Clarissa's life her father's will looms large; he himself remains absent. The dark side of paternal desire is articulated in a curse
"imprecated on his knees" and repeated to Clarissa by Arabella: " 'that you
may meet your punishment, both *here* and *hereafter,* by means of the very
wretch in whom you have chosen to place your wicked confidence' " (II 170).
Clarissa responds to her father's curse with great apprehension and "va-
pourish despondency" (II 169), and her unquestioning belief in the power of
her father's curse is justified in the short as well as the long run, consolidating
the rather tenuous hold Lovelace has had over her to this point. Lovelace
responds to her illness with tender concern and reassurances, and Clarissa
tells Anna that

> his kind behaviour and my low-spiritedness, co-operating with your former
> advice and my unhappy situation, made me that very Sunday evening *receive
> unreservedly his declarations;* and now indeed I am more in his power than ever.
> (II 175)

Her father's curse thus becomes a self-fulfilling prophecy. As for Lovelace, the
immediate effect of the curse is a double one: on the one hand, he is genuinely
moved to "endearments," "vows," and "offers," and considers himself, on
her recovery, as now "more than a father to her; for I have given her a life her
unnatural father had well-nigh taken away . . . "; on the other hand, his pride
is wounded by her acknowledgment that she now "must be wholly in my
protection. . . . More indebted still, thy friend, as thou seest, to her cruel relations, than to herself for her favour!" (II 184). No more willing than Mr.
Harlowe to allow Clarissa what she calls "my own negative" (I 33), her mo-

nogamous (even monomaniacal) seducer wants, Lear-like, this perfect daughter Clarissa to love him without reference to anyone else, to prefer him to all other men—to stop being, in his words, "father-sick!" (II 187).

Writing Clarissa

In spite of the reductive attempts of both friends and foes, Clarissa emerges from a close reading of her history a very complex character: obedient yet determined, highly intelligent yet repeatedly duped, virtuous yet susceptible to a rake's charm, powerless yet strong. She is caught up in a fierce battle over who is to control her person; it is assumed her "will" will also fall to the victor. It does not. Spurned and then cursed by her father, tricked out of herself and then raped by Lovelace, robbed by one and then the other of love, approval, dignity, reputation, and hope, Clarissa never stops saying "nothing but No" as long as she is "able to speak" (I 464).

Clarissa centers on the question of whose version of Clarissa is the correct one—that is to say, who will have the strength to authorize his version of Clarissa as against all others. The James Harlowes share the fundamental patriarchal view that daughters are to be given in marriage to the advantage of the family that has produced them; daughters are to be possessed, that is to say, according to the pleasure of the man by whom she is prepossessed. When Clarissa shows signs of resisting this view, she who has hitherto been the pride of her family for her dutifulness gets rewritten as a willful schemer, spoiled by her sexuality and the allure of a Lovelace. This family fiction is confirmed by Clarissa's flight, and nothing she does thereafter—except dying—can effect any further revision of the Harlowe Clarissa.

Lovelace's Clarissa is a more complicated text: he brings to it a set of commonplaces about the frailty and corruptibility of the sex, a hitherto unchallenged belief in his own powers of seduction and plot making, and an obsession with Clarissa based upon the very qualities that her family claims she has forfeited—purity, submission, vulnerability, and obedience. Anna Howe's Clarissa is the daughter paragon intermixed with a respectable portion of the human frailties the dutiful daughter is expected to extinguish in herself: this Clarissa is prepossessed by Lovelace, has too punctilious a notion of filial piety, and undergoes trials that are suitably in proportion to her virtues. Clarissa writes herself as a variable mixture of all these Clarissas: her incisive analytical and argumentative skills present a persuasive case that she *is,* in intent at least, a dutiful and pious father's daughter even as her very eloquence in argument and rebuttal undercuts her posture of submission and duty; she is remorselessly self-indicting and humble (yet self-inditing and so how humble?), yet always finds an eminently reasonable explanation for her conduct; she is moral enough to dismiss Lovelace as a husband, but susceptible enough to be had—his schemes, stratagems, lies, and force needing a prior interest on Clarissa's part to be put into play (and that very susceptibility is itself a proof that the training of daughterly desire in the patriarchal direction has been singularly successful in her case).

How is it then that most of us remember a whey-faced goody-goody or a two-faced hypocrite when we think of *Clarissa?* (Not only readers, but writers who build upon her story, take one of these Clarissas as their starting point, as Leslie Fielder points out.)[8] My answer to this nonrhetorical question depends upon my own interested reading of *Clarissa*. Like the rest of her readers, I want to use Clarissa's corpus to authorize my own text. We read the *readings* of Clarissa in reading *Clarissa;* the readings of her friends, her relatives, her seducer(s), her traducers, and behind all these, the layers of Richardson's readings, who "edited" his text in an increasingly insistent response to misreadings of his heroine and villain—all of which readings in effect top the father's part in suppressing any Clarissa who is not the prototype of the sentimental daughter. The posthumous text, compiled as a joint project by the man who couldn't have her and the woman who couldn't be her and annotated by the man who couldn't stop writing her, writes the sentimentalized Clarissa, and whether we read it straight or subversively/derisively, we are largely responding to the sentimental tropes with/in which our particular, impossible, ideal Clarissa Harlowe is buried.

Mrs. Howe, with her daughter's concurrence, is one of the first to commission the exemplary version of Clarissa's story:

> You are, it seems (and that too much for your health), employed in writing. I hope it is in penning down the particulars of your tragical story. And my mother has put me in mind to press you to it, with a view that one day, if it might be published under feigned names, it would be of as much use as honour to the sex. . . . she would be extremely glad to have her advice of penning your sad story complied with. And then, she says, your noble conduct throughout your trials and calamities will afford not only a shining example to your sex, but at the same time (those calamities befalling such a person) a fearful warning to the inconsiderate young creatures of it. (IV 46)

But Clarissa is too ill in mind and body to accede to this request, and too close to her final apotheosis as the perfect (i.e., dead) daughter to continue her self-inditings. It is left to others to speak for and through Clarissa's story.

John Belford is the executor of Clarissa's estate, a rake reformed by the spectacle of Clarissa's long passion and dying. Formerly Lovelace's advocate and accomplice in all his schemes, a man who was once capable of affronting and shocking Clarissa on his first meeting her by a suggestive compliment to Lovelace in her presence—" 'You have so much courage, and so much wit, that neither man nor woman can stand before you' " (II 230)—Belford has become Clarissa's warmest advocate and defender, a veritable proselyte of the sentimental Clarissa, who can ask his former companion in vice and rowdiness such floridly self-righteous questions as these:

> Prithee tell me, thou vile Lovelace, if thou hast not a notion, even from these jejeune descriptions of mine, that there must be a more exalted pleasure in intellectual friendship, than ever thou couldst taste in the gross fumes of sensuality? And whether it may not be possible for thee, in time, to give that preference to the *infinitely* preferable, which I hope, now, that I shall always give? (IV 16)

Belford takes Lovelace's desired place as the writer of the accepted version of Clarissa just as he takes Lovelace's place as the father of Lord M.'s heir. For Clarissa's will assigns Belford the task of collecting all of the correspondence that has passed between himself and Lovelace that "relates to my story" and making copies for himself and Miss Howe (IV 425). Belford, in his zealous care and admiration for the reputation of his "inimitable testatrix" (IV 473), performs and exceeds (rewrites) her commission (even Clarissa's *last* will is not the last word). He conducts his own correspondence with Miss Howe, among others, adding his own interpretations and episodes to the writing task originally intended by the subject of it to be limited to transcription. He goes so far, in fact, as to solicit epistolary essays on Clarissa's character and life, as the Editor (Richardson, remember, can't keep his hands off her either) informs us (IV 490). He asks Miss Howe to "give the character of the friend she so dearly loved" (this report is in italics in the text, as are all the "Editor's" addenda):

> "I am more especially curious to know, *says he*, what was that particular disposition of her time, which I find mentioned in a letter which I have just dipped into, where her sister is enviously reproaching her on that score. This information may perhaps enable me, *says he*, to account for what has often surprised me; how, at so tender an age, this admirable lady became mistress of such extraordinary and such various qualifications." (IV 490)

And Anna's answer is innocent of all her former suspicions, is replete with such phrases as "a wonderful creature from her *infancy*," "a sacred regard to truth," "*wisdom* was her *birthright*," "mistress of . . . domestic qualifications," "*Propriety* . . . was . . . her law," and "the nearest perfection of any creature I ever knew"; Anna summarizes her friend's character thus: "All humility, meekness, self-accusing, others-acquitting, though the *shadow* of the fault was hardly hers, the *substance* theirs whose only honour was their relation to her" (IV 490–510).

Clarissa's corpse has become Clarissa's corpus. That which "*will be nothing when this writing comes to be opened and read*" (IV 417) has become not only Clarissa's final love letter to her father (as Shoshana Felman has called Cordelia's "Nothing")[9] but also the occasion of the sentimental rewriting of a far from simply sentimental heroine. Writing upon her coffin, following Clarissa's literal example, against the weeping and the remorse of the father who can't see her even at the last (". . . before the lid could be put aside, O my dear, said the father, retreating, I cannot, I find I cannot bear it!" [IV 405]), Belford (and his literary heirs—Charles Dickens, as we shall see, one of the most faithful) begets "upon the body of the said Clarissa Harlowe" (in the words of Lovelace's marriage settlements [II 471]) a long line, a veritable genealogy of daughters of sentiment.

2

The Fear of the Father:
Dombey and Daughter

Doubtless it is cruel to have to describe, on the one hand, a host of ills overwhelming a sweet-tempered and sensitive woman who, as best she is able, respects virtue, and, on the other, the affluence of prosperity of those who crush and mortify this same woman.

—Justine

She could not speak. But she was not wanted to speak. It was enough for her to feel.

—Emma

The story of Charles Dickens' seventh novel is the story of one man's doomed resistance to his family firm's being "a daughter . . . after all" (893). Paul and Florence Dombey are a particularly interesting father-daughter pair because she is so typical of Dickens' heroines; he, so atypical of their fathers.[1] Like Agnes Wickfield, Lizzie Hexam, and Esther Summerson, Florence is not merely ornamental: in addition to being beautiful, sweet, virginal, and submissive, she is also self-reliant, patient, persistent, intelligent, and genetically programmed to mix perfect glasses of grog (705). Unlike Mr. Wickfield, Gaffer Hexam, and John Jarndyce, Paul Dombey is a successful businessman, a true patriarch at home, and so hard and erect that the "stiff and stark fire-irons appeared to claim a nearer relationship than anything else there to Mr. Dombey" (65). Florence embodies the usual virtues of the hearth angel; Dombey is a powerful father. Dombey's refusal to acknowledge the particular power conceded to his daughter's sentimental attributes generates both the domestic and the sexual discord in the Dombey household.

Dickens' usual practice is to defuse domestic intimacy by housing his daughter-heroines with avuncular, unthreatening father figures. While there is a progression in Dickens' construction of the travails of his heroines, from, say, the melodramatic menace of Quilp to the psychological abuse of the obsessed Bradley Headstone, the potential sexual threats to be found in their worlds are located outside the patriarchal hearth and home. In *Dombey and Son,* however, Dickens hedges no bets. Dombey's difference from all other Dickensian fathers of daughters, like the railway that "let[s] the light of day in on" the "battered roofs and broken windows" (300) of poorer homes, reveals the structural flaw in the church of home and hearth: the angel in the house is constructed to accommodate impotent old father figures and young male ingenus. Only those who need her, those with nothing to lose, those who can't stand up for themselves, love her.

The Clue to Something Secret in his Breast

Paul and Florence Dombey are unlike any other father-daughter pair in Dickens. Father figures like William Dorrit, Noddy Boffin, and Captain Cuttle accept the homely attentions of their daughters, and daughter stand-ins, with patience if not gratitude. Paul Dombey possesses his very own "little mother,"[2] fully endowed with all the virtues and talents of the standard hearth angel, and yet nowhere else in the canon do we find a daughter rebuffed so long and so well by her father. To be sure, Little Dorrit may not be appreciated by her self-centered papa; Georgiana Podsnap receives less paternal attention in her own person than she does in her rhetorical role of "the young person"; Little Nell may find her father figure rather more a burden than a bulwark: none but Florence endures the ordeal that is the story of her journey from child to woman in such unremitting isolation. All of Dickens' heroines undergo more or less arduous ordeals; indeed, the more delicate and virginal she is, the more thrilling to the reader-voyeur is the story which subjects her to the odious behavior her innocence precisely unfits her to counter. *Dombey and Son,* written at approximately the midpoint of Dickens' career, is an intersection of another sort: in this novel the heroine's father is also her tormentor.

Dombey's life is dominated by his "one idea," Dombey and Son: "The earth was made for Dombey and Son to trade in, and the sun and moon were made to give them light. . . . stars and planets circled in their orbits to preserve inviolate a system of which they were the centre" (12). For the first six years of her life, Florence is merely irrelevant:

> But what was a girl to Dombey and Son! In the capital of the House's name and
> dignity, such a child was merely a piece of base coin that couldn't be invested—a
> bad boy—nothing more. (13)

Once his son and heir is born, Dombey's indifference to his eldest child is
transformed into "an uneasiness of an extraordinary kind." Watching the
dying Fanny Dombey embrace the six-year-old Florence is "a revelation and a
reproach to him": he has no part in it; he feels "quite shut out." This consciousness of Dombey's gives rise to his fear that Florence "held the clue to
something secret in his breast" (41).

Dombey's fear turns out to be prophetic. One secret in his breast is the
nature of his response to his wife's imminent demise in childbed:

> He was not a man of whom it could properly be said that he was ever startled or
> shocked; but he certainly had a sense within him that if his wife should sicken
> and decay, he would be very sorry, and that he would find a something gone
> from among his plate and furniture, and other household possessions, which
> was well worth the having, and could not be lost without sincere regret.
> Though it would be a cool, business-like, gentlemanly, self-possessed regret, no
> doubt. (16)

Dombey, hoarding his son to his heart, wants no rivals for his son's attentions: " 'He will make what powerful friends he pleases in after-life. . . . Until
then, I am enough for him, perhaps, and all in all' " (59). Dombey's jealousy
extends to the only class of people who can insure the continuation of his
Firm. He pities his infant son, and himself "through the child" (30), because
Dombey and Son finds itself "endangered in the outset by so mean a want"
(26) as a wet nurse. Each time he is able to reject a candidate for that position,
he is secretly pleased. When he is unable to find a flaw in Polly Toodle's qualifications, he regally instructs her to form no ties that are not incorporated in
their "bargain and sale" contract, and performs the quintessential patriarchal
gesture of control by renaming her "Richards."[3]

Although Dombey's possessiveness is clearly excessive, his antipathy to
mother-women receives a significant amount of sub rosa support from the
text. The two fallen women of the novel are raised and marketed by single
mothers. The comic mother, Mrs. MacStinger, spends her time obsessively
cleaning, tyrannizing over Captain Cuttle, and spanking young Alexander
MacStinger and setting him to cool on the paving stones. When they aren't
odious, mothers are not attentive enough: the "good" mothers in Dombey
and Son are notable mostly for their habit of abandonment. Fanny Dombey
dies, as does Walter Gay's mother. Mrs. Chick leaves her own offspring at

home in order to spend what seems an inordinate amount of time dancing attendance on her brother's son. Even Polly Toodle, that "good, plain sample of a nature that is ever, in the mass, better, truer, higher, nobler, quicker to feel, and much more constant to retain, all tenderness and pity, self-denial and devotion, than the nature of men" (39), even Polly Toodle is an abandoning mother,[4] leaving her own family to tend to Dombey's when summoned and committing the dereliction of duty that moves Dombey to dismiss her from her position as Paul's "second mother—his first, so far as he knew" (96).

Dombey's jealousy of whoever might prove important to his son marks Florence's progress from an irrelevance to a rival. One of the sanctioned ways the daughter can be managed is by positioning her as maternal, to make of her a *little* mother. Dombey responds to Florence in her little mother role just as he responds to the real mothers in his world. His daughter's maternal connection with his son makes Dombey feel left out all over again, reviving the unwelcome revelation of Fanny Dombey's deathbed. Dombey perceives little Paul's love for Florence as a misappropriation which depletes the available supply of affection. When young Paul is enrolled in Dr. Blimber's boarding school,[5] a move calculated by Dombey to wean Paul's affection from his sister, the boy's good-byes are revealing:

> The limp and careless little hand that Mr. Dombey took in his was singularly out of keeping with the wistful face. But he had no part in its sorrowful expression. It was not addressed to him. No, no. To Florence—all to Florence.
>
> If Mr. Dombey, in his insolence of wealth, had ever made an enemy, hard to appease and cruelly vindictive in his hate, even such an enemy might have received the pang that wrung his proud heart then, as compensation for his injury. (164)

If Dombey's general suspicions about mothers are unreprimanded, even supported, by the narrative, his unremitting resistance to Florence's maternal gestures is not. Across the street from Dombey's gloomy house live four rosy little sisters, motherless like Florence. Alone in her home after the death of her brother, Florence pensively watches the workings of that household. The eldest girl is younger than Florence but is, nonetheless, her father's companion: "she could be as staid and pleasantly demure with her little book or workbox, as a woman," and in the evenings after she had made her father his tea, "happy little housekeeper she was then!" (266).

The place of the daughter, particularly in a motherless household, can be managed to everyone's advantage by placing her in a maternal position. The properly placed daughter makes tea and darns stockings. She attends to the home comforts of her father. She can even, as the contrapuntal story of the

Blimber family makes clear, provide a fond father with heirs, if not to his name, at least to his business. Florence attempts to play the role of maternal daughter, shepherding her brother through his short life and last illness, making advances to her father that are coldly, even viciously, rejected out of hand, pervading the house of Dombey leaving nosegays and hand-painted watch stands and tears on her father's desk. Dombey will not cooperate. Her every gesture increases his hostility.

The power struggle that began with little Paul's birth does not end with his death. Dombey's hostility toward Florence is compounded by his reading her as "the successful rival of his son, in health and life," and as "his own successful rival in that son's affection" (274). Haunted by this double defeat, Dombey travels to Leamington, seeking "something to interpose between himself and [Florence]" (302), and comes up with Edith Skewton Granger. Edith is a strikingly handsome and regal woman of a faintly noble and definitely impecunious family. Dombey considers her a consort worthy of his own eminence, as he need not, himself, marry for money. As it happens, far from consolidating his position as patriarch, his second wife's presence in his home increases Dombey's uneasy sense of the threat represented by his lovable daughter.

For not only does Edith oppose her merchant husband's wishes with all of the considerable strength of her character, she also shows a marked inclination to please his daughter, rather than himself. To his horror, Dombey watches a new alliance being formed in his house, against his will, and, as he sees it, against his interest. The night of "the happy couple's" return from their wedding trip is paradigmatic. Agreeably surprised by Florence's beauty, "almost changed into a woman without his knowledge," Dombey "soften[s] to her, more and more." Alone with her for the first time, watching her busy at her workbasket while he pretends to be asleep, Dombey seems about to call her to his side. At this almost pivotal moment, Edith enters the room, an Edith her husband has never seen, a "softened" and "winning" Edith, and his wife and his daughter go "out of the room like sisters" (525). Dombey's reflections on this incident reveal his construction of the power struggle:

> It seemed his fate to be ever . . . humbled and powerless where he would be most strong. Who seemed fated to work out that doom?
>
> Who? Who was it who could win his wife as she had won his boy! Who was it who had shown him that new victory. . . . Who was it whose least word did what his utmost means could not? . . . She had crossed him every way and everywhere. She was leagued against him now. Her very beauty softened natures that were obdurate to him, and insulted him with an unnatural triumph. . . . in his pride, a heap of inconsistency, and misery, and self-inflicted torment, he hated her. (582–83)

The underlying question is, *where* would Dombey be most strong? Both his new wife and his new (in the sense that Dombey here sees her as "young, beautiful, and good"[6] for the first time) daughter have just left the room. The conflation of daughter and wife that will culminate in the blow that sends Florence out into the streets of London begins here. Being like sisters, both women become daughters; both, wives. Most of the "Who" questions are more applicable to the wife than the daughter, as the reader knows (and Dombey doesn't), and Dombey thus combines the obdurate wife with the yielding daughter. And if Florence does soften natures obdurate to Dombey, we should remember that in this passage he has himself been softened and that Florence's "unnatural triumph" which has insulted Dombey certainly refers to his softening to near-capitulation to his daughter's beauty.

Concurrent with her newly blossoming womanhood. Florence has been promoted from her position as rival for his son's affections to a far more threatening position as Dombey's "fate" and "doom." This is a position that refers not only to his wife's perceived preference for Florence over him, but also to a more complex dimension of power and strength. Florence's beauty, her "least word," appears to Dombey to have power that his "utmost means" do not; power that works even on him, until he hardens himself against her after her "triumph." What is this other power that seems, in its very quietude, so effective and affecting?

> . . . Florence grew to be seventeen. Timid and retiring as her solitary life had made her, it had not embittered her sweet temper, or her earnest nature. A child in innocent simplicity, a woman in her modest self-reliance and her deep intensity of feeling, both child and woman seemed at once expressed in her fair face and fragile delicacy of shape, and gracefully to mingle there. . . . (674)

The very reverence of this description covertly invokes Florence's desirability. She feels deeply and intensely; she is sweet and earnest. A graceful mingling of child and woman, her "shape" is delicate and "fragile." It is just this irresistible combination of charms that attracts the odious attentions of a Quilp to a Little Nell, a Bradley Headstone to a Lizzie Hexam, and, on a less melodramatic level, a Captain Cuttle to a Florence Dombey:

> "It's the sweet creetur grow'd a woman!"
> Captain Cuttle was so respectful of her, and had such a reverence for her, in this new character, that he would not have held her in his arms, while she was unconscious, for a thousand pounds. . . . (690)

(In fact, he does hold her in his arms while she is unconscious, and throughout this entire episode of the novel carries her around and about the house and up and down the stairs with remarkable energy and persistence even after she regains consciousness.)

> Yielding to the urgency of the case, the Captain then, using his immense hand with extraordinary gentleness, relieved her of her bonnet, moistened her lips and forehead, put back her hair, covered her feet with his own coat pulled off for the purpose, patted her hand—so small in his that he was struck with wonder when he touched it. . . . (690–91)

Florence's innocence and vulnerability provoke invasive responses. Juxtaposed with Captain Cuttle's delicate violations of Florence's person is her father's violent one, foreshadowed in the homecoming night scene (which appears in a chapter entitled, equivocally enough, "The Happy Pair") by references to Dombey's growing in "height and bulk before her" as she yearns toward but shrinks from him, and by the narrator's exclamation, "Unnatural the hand that had directed the sharp plough, which furrowed up her gentle nature for the sowing of its seeds!" (523). Enraged by his discovery of Edith's elopement with Carker, Dombey expends his frantic desire to beat "all trace of beauty out of [Edith's] triumphant face with his bare hand" in a heavy blow to Florence's breast, "and as he dealt the blow, he told her what Edith was, and bade her follow her, since they had always been in league" (687).

Even the avuncular Captain Cuttle has a hard time keeping his hands off this desirable daughter. How much more difficult it is for her magisterial father, this climax in the difficult father-daughter history reveals. By refusing, in his arrogance, his culture's strategy for managing the place of the daughter, by denying Florence the little mother role he alone has the power to legitimate, Dombey forces his daughter to occupy a very threatening place indeed.

Hollow Alibis

The same fear and animosity that produced fevered visions of the vagina dentata also named the Duke of Exeter's daughter, and Scavenger's daughter (instruments of torture named after their creator's daughters), and the gunner's daughter (the gun upon which erring seamen were flogged). Even the hard sciences are not immune: an atomic species that is the immediate product of the radioactive decay of a given element is named "daughter." When she is not allowed to usurp (or borrow) the place of the mother, the presence of the daughter is a sign of her father's imminent impotence and decay. The "bliss repressed beneath the stereotype" of the sentimentalized daughter is inextricably intertwined with the violence generated by fear and hatred.[7] And where does the fear and hatred come from? In *Dombey and Son* its source is revealed clearly, and the narrative voice's frequent (and provisional) attribution to pride, to arrogance, to emotional awkwardness ought not to divert our attention from it. A son can help Dombey cheat time; the racing watches of the first chapter, while they mark a death, also punctuate the birth that will ensure Dombey's victory over impotence and death, or so he fondly hopes.

A daughter, on the other hand, stands for impotence. Florence, as a "piece of base coin," cannot be invested in the future of the family business. In her little mother guise, Florence could perhaps have circumvented Dombey's bitter struggle, but he is not a man willing to accommodate himself to insulating myths and social compromises. (Witness his rejection of Edith's proposed nonaggression pact: though he values most highly "the world's" opinion, he will not settle for the mere appearance of submission; he wants the real thing [590].) Only external forces can resolve the battle: the bankrupt Dombey docilely submits to retirement and grandfatherhood; Florence becomes a mother in fact.

A daughter is anomalous in the patriarchal nuclear family. Virtually every other daughter-heroine in the canon occupies a place Dickens fudged especially for her by literally or figuratively removing her mother so the daughter can play stand-in as little mother, or by desexualizing the father figure so the daughter plays hearth angel—in either case, the sexuality inherent in her separate desirable qualities is repressed beneath the sanctified asexuality of the maternal, and any leftover eroticism thus appears to be no more problematic than that to which the worshipful Captain Cuttle succumbs. In *Dombey and Son*, Dickens comes as close as he ever does to revealing the hollowness of his fictional, and his culture's ideological, daughter alibis.

Given Dombey's stiff-necked refusal to compromise, his inability to participate in the polite fictions and subtle communal deceits of society, he has no safe place to put his genuinely desirable, dutiful daughter. She's a destabilizing element; if she is handled improperly, all kinds of edifices are subject to collapse. Thus, our sympathy for Dombey survives his arrogance, his cruelty, his meanness. He is a man genuinely at risk. It is certain that Dickens himself sympathized with his character. Apparently stung by a *Blackwood's Magazine* reviewer's scoffing at Dombey's end-of-novel change of heart,[8] Dickens appended a curiously defensive preface in which the line between this fiction and his own reality is blurred.[9] Observing first that in his experience the ability to correctly observe men's characters is rare, Dickens writes, "Mr. Dombey undergoes no violent change, either in this book, or in real life."

Dickens refers to Dombey's struggle in the historical present tense ("A sense of his injustice is within him all along"), but moves to the more immediate present perfect tense in describing its resolution ("but it has been a contest for years").

The shifting tone of the preface necessarily calls up what we know of Dickens' life and his own uncertain adjustment to the necessities of domesticity. Dickens and his daughters seem to have been entangled in their own web of conflicting needs and dubious fulfillment. Mamie Dickens appears to have occupied the place Florence longs for. By her own account, Mamie never had to choose between pleasing her father and being happy: "My love for my father has never been touched or approached by any other love. I hold him in my heart as a man apart from all other men, as one apart from all other beings" (8). This is surely a status inflated enough to frighten all but the most self-assured of men.

Katey Dickens was more active than her sister in her attempts to establish emotional distance from her father. And it was she who was, according to Edgar Johnson, initially "harsh" about her father's infatuation for the young Ellen Ternan:

> But as Katey looked back on the tangled and unhappy story in after years, her judgment of Ellen softened. "She flattered him," Katey said, "—he was ever appreciative of praise—and though she was not a good actress she had brains, which she used to educate herself, to bring her mind more on a level with his own. Who could blame her? He had the world at his feet. She was a young girl of eighteen, elated and proud to be noticed by him." (1007)

Her anger softened, Katey's empathy for Ellen Ternan's situation seems based on something stronger than imagination. (And notice, too, how very Florence-like Ellen Ternan's attempts to be worthy are.)

Dickens began *Dombey and Son* when he had been married ten years (and that's how long Dombey has been married when Paul Junior is born). Dickens' problematic relationship to his wife, his frenetic residence hopping, his susceptibility to the charms of girls young, beautiful, and good—all bespeak a marked personal investment in the fate and fortunes of Paul Dombey, Sr. Even the family names echo one another. The echoes seem particularly resonant when we consider *Dombey and Son* as a kind of deck clearing for *David Copperfield*, as a species of portrait of the artist facing middle age which inspired Dickens to offer his public a sunny version of the fiction of his life—whether to instruct the public in "the faculty . . . of correctly observing the characters of men" or to capitalize on its inability to do so many never be entirely clear.

The Pious and the Perverse

There is no more a real place for the daughter in the paternal domestic space than there is in the paternal bed. In either space, the daughter is present by virtue of usurping (or borrowing) the mother's place. Alexander Welsh, for example, suggests that the Victorian preference for "little mothers" is based upon the uncomfortably close connection between real mothers and birth, therefore death (210). But there really is no inherent quality in little mothers that makes them less evocative of the truth of universal decay and death, as we have seen. Likewise, there is no inherent quality in wife or mother or daughter that dictates that one evokes decay, impotence, death, defeat—or, for that matter, devotion, salvation, redemption, regeneration—any more vividly than either of the other two. The daughter as emblem of forbidden desire, and the daughter as hearth angel, is a daughter, after all. Any way you cut them, the cards are stacked against her. Likewise wife. Likewise mother. Even at our sentimental, romantic, desiring best/worst, even when the adjectives attributed to her are laudatory, " 'girls are thrown away in this house . . .' " (*Dombey* 37).

George Orwell, speaking of Charles Dickens' style, remarks that the "outstanding, unmistakable mark of [his] writing is the *unnecessary* detail" (45), and Dickens criticism has tended to dismiss Florence as a gratuitous piece of not-quite-at-his-best Dickens stylistics. Annoyed by her "incessant" weeping, affronted by her apparently inexhaustible vulnerability, disapproving in general terms of her role in this novel and of the sentimentality of the usual Dickens heroine overall, Dickens scholars have often replicated Dombey's relationship with Florence in their dealings with her.

The general tenor of traditional Dickens criticism is at one with Sylvère Monod's disapproval of Florence's "sentimental blackmail" (265).[10] A. E. Dyson, for example, believes that Dombey is the "natural victim in the novel" who is subjected to an ending the "reader" is "uneasy" about. He then proceeds to lay this ending (and this uneasiness) at Florence's door: she has an "obsessive need to be loved," which, presumably, no one could have satisfied. Dyson's own source of uneasiness with the resolution of the novel and of the father's long resistance to the daughter seems, finally, to be his sympathy with Dombey as a man faced by what seems to Dyson to be an appalling and inexhaustible need: Florence is "resolutely self-centered," and her notion of her problem with her father is too "inward-looking, too obsessive, to be pure love with healing properties." (This because she broods about what she surmises is the fault in herself which must, she concludes, be the reason her father can't seem to love her.) Dyson actually accuses Florence of not knowing her father "as a person," of not showing "any respect for him as the person who, for better or worse, he really is" (131). Dombey's insistence upon what he calls "respect" is, of course, an essential component of his unease in his world, and his one-sided war with his daughter is largely founded upon his definition of that respect—a definition that excludes, as Dyson's does, any possibility of the respectful party's needing to be respected in turn.

The narrative of *Dombey and Son* also reflects—at length—about the lack of communication between father and daughter, but it never suggests that Florence doesn't "respect" her father's personhood. It treats the absence of acquaintance as a fault of the father rather than of the daughter. The fundamental difference between Dyson's reading of the father-daughter relationship that is at the center of this novel and the narrative's reading of it (and, it is probably safe to say, Dickens' as well), is that Dyson regards Dombey's response to Florence as a reasonable one, given her status as an uncontrollable, obsessive, insistent, and wrong-headed representation of need. Where Dyson sees a frightening and threatening demand ("Her need for love blossoms through late childhood and early adolescence into a possessive obsession, which is fulfilled only when Mr. Dombey's manhood is broken in the game of life" [131]), the narrative encourages us to decide that if anything could have averted the tragic end of Dombey's second marriage and the collapse of his business, it would have been his returning Florence's genuine love and disinterested affection. Alone in his empty and abandoned house, Dombey is contemplating suicide, reviewing his past, thinking about the daughter who "would have been true to him, if he had suffered her" (864), and his rejection of that love:

> But that which he might have made so different in all the past—which might have made the past so different, though this he hardly thought of now—that which was his own work, that which he could so easily have wrought into a blessing, and had set himself so steadily for years to form into a curse, that was the sharp grief of his soul. (863)

The agency here is Dombey's, not Florence's, and there is no mitigation of his mistake, no sharing of the blame between equally erring parties (as there is with respect to Edith's share in Dombey's misery).

Adhering to the Dyson line that most of Mr. Dombey's misfortunes are caused by demanding females (Dyson's final pronouncement on this question is that "if Dombey had been luckier [given his own cold temperament] in wife and daughter, he might have settled down as a very ordinary *pater-familias*" [127]), Julian Moynahan complains that Dombey

deserves a complex fate but does not get one. And if we admit that we shall have
to admit further that he had everything to fear and nothing to gain from Florence's love. He was right after all. (127)

Moynahan's argument relies for much of its energy and force upon an assumption that his reader will share his distaste for Florence as "a sentimental heroine upon whom angelic powers and attributes have been arbitrarily grafted."
(I. A. Richards calls "sentimental" one of literary criticism's "polite terms of
abuse" than which there are "few so effective" [255], and Moynahan bran-
dishes it with skill and wit.) Moynahan then anathematizes Florence's
"slackly feminine sphere" of influence. She embodies a sentimental religion
which is neither secular nor divine, but "a set of loose analogies and tropes
employed to conceal faulty argument by analogy: people who act like saints
will be rewarded like saints in the end. The meek shall inherit the Industrial
Revolution" (130).

This dismissive attitude, which duplicates in an unsettling way Dombey's
attitude toward his daughter, is itself based on a set of rather loose critical
tropes and analogies. The basic critical attitude found in readings like those
above is one of self-congratulation that we are no longer so unsophisticated as
to fall for *that*. One sees it applied to other kinds of fictional embodiments of
one thing and another—the Vice, the Don Juan, the courtly lover—but rarely
with such consistent critical sneers and easy assumptions of such a well-
established community of agreement that articulating the argument is unnecessary, if not a bit *de trop*. The loose analogies rest upon a metonymized
reading of the sentimental daughter in fiction: first, her "angelic" qualities
themselves are focused on; then, the reader imagines what the effects of such a
collection of presumptively implausible perfections would be upon him/
herself. What this kind of reading leads to is a two-dimensional version of the
sentimental daughters of fiction based, often enough, on hasty readings generated by the assumption that one needn't, after all, pay too much attention to
the mushy stuff.

Missing from our readings of the daughter-heroine is the "erotic coloration" of the sentimental (Hagstrum 7). Florence Dombey and figures like her
stand at the intersection of the pious and the perverse. Sexual desire, ambivalence, fear, and anxiety are written in *Dombey and Son*, and to focus, at least
for a moment, on that level is also to read desirability back into the sentimental heroine.[11] Until we can read her thus three-dimensionally, we will never
lose our irritation with her. The problem is not limited to our having "forgotten" how to read certain tropes; the sentimental daughter has become so
closely associated with a frightening archetype—the dutiful daughter, the

Desdemona, the Clarissa, the one who despite her apparent filial devotion must inevitably betray her father once she reaches nubility—that we simply cannot read her or any of her stories with any real patience.

The truth of *Dombey and Son,* more than any other, is that even constructed in the images they have prescribed, men don't like women; yet, women seem to like men. What is the difference that accounts for that difference? In the Dombey world, women *have* to like men. Men don't have to like women. Until Dombey loses the last vestige of his patriarchal, socially constructed power, he need not treat his daughter (who is all women) or any other women (who are all daughters) with anything other than a lordly contempt, a contempt that masks the fear generated by any oppressed domestic population. This is an impious suggestion, and one which, if followed to its logical conclusion, would in fact entail dismantling the family business. No more than Moynahan does Dickens, his sentimental dreaming notwithstanding, want to consign the Industrial Revolution to the saintly "Wooman, lovely Wooman."[12] So, having brought *Dombey and Son* to the verge of a radical truth, Dickens brings Dombey himself to the extremity of need in order to effect a proper restoration of the domestic order, and in so doing consigns his story to the proper order of the domestic fiction.

Ceci n'est pas une métaphore?

Moved by the unexpected appearance of her stepdaughter, Edith Dombey confesses the truth she has vowed never to reveal: that she has not, in fact, "committed herself with the deceased person with white teeth" (893). Addressing Florence as her " 'better angel,' " humbled by her love for the pure and innocent young woman before her, Edith confesses to and asks forgiveness for staining Florence's name (892). Florence, returning to her father after the birth of her son, makes confession too. Beginning with the exclamation, " 'Papa, love, I am a mother' " (868), she declares herself guilty of running away, of marrying without the paternal blessing, of not having understood her duty. Begging forgiveness of the father who has never once been kind to her, she repledges her love and devotion to him. Overwhelmed, weak, grateful, Dombey "would have raised his hands and besought her for pardon, but she caught them in her own, and put them down, hurriedly" (868).

Florence confesses her filial sins to her father, who is the sinned against as well as the proper authority. Edith, the (technically) fallen woman and failed mother,[13] makes her confession to the morally superior daughter whom she has unwillingly injured. Dombey's sin, despite the momentary impulse instinctively deflected by Florence, can be confessed only to one more highly placed than himself.

> As she clung closer to him, in another burst of tears, he kissed her on her lips, and, lifting up his eyes, said, "Oh my God, forgive me, for I need it very much!" (868)

With this round of confessions, the proper domestic hierarchies are apparently reestablished. Edith, whose repentance is addressed to Florence, and who will acknowledge even to Florence only a contingent and shared guilt in the "dark vision" of her second venture in the marriage market, is banished to Europe. Florence is received into the paternal bosom, never more to be rejected. Dombey, who has certainly suffered enough to satisfy the most implacable of his enemies, is admitted to the domestic bliss he has been resisting throughout the novel.

The scene of confession requires the presence of a properly constituted superior and a detailed catalog of sins articulated by the one asking forgiveness.[14] Edith positions Florence as this superior and details for her all the offenses to which she is willing to plead guilty and for which she is asking forgiveness. Florence in her turn recognizes her father as the superior to whom she must confess. Both women confess to violating the domestic space with unseemly rebellions against its culturally sanctioned power structure. Dombey's repentance, on the other hand, while as passionate as his daughter's and his wife's, is hardly as explicit as theirs are. In fact, Dombey, in what looks very like a continuation and exacerbation of his original offense, utterly ignores Florence's presence—except for that kiss—and addresses his request for forgiveness to a higher Authority.

Of course, she is his victim, she embodies his sin, and her mere presence in this scene together with the kiss on her lips seems to re-place her in her proper familial role: Dombey's terse acknowledgment of his need apparently legitimizes her at last. Why stickle for a catalog of Dombey's sins when the story of this father's long denial of his daughter stands before him in the figure of his daughter, as it stands before the reader in the pages of the novel? Because an effective resolution of Florence's long supplication for recognition and Dombey's obdurate neglect and hostility requires that Dombey articulate his sins. Without that articulation the reconciliation between father and daughter is accomplished on the same terms as their long estrangement; that is to say, she offers her love and devotion and this time he accepts it, having no more offered a reason for accepting than he had for refusing it.

The domestic order that was disrupted by silence and absence is thereby refounded upon another silence (Dombey as confessant is silent on the nature of his sins) and another absence (Florence as *daughter* is not present in the confession scene). Florence flees her father's house as a despised daughter; she returns after a year's absence as the wife of Walter Gay and the new mother of Paul Dombey, Jr.'s, namesake. So it is that Dombey has no longer to deal with the daughter in his house. Rather, she is received into the paternal bosom as someone else's wife and the mother of Dombey's grandson. Whatever had frightened and enraged Mr. Dombey has disappeared, as has his wealth, his power, his physical strength.

That Dickens has Dombey lose his economic power as a precondition to reconciliation with Florence demonstrates a deep, albeit perhaps only intuitive, understanding of the necessary content of Dombey's inability to love his daughter. Whereas his connection with Edith is forged as a purchase, her beauty bought by his wealth, his daughter has been in his possession as a "base coin" all along—she was "not quite . . . [what] was expected" (19) of Fanny Dombey to begin with. Dombey's rising uneasiness, escalating into fear, arriving at hostility, is rooted in his conviction that something that is *not* straightforward, by his lights, is going on in the transactions between himself and his daughter. Dombey is merchant enough to recognize that his daughter is dealing in an altogether different currency, but Dombey conducts himself as a true British businessman, speaking only his own language, dealing only in pounds and pence. Indeed, there is one near him who is playing precisely the duplicitous role Dombey mistakenly assigns to his daughter—it is Carker, skilled in many languages, economies, and games, who is all love and fealty without, all revenge and rivalry within; Carker, not Florence, who consorts with improper associates; Carker, not Florence, who deliberately makes Dombey look foolish in the eyes of "the World"; Carker, not Florence, who is at last "in league" with Edith, plotting and scheming against his despised employer and her detested husband. For Carker pretends to deal in the currency Dombey understands, that of bargain and sale and speculation. Florence traffics in a very different sort of currency, one which Dickens and his culture needed to believe to be stronger than Dombey and Son's, the power of pure, unselfish, uncalculated (consequently infinite) love.

What critics like Moynahan and Dyson, as interested observers, find so unattractive, so *unbecoming,* is not Dombey's (and Dickens') succumbing to the wrong side in the war between world and hearth—though that's how they put it. What is objectionable in Dombey's surrender to a power sentimentally represented as greater than his, is that we all "know" that domestic influence is not stronger than capitalistic power, that sentimental hierarchies are not superior to patriarchal ones, and, from the standpoint of that knowledge, Dombey's end looks not only like a capitulation, but an unnecessary and rather frightening one. The power dynamic between capitalist and employee, between businessman and society, between rich and poor, between white collar and no collar, is exactly the same as that between male and female, husband and wife, patriarch and family, father and daughter. Love—whether sexual, filial, or domestic (and these are only theoretically distinct categories)—is not a metaphor for power. Love *is* power. When you take it apart it looks just like business. Or politics. Or violence. And as with power, in our culture men (generally and generically) wield it and women ask for it. Any suggestion that the world might well be perceived differently is much too close to a radical re-creation for comfort.

Little Women:
The Legend of Good Daughters

Seldom, except in books, do the dying utter memorable words, see visions, or depart with beatified countenances; and those who have sped many parting souls know, that to most the end comes as naturally and simply as sleep. As Beth had hoped, the "tide went out easily"; and in the dark hour before the dawn, on the bosom where she had drawn her first breath, she quietly drew her last, with no farewell but one loving look and a little sigh.

—*Little Women*

There was [pictures] that they called crayons, which one of the daughters which was dead made her own self when she was only fifteen years old. They was different from any pictures I ever see before—blacker, mostly, than is common. . . . one was a young lady with her hair all combed up straight to the top of her head, and knotted there in front of a comb like a chair back, and she was crying into a handkerchief and had a dead bird laying on its back in her other hand with its heels up, and underneath the picture it said, "I Shall Never Hear Thy Sweet Chirrup More Alas." There was one where a young lady was at a window looking up at the moon, and tears running down her cheeks; and she had an open letter in one hand with black sealing wax showing on one edge of it, and she was mashing a locket with a chain to it against her mouth, and underneath the picture it said "And Art Thou Gone Yes Thou Art Gone Alas." These was all nice pictures, I reckon, but I didn't somehow seem to take to them, because if ever I was down a little they always give me the fantods. Everybody was sorry she died, because she had laid out a lot more of these pictures to do, . . . But I reckoned that with her disposition she was having a better time in the graveyard.

—Huck Finn

As the case of Dombey illustrates, spurning the sentimental can be impelled by a foredoomed attempt to stake an exclusive claim to the masculine, if not the patriarchal, position—a claim that longs to be untainted by the feminine. A few decades later, on another continent, from his position as American boy-hero running away from Aunt Sally and sivilization, Huck Finn also repudiates sentimentality—but successfully, easily, even automatically. Huck's freedom to do so has been guaranteed, as it turns out, by the death of his voracious, overbearing, vicious father. Huck can raft down the river, he can elude the maternal hands of sivilization, he can light out for the Territory—Pap is dead, no one can touch him. On the other hand, when Huck is a girl—when, that is to say, the one growing up (or trying to refuse to) is feminine—she will stay untouchable (and survive her passage into heterosexuality) only if her father remains diligently present. And if her father is diligently present, there's no escaping adult heterosexuality. Stories about daughters who survive—and most especially stories about fathers' daughters—are inevitably stories about the passage from childhood to sexuality, about *starting* from the Territory (from Nature, the Old World, latency) and ending up in the stern domestic world of Aunt Sally.[1]

Perhaps the earliest American father-daughter story is *The Tempest*,[2] in which daughter Miranda's place is established in her first seven words. "If by your art, my dearest father . . ." (I.ii.1), begins this dutiful daughter of a father with unnatural powers over Nature. Her place, and Nature's, is in the hands of the patriarch-magician Prospero. If Miranda knows her place, she does not, however, know her genealogy—which is to say, she doesn't know who she is because she doesn't know her father's story. And now, at the (biologically significant) age of fifteen, she is about to find out:

> I have done nothing but in care of thee,
> Of thee my dear one, thee my daughter, who
> Art ignorant of what thou art, naught knowing
> Of whence *I* am, nor that I am more better
> Than Prospero, *master* of a full poor cell,
> And thy no greater father.
>
> (I.ii.16)

Miranda, being a good girl, has not indulged in untimely curiosity: "More to know, did never meddle with my thoughts." But now " 'Tis time," says Prospero, and he asks her to help him disrobe, transforming himself from magician to father. "Sit down," he says, "For thou must now *know farther*" (I.ii.21–22, 33).[3]

Prospero's tale of woe is marked, interestingly, by his anxiety about being listened to. At least eight times in less than a hundred lines, Prospero makes explicit his command of Miranda's attention—"Obey and be attentive," "Thou attend'st not?" and so on—marking the importance of what he has to say, exhibiting the autocratic nature of his relationship with Miranda, punctuating her unquestioning obedience to him, and, most important, revealing his strange suspicion that at this moment in her life, when it is "Time," she will somehow slip out of his power (out of his story).

Miranda's lineage is insistently patriarchal; her mother is mentioned only to be dismissed in one of the few witty remarks Prospero makes:

> *Miranda:*   Sir, are you not my father?
> *P:* Thy mother was a *piece* of virtue, and
> She said thou wast my daughter; and thy father
> Was Duke of Milan; and his only heir
> And princess, no worse issued.
>
> (I.ii.55–60)

If Miranda's lineage is patriarchal, her character is composed by her heavenly Father:

> *P:*   O, a cherubin
> Thou wast that did preserve me! Thou didst smile,
> Infusèd with a fortitude from heaven
>
> (I.ii.152–54)

and her temporal paternal pedagogue:

> *P:*   Now I arise.
> Sit still, and hear the last of our sea sorrow.
> Here in this island we arrived; and here
> Have I, thy schoolmaster, made thee more profit
> Than other princess' can, that have more time
> For vainer hours, and tutors not so careful
>
> (I.i.169–74)

Prospero's care, directed at preventing those idle hours, has produced a perfect daughter: sweet, submissive, virginal, and ready when the time comes for reckoning up exchange value to make *him* some profit.

Miranda is not alone; Prospero names and places Caliban too. Caliban, with his matrilineal claim to the island, never stands a chance against Prospero's colonizing incursion:

> This island's mine, by Sycorax my mother,
> Which thou tak'st from me. When thou cam'st first,
> Thou strok'st me . . .
>
>   and teach me how
> To name the bigger light, and how the less
> . . .
>   And then I loved thee
> And showed thee all the qualities o' th' isle,
> . . .
> Cursed be I that did so! . . .
> . . .
> For I am all the subject that you have,
> Which first was mine own king; and here you sty me
> In this hard rock, whiles you do keep from me
> The rest o' th' island
>
>   (I.ii.330ff.)

Where Caliban has apparently pursued his possession only so far as *use*—in the noble savage tradition—Prospero introduces language and succession to him as well, subjecting Caliban, as he has his daughter, to the discourse of the fathers. The one with the power to name is the one with the power to rule. And his pedagogical reign is founded in the first instance upon the love and loyalty of his students.

Miranda, like the island, is unpossessed and untilled. And like the island she is created and governed solely by Prospero. She will be the cause of her father's issue (her sons) being kings (of Naples *and* Milan) rather than merely dukes (or permanent exiles). As with the island (and Caliban), her accession to language (which is enacted as her willingness to learn it) initiates her availability to conquest; her acceptance of the patriarch's discourse means that she makes herself available to the system of exchange of which it is an integral part. She becomes, that is, instrumental in the patriarchal scheme of naming and genealogy, conquest and profit.

Ferdinand, heir to the throne of Naples, acknowledges her father's authority:

>   Let me live here ever!
> So rare a wond'red father and a wise
> Makes this place paradise.
>
>   (IV.i.122–24)

Prospero accepts this exemplary suitor, but anxiously hovers over the lovers, warning them against the incitements to intimacy the lush island constantly

offers. Prospero's anxiety about the young couple's chastity exceeds the
merely conventional for good reason: while his linguistic initiation of her
makes her vulnerable to masculine incursion, Prospero's re-placement in the
old patriarchal hierarchy depends upon Miranda's vendibility (solely determined by her status as virgin territory).

With Miranda's transfer from father to approved successor, Prospero's
power (his bargaining power, his supernatural power, his paternal power) is
safely spent, and wild, dangerous Nature is appeased; both father and daughter survive this orderly return to "sivilization." This sentimentalized good
daughter is taken back to Europe, whence she came, to the ordered society
that has always had a particular place for her in the hierarchy. Having reached
the age of nubility, she is safely introduced to language and to desire by her
father, graduating under the hand of her "schoolmaster" to a world far re-
moved from the island with its lusty green grass, its strange and wondrous
spirits and music, and the temptations presented by what Ferdinand calls "the
murkiest den, / The most opportune place, the strong'st suggestion / Our
worser genius can . . ." (IV.i.25–27). The Bad, Younger Brothers are likewise
hauled back to Europe and to their proper (subordinate) place in the social
order. But what happens when the Bad Brother goes west, abandoning the
Old World and its fathers? What happens when Daddy's Girl leaves the safety
of the Old World and comes—without Daddy—to the New? America's first
native father-daughter romance, Susanna Rowson's *Charlotte Temple: A
Tale of Truth,* poses these questions—to no good end for the Good Girl.[4]

In her preface Rowson defends herself against possible imputations of harboring active, writerly designs upon the literary canon, declaring that she
writes not for "the applause which might attend the most elegant, finished
piece of literature" but rather for the use of "the many daughters of Misfor-
tune who . . . are thrown on an unfeeling world without the least power to
defend themselves . . ." (36, 35). She wants, that is to say, to defeat the ma-
rauding son and his love posturings by supporting the father's claims to the
daughter, to advocate the paths of virtue as sentimentally encoded in the doctrine and duty of filial piety.

When we first meet Charlotte Temple, "the only pledge" of her parents'
"mutual love" (56), she is a student at Madame Du Pont's school. Through
the baleful manipulation of "the artful French woman" (61), Mademoiselle
La Rue, Charlotte falls into intercourse with Lieutenant Montraville. Her
first mistake—not immediately reporting his advances to her mother—leads
inevitably to the slippery slope which terminates in her fainting "into the arms
of her betrayer" (82), who has promised undying love and also marriage (as
soon as they get to the other side of the Atlantic). As imprudent as she is,
Charlotte is acting in good faith and in love. She is herself the product of a

romantic love match: her father and mother married, in fact, in the face of Mr. Temple's disinheritance by his own father. The novel is not, therefore, a crusade against romantic love per se. The female Temples are virtually indistinguishable sentimental heroines, but falling in love brings unmitigated disaster to only one of them. The didactic difference must then reside in their respective love stories.

As a young woman, Lucy Eldridge also receives inappropriate attentions from a young man. Unlike her daughter after her, she reports it to her parents. Her father receives an unsatisfactory answer to his inquiry into the young Lewis' attentions and forbids him the house. The vengeful Lewis calls in an I.O.U., and the bankrupt Mr. Eldridge is imprisoned.

But worse comes of these improper attentions appropriately reported to the proper authority: Lucy's brother, now the sole support of his family (a practical matter which doesn't, for some reason, seem to catch his attention), challenges Lewis, fights, loses, and dies in his sister's arms. Their mother dies shortly thereafter. Lucy goes to her father, who awakens from a three-week fever inquiring for the rest of his family. Mr. Eldridge tells the story to young Temple:

> "I was so weak as to be almost unable to speak. I pressed Lucy's hand, and looked earnestly round the apartment in search of another dear object.
> 'Where is your mother?' said I, faintly.
> "The poor girl could not answer: she shook her head in expressive silence; and throwing herself on the bed, folded her arms about me and burst into tears." (47)

Lucy throws herself into her mother's place in other ways as well. She spends every day at her father's side, supporting him through her sentimentally approved true woman talents for fine needlework and painting fan mounts. She refuses a place in a benevolent lady's family, asserting that she will never leave her father. This picture of perfect filial piety dressed in a plain white linen gown captivates Henry Temple. He mortgages part of his small income to rescue the father, and is rewarded by the "exquisite transport" of seeing "the expressive eyes of Lucy beaming at once with pleasure for her father's deliverance and gratitude for her deliverer" (50).

Lucy Eldridge's charms, the generic charms of the sentimental daughter, mark her as an object of desire for the honorable man and the "man of honor" alike. Her allure, innocently radiated and artlessly displayed, wreaks all kinds of havoc. The presence of his nubile daughter indirectly robs Mr. Eldridge of wife, son, home, and sustenance. What makes her a good woman, rather than a fallen one, however, is precisely her paternal monogamy. Her attachment to

Temple is never imagined as excluding her father from his place in her life; in fact, her father himself solicits Temple:

> "... I am a poor weak old man, and must expect in a few years to sink into silence and oblivion; but when I am gone, who will protect that fair bud of innocence from the blasts of adversity, or from the cruel hand of insult and dishonour?" (42)

As in *The Tempest,* an orderly succession is crucial. When the father is willing to acknowledge that he needs a successor, then and only then may the virtuous daughter of sentiment be bestowed on a paternally sanctioned suitor.

Charlotte's inexpiable sin is not so much the loss of her chastity as her betrayal of what she herself calls her "filial duty" (76). Her father is man enough to forgive her for her sexual indiscretion (she dies with the paternal blessing) and to rescue the newest addition to virtue in distress (he takes her infant daughter home to raise and cherish), but there is no place in the narrative for this kind of prodigal to return to the patriarchal hearth.

The westering son and the family patriarch, then, each lay claim to the daughter of sentiment. Where the patriarch dissolves conveniently for the likes of Huck (and his brothers Natty Bumppo and Dan'l Boone), the daughter of the New World, like the daughter of the Old, must remain faithful to her father—or suffer the dire consequences exemplified by Charlotte Temple's fall.

When we move from the world of *Charlotte Temple* to the world of *Little Women,* we move from a fictional world in which the daughter is somehow expected to be born good, to one in which the father actively instructs and guides the daughter's arrival at Good Womanhood. The daughter who takes the most time getting there, the one at the narrative center, is the awkward, thorny, difficult Jo, a tomboy who at the outset would certainly be right at home on Huck and Jim's raft. But Jo makes it to True Womanhood—and she not only gets there, she ends up *liking* it. And therein lies the book's long-lived appeal. *Little Women* could serve as a handbook for daughter composition: it illustrates the processes by which even the most disorderly of raw materials, the most unorganized of rough drafts, the most excessive of daughters, can be arranged, reduced to a manageable minimum, and settled into proper proportions.

When we first meet Jo, she seems unpromising material indeed:

> Fifteen-year-old Jo was very tall, thin, and brown, and reminded one of a colt, for she never seemed to know what to do with her long limbs, which were very much in her way. . . . Her long thick hair was her one beauty, but it was usually

bundled into a net, to be out of her way. Round shoulders had Jo, big hands and feet, a flyaway look to her clothes, and the uncomfortable appearance of a girl who was rapidly shooting up into a woman and didn't like it. (14)

But Jo does become a good daughter, and she gets her reward: love and approval, a husband, and a home of her own.

Little Women begins with the four March girls resolving to rid themselves of their chief faults in order to present four finished little women to Father when he returns from the war. Father sets them this task in a letter to their mother:

> I know they will remember all I said to them, that they will be loving children to you, will do their duty faithfully, fight their bosom enemies bravely, and conquer themselves so beautifully that when I come back to them I may be fonder and prouder than ever of my little women. (19)

Marmee duly seconds it: " 'Now, my little pilgrims, suppose you begin again, not in play, but in earnest, and see how far you can get before Father comes home' " (20). Jo's private response to this challenge, after she announces her intention to give up her roughness and wildness and restlessness, is that it is a much harder job than facing a rebel or two down south. But she tries hard, motivated by her desire to be loved and by her fear of love withdrawal. Her first experiment in self-control is a failure: after Amy burns the only copy of a manuscript Jo has been hoping will be "good enough to print" (91), Jo cannot forgive and forget fast enough to forestall disaster. Amy nearly drowns because, according to the narrator, Jo let the sun go down on her anger. The mishap serves to call forth Jo's deepest fear: " 'I'm afraid,' " she says to Marmee, " 'I *shall* do something dreadful some day, and spoil my life, and make everybody hate me' " (95).

Joe acquits herself with honor, however, during her next serious trial, Beth's illness, and earns the coveted fatherly praise. Upon his return from the war, he holds a domestic review of his troops. He notes that "son Jo" has mostly disappeared; she doesn't whistle, lie on the rug, or talk slang.

> "Her face is rather thin and pale just now, with watching and anxiety, but I like to look at it, for it has grown gentler, and her voice is lower; she doesn't bounce, but moves quietly, and takes care of a certain little person in a motherly way which delights me. I rather miss my wild girl, but if I get a strong, helpful, tenderhearted woman in her place, I shall feel quite satisfied." (250)

Jo's further journey toward fatherly approval through daughterly virtues can be traced in the fortunes of her writing career and aspirations. Her "scribbling" as she calls it started as a gift for Father, in the shape of the fairy tales Amy burned. Her next venture is a bit more fortunate: she is allowed to publish (gratis) her first Gothic tale in a local story paper. So Jo pursues this avenue and makes enough money to begin "to feel a power in the house, for by the magic of a pen, her 'rubbish' turned into comforts for them all" (302). Her success, she is sure, is due to her working for the money, for others, rather than for herself and fame.

"[R]esolved to make a bold stroke for fame and fortune" (303), her ambition grows; Jo's next project is a novel. She tries to ensure success by editing it to please *everybody* and ends by displeasing nearly everyone. She is aiming too high. Next comes her winter in New York, and her sensation story period. She writes progressively more lurid prose, and is saved just in time by the warning of Friedrich Bhaer.

Jo's quest for independence through writing is put on hold when she is called back home to nurse Beth through her lingering illness. Jo is chastened by Beth's death, not simply because of sorrow, but also because of her own helplessness. Her lessons in submissiveness are not over until she accepts— cheerfully—the dictates of her heavenly father, always with Father March's aid and counsel. A hard fate, to watch a beloved sister die, and the tragedy is compounded for Jo by the shape her duty takes after that death. She is assigned by her family to fill Beth's place, to settle into the dull round of home duties, "trying to make home as happy to them as they had to her" (480). She strives to do that duty cheerfully, to accept the shrunken horizons of her dream of doing "something splendid, no matter how hard. . . . [and] what could be harder for a restless, ambitious girl than to give up her own hopes, plans, and cheerfully live for others?" (480).

It is not grief that compels Jo's surrender to the demands of domestic self-abnegation, as Beth's final admonition to her sister makes clear:

> "You must take my place, Jo, and be everything to father and mother when I'm gone. They will turn to you—don't fail them; and if it's hard to work alone, remember that I don't forget you, and that you'll be happier in doing that, than writing splendid books, or seeing all the world; for love is the only thing that we can carry with us when we go, and it makes the end so easy." (513)

The sentimentality of Beth's death, over which generations of readers have (pleasurably, guiltily) cried, underscores the desirability of the dying daughter while it slyly adumbrates one possible consequence of extreme daughterly compliance to the father's demand for self-conquering. Compare the similar deaths of Little Nell and Little Eva: both resulting, in a sense, from impossibly perfect conformity to the patriarchal daughter of sentiment fiction; both, in another sense, allowing the reader a certain amount of comfort in her own failure to measure up to paternal desires.

Finally, broken by Beth's death, Jo pours her heart into a story—at her mother's suggestion—without thought of fame or money. Her father, not Jo, sends it to a magazine, which accepts it and asks for more of the same. It is at this point that Jo's composition is finally complete, and she graduates from striving, desiring daughter to accomplished, complacent "mother":

> So taught by love and sorrow, Jo wrote her little stories, and sent them away to make friends for themselves and her, finding it a very charitable world to such humble wanderers; for they were kindly welcomed, and sent home comfortable tokens to their mother, like dutiful children whom good fortune overtakes. (481)

The reward promised to the successfully composed daughter is a husband and happy home. Before her apprenticeship is quite over, Jo refuses Laurie's offer of marriage—to the undying ire of many readers to this day. But Jo understands what many of her adherents do not: Laurie would not make her happy; he is not the appropriate reward for the daughter course she's been enrolled in. He needs a lady, she tells him, " 'some lovely accomplished girl, who will adore you, and make a fine mistress for your fine home. I shouldn't. . . . you'd be ashamed of me . . . I shouldn't like elegant society and you would, and you'd hate my scribbling . . .' " (403).

Besides, Laurie is a boy; Friedrich Bhaer is a man of forty. Like the Princesse de Clèves, Jo rescripts romantic love. Her choice may not be what we initially expect from the heroine of a novel, but it certainly makes sense in Alcott's story.[5] Jo retains her ideal (or illusion) of independence, declaring that she marries as a full partner: " 'I'm to carry my share, Friedrich, and help to earn the home. Make up your mind to that, or I'll never go' " (531). She doesn't have to squeeze herself into the role of a lady; she will have a profession. And whereas spinsters must worship at the shrine of other people's children, Jo gets to have her own and to take over other people's children as well. Finally, Papa Bhaer is basically an avatar of Father March—both are bookish, admonitory men and both have played a role in composing this particular daughter; Jo promotes herself from student to "professorin" by refusing the boy and marrying the man.

What has made her marriageable, what has made her desirable, is what makes her indistingushable from her sisters in sentiment, Miranda and Charlotte Temple. She has offered herself to the father's teaching and has successfully conformed to the mandate of his letter. The transformation of the daughter's desire can be traced in the transformation of her relation to writing. Jo's first moneymaking sensation story belongs to the era of the daughter active in desire:

> . . . when the writing fit came on, she gave herself up to it with entire abandon, and led a blissful life, unconscious of want, care, or bad weather, while she sat safe and happy in an imaginary world, full of friends almost as real and dear to her as any in the flesh. Sleep forsook her eyes, meals stood untasted, day and night were all too short to enjoy the happiness which blessed her only at such times, and made these hours worth living, even if they bore no other fruit. The divine afflatus usually lasted a week or two, and then she emerged from her "vortex," hungry, sleepy, cross, or despondent. (298–99)

This kind of writing, with its vortex of jouissance, is precisely the unauthorized career that Professor Bhaer puts a stop to.[6] (And the narrative admonishes us to notice that Jo becomes wife material for Bhaer because "she stood the test, and he was satisfied . . . he knew that she had given up writing"; Jo's willingness to "profit by the reproof . . . lay[s] a foundantion for the sensation story of her own life" [395]). Not a divine wind but a mother's advice propels the production of Jo's "real" writing success—a domestic sentimental tale with a suspicious resemblance to *Little Women*:

> Jo never knew how it happened, but something got into that story that went straight to the hearts of those who read it. . . . For a small thing it was a great success, and Jo was more astonished than when her novel was commended and condemned all at once.
> "I don't understand it. What *can* there be in a simple little story like that to make people praise it so?" she said, quite bewildered.
> "There is truth in it, Jo. . . . You wrote with no thought of fame or money, and put your heart into it, my daughter; you have had the bitter, now comes the sweet. Do your best, and grow as happy as we are in your success."
> "If there *is* anything good or true in what I write, it isn't mine; I owe it all to you and Mother and to Beth," said Jo, more touched by her father's words than by any amount of praise from the world. (481–82)

Jo's relation to her text is now neither physical nor direct. She may have written it, but she can't read it: it is a measure of her successful daughter-indoctrination that she needs her father as much to tell her what she has said as to tell her that it is good.

Thin Ice

Two devils, as yet, I am not quite divine enough to vanquish—the
mother fiend and her daughter.

—Bronson Alcott

Little Women is most often read and remembered as a celebration of idealized
matriarchy and/or independent sisterhood; Father March's general absence
from center stage is taken to be equivalent to nonpresence in the story.[7] Consequently, when she finally accomplishes the transformation called for by her
father's letter, Jo is often seen as betraying her real self, and Alcott, the *real*
story of *Little Women*. In her introduction to the Modern Library edition of
the novel Madelon Bedell objects to Jo's fate in terms that echo such readings
of the book she calls "*the* American female myth" (xi); she sees Jo as sacrificing "both romance and independence in taking for a husband a man who is
her mentor" (xxiv). Patricia Meyer Spacks reports a similar response she and
her students had in reading the book together:

> But my students felt—rightly, I think—that this was something of a sell. Why,
> after all, shouldn't Jo have charming, rich Laurie? Why should she be subjected
> to a father figure? Would she really be as happy as the author claims? (12)

Nina Auerbach is not so much distressed by Bhaer ("Professor Bhaer, an edu-
cator, can make her a cosmic mother—the greatest power available in her
domestic world" [24]), as interested in what she considers the novel's inadequate explanation for Jo's rejection of Laurie.

What these responses and others like them have in common is their inclination to see the adolescent (pre-Bhaer) Jo as rebelling against the father, and
therefore, as being on the right track. Consequently, the adult Jo precipitates
discussions centering either on the betrayal of the "real" Jo or on what is
perceived as a now dated (in narrative and in real life) necessity: the implicit
assumption is that Jo's particular marriage wouldn't be at all necessary or
appealing if the story were written today. Bedell, for example, goes on to point
out that "if Jo must marry, what better choice than the professor" who is
"intellectually superior" to the indolent, though handsome and charming and
rich, young Lawrence (xxv). On the whole, however, Bedell sympathizes with
the "unease and dissatisfaction" of "the reader" who, as Cynthia Ozick
(quoted by Bedell) puts it, persists in identifying with " 'some Jo of the future.' " It is this Jo who justifies the " 'thousand, ten thousand times' " Ozick

(and probably Bedell's gen[d]eric reader) has read *Little Women* (xxiv–xxv)—the adolescent Jo, that is, who thus describes her "castle in the air":

> "I'd have a stable full of Arabian steeds, rooms piled with books, and I'd write out of a magic inkstand, so that my works should be as famous as Laurie's music. I want to do something splendid before I go into my castle—something heroic or wonderful that won't be forgotten after I'm dead. I don't know what, but I'm on the watch for it, and mean to astonish you all some day. I think I shall write books, and get rich and famous: that would suit me, so that is *my* favorite dream." (178)

But this wish list can't be read simply as a defiance of the father, as expressing the "real" Jo. Jo's dream is set over against Meg's, which centers on " 'a splendid, wise, good husband, and some angelic little children' " (177). In elaborating this version of her desire, Jo is not so much denying the father as expressing an aversion, in spite of her worship at Alcott's maternal shrine, to becoming her mother: Jo's means of defiance is rejection of the pattern set by her father's *big* woman. This distinction is difficult for many feminist readers to see, eager as we often are for our girl in the story to reject the father, if not patriarchy in general.

When Jo takes Beth's empty place for her own, she crosses the final threshold into womanhood:

> Then, sitting in Beth's little chair close beside him, Jo told her troubles. . . . She gave him entire confidence,—he gave her the help she needed, and both found consolation in the act; for the time had come when they could talk together not only as father and daughter, but as man and woman, able and glad to serve each other with mutual sympathy as well as mutual love. (532)

Jo is now truly Daddy's girl. But this is, of course, precisely the position for which Marmee has been training her. When Jo succumbs to her father's letter, she gives up all of her "son Jo" desires—writing, marrying Meg, traveling—to become even more than a little woman; she becomes a little marmee. She has learned to do so through an ingeniously coded process, one which we can begin to examine by rereading the filial pieties of *Little Women*.

An inquiry into the problematic position of the maternal might well begin with perhaps the most melodramatic scene in the novel: Jo March's "heart stand[s] still with fear"; "her voice [is] gone." Blue-eyed, golden-curled, artistic, baby-of-the-family Amy has crashed, her sister watching all the while, through the rotten river ice, and Jo can "only stand motionless, staring, with a terror-stricken face, at the little blue hood above the black water." This is the second time in this episode Jo stands silent and still: the first time she watches her sister skate out to the center of the river and does not relay Laurie's warning about the dangerous condition of the ice. Jo is angry at Amy, and the "little demon she was harboring said in her ear,—'No matter whether she heard or not, let her take care of herself' " (99).

Little Women valorizes the maternal and elevates the principles of domestic true womanhood to heights matched only, perhaps, by Harriet Beecher Stowe's apotheosis of maternity in *Uncle Tom's Cabin*.[8] The March household is everyone's favorite matriarchy, and Jo is the daughter destined for multiple motherhood and a matriarchy of her own. What has precipitated the astonishing spectacle of Louisa May Alcott's protagonist proposing to let someone smaller and weaker "take care of herself"? The smooth surface of this "children's" story would have it that Jo willfully " 'let the sun go down on her anger,' " causing her little sister's mishap.

The first clue we get that Jo's anger will be treated as culpable is its effect on the maternal nest: "It was not a happy evening; for, though they sewed as usual, while their mother read aloud from Bremer, Scott, or Edgeworth, something was wanting, and the sweet home-peace was disturbed" (97). When Jo confesses her sins to her mother, neither Marmee nor the narrative absolves her. Instead, her responsibility is taken for granted, and Marmee's comfort takes the form of admonishment and example:

> "Mother, if she *should* die [Marmee has just asserted that Amy won't even take cold], it would be my fault;" and Jo dropped down beside the bed, in a passion of penitent tears, telling all that had happened, bitterly condemning her hardness of heart, and sobbing out her gratitude for being spared the heavy punishment which might have come upon her. . . .
>
> "Watch and pray, dear; never get tired of trying; and never think it is impossible to conquer your fault," said Mrs. March. . . . "You think your temper is the worst in the world; but mine used to be just like it." (100–101)

A fault in the ice caused the accident; the accident is Jo's fault; Jo's fault is her temper. In addition to being a "moral weakness less serious than a vice," *Webster's* tells us that a fault is "a fracture in the earth's crust accompanied by a displacement of one side of the fracture with respect to the other." The fault line here is accompanied by a displacement of the familial harmony; the other side of that fracture is Jo's improper attempt to locate herself outside the maternal economy of the March household. This chapter, "Jo Meets Apollyon," starts with a quarrel between Jo and Amy. Little sister Amy wants to tag along on a trip to the theater with the two oldest girls and Laurie. Meg tries to talk Amy out of her desire; Jo responds like a bad mother. She speaks "sharply," "mortifying" Amy by telling her that " 'little

girls shouldn't ask questions' "; "impatiently" breaks in on Meg's attempt at
gentle dissuasion; and finally refuses "crossly, for she disliked the trouble of
overseeing a fidgety child, when she wanted to enjoy herself" (92–93). They
go without Amy, but the price of her victory is that Jo feels like a selfish,
guilty mother. Her pleasure in the play has "a drop of bitterness in it" as "the
queen's yellow curls reminded her of Amy," and she spends the intervals
between the acts wondering about Amy's threatened revenge. A rejected
child always knows exactly where to find its nearest rival: Amy burns the
only copy of Jo's nearly finished manuscript, "the loving work of several
years" and "the pride of her heart" (96).

Jo's twenty-four hours of anger hardly seem disproportionate to Amy's act.
But the narrative takes a disapproving stance; on balance, and considered
over against the "sweet home-peace," her reaction is excessive:

> It was only half a dozen little fairy tales, but Jo had worked over them patiently,
> putting her whole heart into her work, hoping to make something good enough
> to print. She had just copied them with great care, and had destroyed the old
> manuscript, so that Amy's bonfire had consumed the loving work of several
> years. It seemed a small loss to others, but to Jo it was a dreadful calamity, and
> she felt that it never could be made up to her. (91)

Well, yes. How could it be made up to her? But a whole series of more intrigu-
ing questions subtend this passage: How could this possibly seem "a small
loss to others"? What does it mean that the committed writer Louisa May
Alcott could use such a belittling description as "only . . . little fairy tales" for
poor Jo's "literary sprout"? Why does this episode set literary ambitions
against good mothering? Are good little women the ones who become their
mothers? Do they have to practice first by being "little mothers"? If good
daughters are supposed to be like their mothers, can writers ever be good
daughters? What does it mean that Jo shares Marmee's only character flaw? If
she replicates her mother, what then constitutes a good daughter's proper
relation to her father? What kind of father-daughter story is possible for an
aspiring "good daughter" who includes both mother and father in the legend
of good daughters?

This story written by an ambitious woman writer valorizes pleasing the
father (by being like mother) over being an ambitious woman writer. But
these values are neither presented nor enforced straightforwardly: in this instance Jo's writing is not prohibited by the father, it is destroyed by her sister,
and that destruction is trivialized—if not authorized—by both her mothers
(Marmee's position being seconded, as we have seen, by Alcott's narrative
voice). Issuing from the maternal position is the paternal lesson, distressingly

and paradoxically written and underwritten by the aspiring good daughter Alcott and her inspiring good mother Mrs. March: ambition, self-assertion, and the anger they inevitably produce in the context of familial proprieties will destroy your *real* desire, love and approval.

Thus the fault lines that riddle the shining surface of Alcott's story—individual ambition, authorial desire, self-authorizing fictions—are frozen in place only as long as Jo the aspiring writer stays voiceless and still, "near the shore" of the treacherous flow of familial love and desire. It is difficult for women to place in question our asserted community with someone like Alcott. We want her to rebel, reverse, reject. But in reading a story in which motives speak more loudly than actions, we must be willing to countenance the motivating assertions of the story itself. It is a temptation to read, as Madelon Bedell does in *The Alcotts*, the ice incident as a redaction of real-life sisterly jealousy and consequent guilt, but it is important not to stop there. The novel enacts, in its own twisty way, an allegory about the power of a writer's anger. Its solution is to eliminate the writing, and to punish Jo's desire to be something other than a little woman, a little mother, a mother's daughter. And the most elusive link in this sentimental narrative chain is that Jo (Alcott?) thinks she learns to want to be like Marmee for *Marmee*'s sake: " 'Oh, mother, if I'm ever half as good as you, I shall be satisfied,' cried Jo, much touched" (102). With the admonition to " 'go to God with all your little cares, and hopes, and sins, and sorrows, as freely and confidingly as you come to your mother,' " Marmee closes the evening conversation.

> Jo's only answer was to hold her mother close, and, in the silence which followed, the sincerest prayer she had ever prayed left her heart, without words; for in that sad, yet happy hour, she had learned not only the bitterness of remorse and despair, but the sweetness of self-denial and self-control; and, led by her mother's hand, she had drawn nearer to the Friend who welcomes every child with a love stronger than that of any father, tenderer than that of any mother. (104)

Even if a feminist revisionist reading could make this female bildungsroman come out "properly" (that is, as a celebration of maternal/sisterly community, albeit with a "flawed" ending), we'd still be up against the inevitable problem of the source of Marmee's discourse—the discourse which includes not only her motherly advice and love but also her silence. The anger she experiences " 'nearly every day of [her] life' " (101) is dammed behind her "folded" lips.[9] The dam is constructed by her teacher/husband, the Reverend March, who has made her an exemplary mother: " 'He helped and comforted me, and showed me that I must try to practise all the virtues I would have my little girls possess, for I was their example' " (102). And having taught her to want to be silent, Father continues the lesson whenever necessary by placing his finger over his lips to enjoin maternal forbearance, silence, endorsement (103).

Who's(e) Mother?

"Hope, and keep busy; and, whatever happens, remember that you never can be fatherless."

—Marmee

We employ sentimental narratives in order to avoid having to acknowledge certain adverse implications of the stories we like to tell. The sentimental strategy is not limited to novelists and television scriptwriters: readers and critics also adopt the essential sentimental strategy in order to elide problematic moments in our own "familial fictions." If we read from a feminist position, for example, we may hope that we can extirpate the father-daughter romance by cheering for the other side, but when we object to Jo's end and then read her relationship to Marmee as unproblematic, we reproduce the same elisions Alcott herself had to deploy. Feminist critical and theoretical inscriptions of mothers and of the maternal constitute the most important current versions of such sentimentalization—and they are enforced by the same implicit threats the father-daughter romance generates. Break ranks and lose love.

This is the implicit subtext, for example, of two of the articles in the "Feminist Issues in Literary Scholarship" number of *Tulsa Studies in Women's Literature*. Jane Marcus urges that we be unafraid of publicly criticizing our own, and then proceeds to follow her own advice. Speaking of certain "theoretical feminist criticisms" as refusing Virginia Woolf's call in "A Room of One's Own" to think back through our mothers, Marcus diagnoses their faults as stemming from choosing the wrong parent: "But these critics deny the authority of the female text. By taking father-guides to map the labyrinth of the female text, they deny the motherhood of the author of the text. . . . The critic takes a position which is daughter to the father, not daughter to the mother" (89). In "The Madwoman and Her Languges: Why I Don't Do Feminist Theory," Nina Baym takes this either/or choice up one level of abstraction: for her, choosing any kind of "theory" is choosing the wrong parent: "These grounding theories manifest more than indifference to women's writing; issuing from a patriarchal discourse, they exude misogyny. Mainly, feminist theorists excoriate their deviating sisters" (45).

If *Little Women* has anything to offer us beyond the pleasures of sentiment, it surely offers us the opportunity to interrogate the deceptiveness of such dichotomizing: we cannot always be confident of locating either a theoretically or an empirically clear distinction between patriarch and matriarch, father and mother, daddy's girl and mommy's girl. It is true that Jo's disapproved and destroyed book of fairy tales was intended to be a gift for her father, and that it represents a fearsome (and feared) potentially murderous power. And as an assertion of power and nonmaternal creativity, it is also Jo's difference from her mother. But Alcott's text, which sentimentalizes the mother, proscribes Jo's text, which inscribes daughterly difference. And that means, among other things, that in this female bildungsroman the prescription "Be your mother" is indistinguishable from the patriarchal "Be good for daddy." The question for feminist readers thus becomes: How far should *we* go to protect a version of the Mother which, after all, has been incited by, if not produced by, patriarchal discourse to begin with?[10]

Louisa May Alcott faced what she apparently perceived as just such a choice when she took up the task of editing her mother's journals for publication. She had to choose between the mother she had enshrined in the March novels, in *Transcendental Wild Oats,* and in her own diaries, and the Abbie May March evidently inscribed in the maternal journals. She chose the sentimentalized mother and burned the maternal text—it was, she said, too sad to read (Saxton 367, Stern 273).

It has become something of a truism in some feminisms to ascribe motherhood to certain texts. The danger in such a perspective is it occludes the certainty of the texuality of motherhood. In a section subtitled "The Mother," Nina Baym draws together the various threads of her *TSWL* essay. Baym chooses to speak from the position of the mother, a construct she grounds (theoretically) in "our rational moments," and (empirically) in her own experience (e.g., "we who have been mothers know"). It is her project to demonstrate that "mothers are demonstrably unlike the mothers of their theories" (55). The immediate grammatical referent of the possessive pronoun is "the patriarchal social world of Freud and Lacan," but feminists using any kind of nameable theory have been so thoroughly otherized at this point in the essay that it also applies to such diversely positioned people as Adrienne Rich, Sandra Gilbert, Susan Gubar, Mary Jacobus, Jane Gallop, Nancy Chodorow, Domna Stanton, Julia Kristeva, Hélène Cixous, or Luce Irigaray (all of whom are cited by Baym as being of the mother-betraying party).

Baym reads recent work on mothers and daughters to find deep-seated hostility of daughters toward mothers. She figures Bertha Mason as the victim of literary and theoretical matricides perpetrated by Gilbert and Gubar, by Jane Eyre, by Charlotte Brontë, and accuses the theoretically inclined

daughters of feminist literary criticism of harboring the same intentions toward their literary, academic, and "real" mothers. But her verdict that "feminists do not like their mothers" might well be reversed to ask how Baym likes
her daughters. Baym states that there "is no future for a commonality of
women if we cannot traverse the generations" (57), but failure to traverse the
generations is an insistent subtext of Baym's polemic against a whole genera-
tion of feminist critics and theorists. When she declares that "the family
model of daddy, mommy, and me, is inimical to the human future" (57), I am
moved to apply the observation to her essay's unstated model—daddy,
daughter, and me.

With her faith in the "real," and her evangelical distrust of the theoretical,
Baym very much resembles the author of *Little Women*. In our eagerness to
construct nonpatriarchal genealogies, to remember and even valorize our maternal roots, it is easy to replicate Alcott's gesture of reifying the patriarchal
ideal(ized) mother. But if Baym's essay is any guide, it would appear that
assertions of love and respect for the ("real") maternal do not guarantee that
"deviating sisters" will not be "excoriate[d]" any more than that Marmee
worship guarantees the preservation of the matriarchal nest.[11]

Sentimentalizing the mother is always already a patriarchal ploy—it
doesn't matter whether it's Alcott, Dickens, Baym, or I who do it. We've all
grown up in this discourse; we've all watched television, gone to the movies,
fallen in love, read *Little Women*. The sentimental is only a surface—often a
brittle one—even though, or precisely because, we conduct our most important business in the space thus conveniently suspended over flaws and fault
lines we prefer not to see.

Alcott's plots enlist in the service of the sentimental proprieties, but to be a
writer is to occupy the paternal (pedagogic, seductive, punitive) position, and
to write as a daughter is therefore to disrupt the proper hierarchies, to name
names, to give (and take) offense. Perhaps to make up for that improper sei-
zure of power, perhaps in order not to recognize it herself, Alcott's life, her
literary daughterhood(s), and her archetypal good daughters are all devoted
to disguising the defects of the father. And that gesture, as it turns out, also
justifies, if not makes palatable, the inevitable lifework of the mother—and
the mother's apprentice, the good daughter—of placating, pleasing, soliciting, and editing the patriarch. At the end of her story, Jo March Bhaer credits
her success to Marmee's teaching; the daughter now occupies the matriarchal
place as female center of her own and Marmee's families. That this happy
ending is fueled by active (therefore proscribed) daughterly desire, that it demands first the production and then the displacement of a mother equally
desired and betrayed by both the fathers and the daughters of patriarchal
discourse, that it consequently fails as either escape from or vengeance upon

those same fathers—these suspicions haunt feminist criticism and Alcott's writing alike.

To read the father-daughter romance as a question of misplaced parental loyalties is to miss, perhaps to reinforce, the always-disembodied source of the mother's voice. Alcott's sensation story "A Whisper in the Dark" figures this predicament. A typical Alcott Gothic in its mild flirtation with evil, its avaricious uncle-guardian, its too-confident heroine, Sybil's story ends "happily." She has escaped the advances of her avaricious uncle, been rescued by the strong arms of his son Guy, and deciphered the mystery of the whispered warnings of a fellow inmate (her dying mother, as it turns out) of the asylum in which she has been incarcerated. But the happy ending is haunted by the Gothic ghost of the mother who like her daugher was imprisoned by the patriarchal powers of her world, but properly so (she was in fact insane):

> Home received me, kind Madame welcomed me, Guy married me, and I was happy; but over all these years, serenely prosperous, still hangs for me the shadow of the past, still rises that dead image of my mother, still echoes that spectral whisper in the dark.

Making the Story Work

"If she had loved me it would have saved us both, for affection can win and hold me as nothing else has power to do. It has done much for me already, because, since I knew you, my darling, I have learned to repent and, for your sake, to atone, as far as may be, for my wasted life."
—"A Marble Woman: or, The Mysterious Model"

"Her art is wonderful; I feel yet cannot explain or detect it, except in the working of events which her hand seems to guide. She has brought sorrow and dissension into this hitherto happy family. We are all changed, and this girl has done it."
—"Behind a Mask, or, A Woman's Power"

As far as we have taken her, the daughter figure as inscribed in the bourgeois novel accepts her father's word as law and solicits its (his) approval only to learn that her approach to the father as word is always mediated by someone's body. The father-daughter romance of *Clarissa*, perpetrating and perpetuating itself through the death of the desired daughter, is mediated by the finally triumphant patriarchal version of the daughter's body (corpse and corpus);

Dombey and Son's dreadful father-daughter courtship remains active only while the paternal body is viable. And whatever they do for the fathers, neither the sad ending of *Charlotte Temple* nor the happy ending of *The Tempest* resolves the problem of the daughter's desire. Designed to exacerbate desire rather than to satisfy mere need, the sentimental daughter must remain provocatively passive, submissive, composed by the language and stories of the fathers. Daughters who would write, then, have a formidable and forbidding set of fictional prescriptions to contend with when they choose to write a version of the father-daughter romance. The writerly daughter reads her world and her father with perhaps too perceptive an eye and certainly too active a pen. She can't, therefore, cast herself as the daughter of whom the father she solicits will approve—without, in any event, some decidedly undaughterly intervention on her part.

The first of the quotations above is addressed to apprentice sculptor Cecilia Bazil Stein Yorke by her dying father; the second refers to Jean Muir, a governess whose "art" enables her to walk off with the elderly—and grateful—family patriarch, Sir John. Louisa May Alcott's anonymous and pseudonymous sensation stories, with their barely submerged authorial anger and explicit interest in sexuality, suggest hidden complexities in a writer sometimes dismissed as a good girl writer of good girl stories. These stories look at first glance very unlike those compendiums of bourgeois family pieties, *Little Women* and its descendants; in her "trashy" fiction Alcott toys with such middle-class titillations as drugs, daggers, dangerous women, and, often enough, the additional fillip of a scandalous reversal of proper gender hierarchies.[12]

It is precisely by manipulating filial pieties that Cecil Yorke and Jean Muir both step out of their places to teach their (paternal) superiors a lesson or two. Cecil is twelve when she arrives on the doorstep of her thirty-year-old guardian, a sculptor who becomes her "master" when he undertakes to teach her his art. The boy next door falls in love with her, but he cannot compete with the master, and Cecil and her guardian marry—a companionate marriage, to prevent scandal. In love with her cold and distant husband-in-name-only, Cecil contrives to put him through a series of object lessons in order to teach him that he does, in fact, love her passionately. In order to do so, she conducts a not very discreet *pas de deux* with a mysterious and attractive dark man (the "Mysterious Model" of the subtitle) who reveals, as he is dying, that he is her father, and that he and her husband had been rivals for her mother's affections. The happy ending has Cecil winning the love of the man her mother wanted (as well as reforming the husband—that is, Cecil's father—her mother could not save).

Governess Jean Muir, an obvious descendant (bend sinister) of Jane Eyre, is a mistress of illusion and improvisation. She uses braided hairpieces, rouged cheeks, several false teeth, and an array of artfully simulated true woman skills to seduce the susceptible, confound the wary, and marry the hale, hearty, fiftyish Sir John, to whom she defers "like a dutiful daughter" (47). Her powers resemble those of a writer of trashy stories: Jean improvises whatever scenarios she requires under the very noses of her victims.[13] She is perhaps both the most artful and the most successful of all Alcott's daughter figures. She not only marries the lord of the manor (having first captured and then abandoned both the cadet and the heir), she asks him for an advance guarantee of immunity and forgiveness. The paternal bridegroom replies "yes" to Jean's petition that he " 'be faithful to the last—to believe in me, to trust me, protect and love me, in spite of all misfortunes, faults, and follies' " (83).

With that "yes" Jean gets what all of Alcott's women—good girls and shady ladies alike—want: unconditional patriarchal love and approval. In *Work* (1873), Christie Devon tries her hand at every feminine vocation (but writing). But a job alone is neither sufficient nor sufficiently trustworthy, and Christie is driven to the brink of suicide by her inability to make a place for herself. She is rescued by a man: the relationship between Christie Devon and David Sterling, characterized by Christie's willingness to learn and serve and by Sterling's grave paternalism, provides Christie with the emotional and vocational home base for which she has been searching. Because of his avocation as rescuer of fallen and about-to-fall women, David is known as a "brother to girls"; Christie's relation to him requires a more intimate familial adjective: "He . . . bent a little as if he was moved to add a tenderer greeting. . . . the paternal expression unusually visible . . ." (259). Alcott, from her position as the daughter-who-writes, returned again and again to the attempt to invent a story in which the daughter's double desire—to be *and* to have (the object of desire)—might be figured. The heroines of such rather timidly transgressive stories as "A Marble Woman: or, The Mysterious Model," "A Whisper in the Dark," "Behind a Mask, or, A Woman's Power," and "The Abbot's Ghost, or, Maurice Treherne's Temptation" seek in one way or another to try their powers of self-assertion and self-inscription. When the heroine's arts are not strong enough—when, that is, her daring is exceeded by his evil, as in "A Whisper in the Dark"—she loses the father figure (though Sybil, her "little arts" having failed with her guardian-uncle, succeeds with his less powerful son). And when the desiring daughter succeeds in capturing the pursued father, her reward is a flawed one: a patriarch who can be manipulated by feminine arts is hardly worth the having, as the "pity and respect" with which the family of the newly married "deceived man," Sir John, implies ("Mask," 103).

A father who can be ruled by his daughter is not only no great prize, his incapacity as pedagogue disrupts heterosexual exchange. In *Moods* (1864), Alcott's first novel and a curious mixture of the sensational and the domestic plots, the motherless Sylvia Yule yearns for a "true friend" who can teach and guide her. She has been able to overmaster her ineffectual father, largely because he has failed to teach her to be a dutiful daughter. When she falls in love with a strong, silent, older man her willfulness helps precipitate a series of misunderstandings which results in her marriage to his best friend, another older man (fifteen years her senior) whom she does not love. Unable to learn to love him, Sylvia leaves her husband and returns to her father to whom she devotes herself in a successful effort to repair the flawed father-daughter relationship. There is no passing of this finally teachable daughter to the father's rightful successor: having achieved her filial apotheosis, Sylvia dies shortly after her father's demise.

Moods was reissued in 1882 with substantial revisions.[14] In this version, Alcott deleted the flirtation with endogamous domesticity, summarily dispatching Mr. Yule rather early in the story and reconciling Sylvia and her husband in the name of mature, adult, nonpassionate love (a love, in fact, very like that of Jo March and Professor Bhaer). Alcott's 1882 preface describes the novel as "an attempt to show the mistakes of a moody nature, guided by impulse, not principle" and explains that "the instinct and imagination of the girl" who wrote it were responsible for the fictional material therein. But in a November 1864 journal entry, Alcott had located the source of her story in " 'my own life and experiences and hope it may suit some and at least do no harm' " (Saxton 280). The revision of the novel may represent an attempt to deflect the kind of biographical reading *Moods*, republished by the author of *Little Women*, would inevitably attract. But her re-vision of the novel's impetus may point to a motive more fundamental than a desire for privacy (and the privacy issue is complicated anyway by the fact that the Alcotts' journals were open to any interested family reader). Abba Alcott's birthday gift for eleven-year-old Louisa was a new journal with this maternal inscription: " 'Remember, dear girl, that a diary should be an epitome of your life. May it be a record of pure thought and good actions, then you will be the precious child of your loving mother' " (Saxton 148). The Louisa May Alcott of 1882 may well have hoped and believed that her edited story more accurately represented the inner Louisa of 1864. In deleting the sensation story aspects of this hybrid novel, in disavowing her own connection with its transgressive elements, Alcott unwittingly makes clear the crucial similarities masked by generic labels. For all of Alcott's fiction, whether "family" or "sensation" texts, inscribe domestic (and domesticated) heterosexual relationships. Alcott's bad girls are supposed to be shocking, but their desire does not differ fundamentally from that of the good girls: in both cases domestic heterosex is inscribed as fundamentally paternal along the male axis; as filial, along the female. The sentimental wrapping makes the story decent by suggesting that the daughter is simply learning to be Daddy's Good Girl. But the sentimental alibi belies the amount of revisionary inscription the sensation story daughter (the desiring daughter, the active daughter, the daughter who writes) must perform—on the sly, quietly—in order to make the story work.

Louisa May Alcott chose neither children nor a home of her own, but thought she had a great longing for both. Alcott fully subscribed to the sentimental daughter text, but did not make the compositional choices it demands: she chose fame, (relative) independence, and a writing career, but she continued to believe that she really wanted the sentimental desiderata that reward her good girls (and her reformable bad ones). And while her heroines can arrive at the happy ending only by dis-placing the mother and re-placing her with the paternal rhetoric of desire that writes both mother and daughter, Alcott herself seems never to have given up the wish she inscribed in her mother's copy of *Moods:* "I hope success will sweeten me and make me what I long to become more than a great writer—a good daughter." A reading of Louisa May Alcott's life-text, suggests that, Jo-like, she hoped to retain some of her ambition even while paying much more than lip service to the sentimental daughter story. Her sanctioned versions of domestic love, in which filial pieties and respect for power are observed, invite us to take Alcott's "good daughter" wish as having been granted. But both the biographical and the fictional texts insistently reveal this as an eat-your-cake-and-have-it-too fantasy: success as a writer, even as a writer of and for daughters, does not make a good daughter—fathers do.

Skewed Confessions

"Which, namin' no names, no offense could be took."

—Sairy Gamp

Based on her often horrific experiences as a Civil War nurse, Alcott's *Hospital Sketches* could well have named names (for example, that of the nurse who coerced dying soldiers to name her their sole beneficiary). Yet it presents itself as resolutely upbeat, offering its reader gentle humor and quiet, heartrending deaths. But before we accuse it out of hand of rank hypocrisy, we should remember the supple multivocality of the sentimental strategy. The text itself tips us the wink: it takes as its epigraph (as I have, above) the cautious disclaimer of Charles Dickens' notorious dark-comic soother of brows and devourer of "cowcombers." Alcott probably learned from

Charles Dickens the trick of sentimentalizing the dangerous elements in the domestic fiction of hearth and home; she was a fervid admirer of Dickens' fiction from her early childhood, allusions to which predominate in her notably allusive corpus. These tend, like the Gamp epigraph, to evade yet name the dark side of Dickensian fictions. *Little Women,* for example, includes allusions to Dr. Blimber and Mr. Toots, a mordantly pedagogical configuration.[15] And when Jo laughingly declares that her guiding light will be "Prunes and prisms," the reader remembers that *Little Dorrit* is another father-daughter love story, one in which the dutiful daughter struggles valiantly to underwrite her father's largely pathetic pretensions to patriarchal, pedagogic authority.

Taking no offense, and giving none, was a particularly important stance for Alcott, but like the hints of the remarkably unsubtle Sairy, Alcott's allusions are sufficiently directional. These allusions to Dickensian pedagogues occur in a novel in which the father/husbands are teachers: Alcott's intertextual father-daughter network may be a web of indirection, but her writings name, insistently, one name.[16] *Little Women* is a fiction of feminine desirability as process and as processed. That March functions as both teacher and reward for Marmee (and that his virtual double, Papa Bhaer, does so for Jo) directs us to what the sentimentalized father-daughter dynamic is designed to disguise: the paternal, the pedagogic, and the erotic are coterminous. These authority-based and authorial relations—father/daughter, teacher/student, mentor/protégée—are erotic coverups.

What Charles Dickens inscribed as the ideal in his fiction, Bronson Alcott typically took to be an achievable literal goal. His methods should sound familiar to readers of such novels of the family as *Clarissa* and *Dombey and Son.* He trained his daughters by way of emotional pain, making frightening faces at baby Anna, for example, to make her start crying and stop pulling his hair (Saxton 73). Anna responded properly, but the young Louisa was not so amenable to paternal discipline. Consider his report of an early battle of wills: the three-year-old Louisa having acted out at table,

> I took her from the table, undressed her, and put her to bed, shutting the door of the bed-chamber, and leaving her to self-isolation, without the usual story or parting caress . . . I shall anticipate a suppleness of will to result from this; if not the same punishment, or similar, must be repeated till her obstinacy is effectually checked. (Saxton 90)

Louisa was expected not only to modify her behavior, but to welcome the demand to do so: " 'There is a self-corroding nature—a spirit not yet conformed to the conditions of enjoyment . . . She does not, I think, fully comprehend the object of punishment: she is awed into obedience by the fear of results not *love* of yielding' " (Saxton, 89).

This battle of wills was intimate, intense, unremitting—and paradigmatic. Whether we read it in Bronson Alcott's journals or in Richardson's, Dickens', or Alcott's novels, it resembles nothing so much as a true romance courtship, one which aims to train a daughter to solicit this kind of attention and to long for its particular rewards. Like her creator, the most resonant of Alcott's fictional daughters also begins by railing and rebelling against every aspect of her socialization into a "little" woman. In a revealing study of frequent and regular readers of contemporary romances, Janice Radway discovers reader preferences for plot and character marked by this same dynamic.[17] Her informants discriminated between "good" and "bad" romances, the former characterized by a tight organization around a single couple "composed of a beautiful, defiant, and sexually immature woman and a brooding, handsome man who is also curiously capable of soft, gentle gestures":

> the quality of the *ideal* romantic fantasy is directly dependent on the character of the heroine and the manner in which the hero treats her. The plot, of course, must always focus on a series of obstacles to the final declaration of love between the two principals. However, a good romance involves an unusually bright and determined woman and a man who is spectacularly masculine, but at the same time capable of remarkable empathy and tenderness. Although they enjoy the usual chronicle of misunderstandings and mistakes which inevitably leads to the heroine's belief that the hero intends to harm her, the Smithton readers prefer stories that combine a much-understated version of this continuing antagonism with a picture of a gradually developing love. (64)

Like the preferred Smithton heroine, Jo March is "sexually immature," clinging to the boyish behavior of the latency period; she is also "defiant," "bright and determined," and beset by a long series of obstacles. For the romance heroine, for Jo, and for Alcott herself, it is precisely the long process of rebellion, the intricate, mutually responsive steps of a courtship dance, which inevitably produces the "love of yielding" that her antagonist/suitor aims at. The Smithton heroine learns to overcome her initial hostility, learns that she has initially misread the hero's intentions, and learns how to love and submit to this dominant presence in her life. The erotic dynamic between the true romance hero and heroine is pedagogic—which is to say, paternal (and it includes enough of the "maternal" to suggest once again that analysis is better served by determining in whose service such qualities are enlisted than by valorizing them out of hand).

One of Bronson's Conversation topics was "Woman," and it is "Woman" he wants his own little women each to become: " 'I consider the ideal woman to be a person in whom the sentiments predominate over the intellect: the heart leading the head, the affections the reason . . .' " (Saxton 303). A dual transformation is directed/effected/policed by and inscribed/subtexted/eroticized in the fiction of the father-daughter romance: the daughter must learn to submit; she must also become a sentimental reader of the force that dominates. In the course of arranging for her "sentiments to predominate over the intellect," Louisa May Alcott was required to transmute certain base facts into gilded fictions; some of these can be found in *Little Women*.

Beth March's illness and death are quietly, nobly suffered in the peaceful center of a loving family; Jo's shirking a task assigned by her mother indirectly brings Beth into contact with the scarlet fever that weakens her heart irreparably. Lizzy, the Alcott sister who was Beth's real-life counterpart, also died tragically young. Abby, like Mrs. March, worked to earn money (unlike Mrs. March, when she worked she was the sole wage earner of the family). She sometimes brought her social work clients—poor, derelict, sick—into her home; one of these clients apparently brought contagion to the Alcott household. Elizabeth Alcott died messily, noisily, taking drugs and drinking alcohol and refusing to speak to her mother, whom she held responsible for her illness (Saxton 215). The fiction removes the mother from even indirect responsibility and installs her in her proper place at the bedside of the invalid. Reverend March, too old for the army, bravely volunteers for wartime chaplain duty, and is brought home valiantly recovering from a near-fatal illness; Jo sells her hair, her "one beauty," to contribute money (which is not spent) for his recovery. Louisa May Alcott, on the other hand, marched bravely off to war, leaving Father at the hearth; she was brought home to recover valiantly from a near-fatal illness (it—or the treatment for it—did finally kill her) which had as one of its side effects the loss of her one beauty, her long, chestnut hair. In this instance a complex sentimental transformation puts the daughter in her proper place at the home fires, the father in his proper place as the man of action, and the loss of beauty becomes a funny and touching sacrifice to filial piety rather than a slightly ridiculous but deeply symbolic wound. Finally, the autobiographical dimension of Jo's writing career is obvious—both Alcott and Jo start with "trash" and progress to sentiment. But in domesticating her improper, not to say impious, imagination, the fictional daughter becomes little more than a transcriber of domestic events; Bronson's daughter more nearly resembles a mythographer.

While the biographical echoes in much of Alcott's writing are flagrant, they are revisions rather than transcriptions of the family history, and therein lies the sentimental paradox for the family scribe. Take, for instance, her fictionalized (not to say allegorized) account of Bronson's ill-fated "utopian" community at Fruitlands, *Transcendental Wild Oats: A Chapter from an Unwritten Romance:* Alcott spoofs her father's utopian fads ("No teapot profaned that sacred stove, no gory steak cried aloud for vengeance from her chaste gridiron . . ." [38]), while valorizing his motives—

> Here Abel Lamb, with the devoutest faith in the high ideal which was to him a living truth, desired to plant a Paradise, where Beauty, Virtue, Justice, and Love might live happily together, without the possibility of a serpent entering in. (28–29)

—and minimizing the irresponsibility of a man who could not only transplant his entire young family to such circumstances but also be off rambling ("some call of the Oversoul wafted all the men away" [53]) when it came time to house the community's scant harvest. Her mother's acquiescence in the arrangement is attributed to good nature and wifely loyalty ("here his wife, unconverted but faithful to the end, hoped, after many wanderings over the face of the earth, to find rest for herself and a home for her children" [29]). Thus acquitting her parents of any culpability in this uncomfortable experiment, Louisa reserved her anathemas for the only other woman at Fruitlands: Jane Gage "was a stout lady of mature years, sentimental, amiable, and lazy. She wrote verses copiously, and had vague yearnings and graspings after the unknown which led her to believe herself fitted for a higher sphere than any she had yet adorned . . ." (46–47). In a wonderfully acrobatic narrative maneuver, Alcott's text fixes moral blame for the community's exploitation of the overworked "Mrs. Lamb's" labor solely on Miss Jane Gage:

> Sleep, food, and poetic musings were the desires of dear Jane's life, and she shirked all duties as clogs upon her spirit's wings. Any thought of lending a hand with the domestic drudgery never occurred to her; and when to the question, "Are there any beasts of burden on the place?" Mrs. Lamb answered, with a face that told its own tale, "Only one woman!" the buxom Jane took no shame to herself, but laughed at the joke, and let the stout-hearted sister tug on alone. (47)

What Alcott does here is typical of her texts and subtexts: her humor is both conservative (in effect it defends the domestic separation of the spheres) and displacing (the implied criticism of the men who set up this utopia is lost in the explicit criticism of the erring Miss Gage).

The writing daughter answers for the father; she lays filial hands upon him in order to transform him into the father she was trained to see when she looked at him. Alcott's literary relations with the figure of her own father are allusive, evasive, a deft quarter turn away from the biographical. Madeleine

Stern, groping for a metaphor to encompass both Alcott's often-proclaimed and acclaimed loyalty to her father and her assumption of the right to edit and revise him, figures Alcott's textual father as a kind of dilution of Bronson Alcott: "Father must be muffled, for the author realized that he would be atypical in a book on the American home. Father, with his vegetarianism, his fads, and his reforms, must be a shadow on the hillside hearth" (176). But neither the real father nor the fictional one is a "shadow"; precisely to the extent that the novel successfully solicits our reading March as a stand-in for Bronson, he is not only present but active, not only active but revised, not only revised but sentimentalized. Alcott's fiction retools him just enough to make her fairy tale father—they are not called Marches (*Märchen*) for nothing— both palatable as fantasy and recognizable as (auto)biography.

How much "farther" could she actually see, after all this training and investment? Charles Dickens, Alcott's father in fiction, was, like Bronson, a remarkably magnetic, physically attractive man. But after a lifetime of hero worship, Alcott could (she thought) see through the emperor's new clothes of her literary father:

> Miss Alcott writes this about Dickens, as he appeared at his readings: "At the first glance I received a shock, and my idol tumbled off the pedestal where I placed him long ago, when I wore his hair in a locket, and thought Shakespeare was an idiot beside him. I did not expect to see the handsome, foppish young man who once paid us a visit, and caricatured us so capitally afterward; but I did think some sign of genius would be visible—some glimpse of the genial creator of *Little Nell, Tom Pinch* and the *Cheerable* [*sic*] *Brothers* would certainly appear. Far from it; youth and comeliness were gone, but the foppishness remained; and the red faced man, with false teeth, and the voice of a worn out actor, had his scanty grey hair curled; a posy in his button-hole; diamond-ring, pin, and studs; a ruffled front, and wristbands *à la* 'Cousin Fenix.' "

Her former hero is now merely foppish, ruffled, and bejeweled—quite impotent, that is, to command the respect of an aspiring good daughter. The hatchet job performed on her erstwhile idol might equally have been turned on her father (similar things were in fact said of Bronson, see T. Beer), but Alcott very decisively chose denial as her approach to the father of her lifetext. Published several months before she began the novel that enshrined Reverend March as the fabulous father capable of both paternal dominance and maternal nurturance, the newspaper filler (reproduced above in its entirety) punctuates a shift in the rhetoric of Alcott's fiction: with the exception of *A Modern Mephistopheles* (1877), written for a series featuring anonymous thrillers by famous authors, Alcott wrote no more of her lurid fictions after the publication of *Little Women*.

Bronson Alcott died on March 4, 1888, at the age of eighty-eight; the daughter he once dubbed "Duty's faithful child," uncannily reprising the un-revised Sylvia Yule's story, died on March 6.[18] Dr. Cyrus Bartol, presiding over their joint funeral, assured the mourners that " '[a]s the young mother in classic story gave her breast to her famished sire in prison, so this daughter, such a support to her father on earth, was needed by him even in heaven' " (Saxton 374). However far she allowed herself to see through the fictions that created and sustained the fictions of her life and work, Alcott herself would probably have preferred the Euphrasia allusion as sentimentally embodied by Dickens' most lugubriously dutiful daughter: "Little Dorrit, though of the unheroic modern stock and mere English, did much more, in comforting her father's wasted heart upon her innocent breast, and turning it to a fountain of love and fidelity that never ran dry or waned through all his years of famine" (*Little Dorrit* 275). For whatever rhetorical trappings are chosen to disguise it, the legend of good daughters invariably nurses the plot of true romance, the plot of sentimental fiction, and the plot, above all, of heterosexual desire—plots constructed by and for the father, and all "nothing but in care of thee, Of thee my dear one, thee my daughter . . ." (I.ii.16–17).

"She couldn't say yes, but she didn't say no": The Daughter *Viva Voce*

And it is odd that, in the whole adventure of female sexuality as described by Freud, the father makes his appearance only at the end and in such a dim, secondary, even "passive" role. With no desires, no instincts, no dealings, of any kind, in regard to his daughter. Neutral and benevolent. But why?

—Luce Irigaray

On two occasions readers of *The Golden Bowl* witness a heterosexual embrace between people married, but not to each other. The first time, the Prince and Charlotte come together: "Their lips sought their lips, their pressure their response and their response their pressure; with a violence that had sighed itself the next moment to the longest and deepest of stillnesses they passionately sealed their pledge" (I 312). The second embrace seals a different kind of pledge. Maggie and her father have just formed their separation agreement. "His hands came out, and while her own took them he drew her to his breast and held her. He held her hard and kept her long, and she let herself go; but it was an embrace that, august and almost stern, produced for all its intimacy no revulsion and broke into no inconsequence of tears" (II 275).

The first embrace is easy enough to discuss, analyze, mythologize; it belongs to an old and prolific literary theme: adultery is the cornerstone of courtly love. And there is an even older tradition for the faint whisper of improper familial relations behind this same embrace of son(-in-law) and (step)mother. About the second embrace it is harder to speak. Affectionate fathers often play marital or sexual obstacles in their daughters' love stories: Lear's favorite daughter may marry, so long as she loves him best; James Harlowe wants his daughter to marry someone she dislikes; fairy tale father-kings assign impossible feats of valor to young suitors.

But Adam Verver plays an altogether different kind of obstacle: he allows his daughter to marry and he keeps her—literally and figuratively—too. Maggie Verver, "one of the beautiful, the most beautiful things" (I 11), answers to all the sentimental daughterly adjectives; she is "the dearest little creature in the world" (I 316), whose proper function is to pick up her stepmother's dropped domestic stitches—"homely work, but that was just what made it Maggie's" (I 319).[1] The most important love in her life is her father, and their relation—glossed, gilded, half submerged as it is in diminutive accolades—is the enigma which centers the novel. Henry James could, after all, have written a compact, geometrically perverse story of adultery, betrayal, and beautiful behavior without including a father-daughter pair. Had he intended merely to explore the particular perfidies and claustrophobic passions of four closely related people who have something to learn about love and passion, the Verver parts could have been played by a pair of friends, cousins, siblings, even mother and son. But he chose, surely not at random, to make the nonadulterous pair a widowed father and his devoted daughter.

The reader of James (especially of late James) always finds it her job to read the story that is not told. That James understood, even preferred, the impact of the story *behind* is axiomatic. In his preface to "The Altar of the Dead," he points to the way "the prodigies . . . keep all their character . . . by looming through some other history—the indispensable history of somebody's normal relation to something" (256).[2] We find the relevant prodigies by rereading, revising, reappropriating:

> To revise is to see, or to look over, again—which means in the case of a written thing neither more nor less than to re-read it. . . . the act of revision, the act of seeing it again, caused whatever I looked at on any page to flower before me as into the only terms that honourably expressed it. . . .
>
> What it would be really interesting, and I dare say admirably difficult, to go into would be the very history of this effect of experience; the history, in other words, of the growth of the immense array of terms, perceptional and expressional, that, after the fashion I have indicated, in sentence, passage and page, simply looked over the heads of the standing terms. . . . (Preface, *Golden Bowl* xvi–xvii)

While James is discussing his own revision of his collected works, the process he describes is particularly applicable to *The Golden Bowl,* a novel which itself centers on the act of reseeing. Shoshana Felman suggests that in our pursuit of "a reading's 'truth,' " we ask the question that Freud "taught us" to ask: "what does such 'truth' (or any 'truth') leave out? What is it *made to miss?* What does it have as its function to overlook? What, precisely, is its residue, the *remainder* it does not account for?" ("Turning," 117). Reading Maggie's story requires "perceptional and expressional" re-vision; it requires, too, attention to what the Freudian account of heterosexuality is made to miss.

The "indispensable history of somebody's normal relation to something" is the focus of the Irigaray essay from which I take my epigraph; it is an extended and brilliant excavation of the ways in which Freudian (and Lacanian) normalizing theoretical fictions attempt to finesse the irremediable, unspoken assymmetry between the sexes (and genders). Apropos of the task of examining other fictions, Irigaray calls for the "examination of the *operations of the 'grammar'* of each figure of discourse, its syntactic laws or requirements, its imaginary configurations, its metaphoric networks, and also, of course, what it does not articulate at the level of utterance: *its silences*" (*This Sex* 75). Maggie Verver is a representative of a particular figure of fictional discourse, the sentimental daughter; my project here is to articulate the silences enabled by that figure.

Marrying a parent is a favorite childhood story, and that Maggie and Adam are so "married" is consigned to the cute stuff of childhood by their fellow combatants—as well as by many of their other readers. But re-vision can locate the hidden dimension of the sentimental. We must not forget, as we consider the childlike qualities imputed to the Ververs, that children are often enough sentimentalized for the same reason filial relations are: to cover the sexuality we would rather not see. This kind of cover-up applies to stories and narratives wherever they are found—literature, movies, television, even the narratives implied by representations in advertising wherein the heterosexualization of suggestively dancing children is more or less hidden behind preinscribed sentimental views of them as innocent and prelapsarian.[3] The sentimental gloss offers terms with which to treat the forbidden desire it veils; the seduction of the diminutive lies in its surreptitious invitation to those who, like Maggie, can't say yes, but don't say no (II 251).

Read from this perspective, *The Golden Bowl* is the story of a possible (though relatively short-lived) love screening an impossible (and therefore undying) one; the participants in this familial saga of desire rely upon sentimental alibis to cover and justify their various passions. The sentimental trope, in turn, enables James to tell a more fundamental love story to those who would hear: the story that structures all hetereosexual relations of desire, the story which is built upon the unarticulated, unspeakable, and finally, perhaps, unknowable relation between the impassive desiring father and his acquiescent desirable daughter. If we can learn to resee James's story, it will be by learning to reread Maggie. If we can learn to reread Maggie, we can perhaps begin to answer Irigaray's question: why did Freud's theory of heterosexual desire require an undesiring, passive, "neutral and benevolent" father?

The Seduction of the Diminutive

The "deeply involved and immersed and more or less bleeding participants" James refers to in the preface (vi) share a version of Maggie: she is dear, sweet, good, innocent, and—the representative, summary adjective—little. Fanny and Bob Assingham's choral conversations are laced with the sentimental diminutive: she is " 'astonishing little Maggie,' " and a " 'dear little person' " (I 280–1). In the dialogue which ends Volume I, Fanny calls Maggie a " 'poor little dear,' " and a " 'passionate little daughter,' " who, with " 'her little scruples and her little lucidities' " and her " 'feverish little sense of justice' " lands in a nearly preposterous imbroglio. When Bob suggests that she will emerge " 'a little heroine,' " Fanny gives it back, " 'Rather— she's a little heroine' " (I 397).

The Prince, for his part, feeling rather outnumbered by "capitalists and bankers, retired men of business, illustrious collectors, American fathers-in-law, American fathers, little American daughters, little American wives" (I 293), patronizingly reflects that his wife has "in perfection her own little character," and that at fifty she will perhaps "suggest a little but a Cornelia in miniature" (I 322). Maggie herself accepts the general assessment quietly enough; she is "of a nature to accept with modest gratitude any better description of a felt truth than her little limits—terribly marked, she knew, in the direction of saying the right things—enabled her to make" (I 163). She is acquiescent to the point of abnegation; she has "no small self at all as against her husband or her father and only a weak and uncertain one as against her stepmother" (II 163).

The sentimental view of the daughter is extended to the paternal-filial relation. Paying a weekend visit with Charlotte, the Prince reflects on his wife and her husband "moping" at "monotonous Eaton Square":

> The knew . . . absolutely nothing on earth worth speaking of . . . and they would perhaps sometimes be a little less trying if they would only once and for all peacefully admit that knowledge wasn't one of their needs and that they were in fact constitutionally inaccessible to it. They were good children, bless their hearts, and the children of good children. . . . (I 333–34)

Charlotte also likens Maggie and her father to a pair of children:

> the two were doubtless making together a little party at home. But it was all
> right—so Charlotte also put it: there was nothing in the world they liked better
> than these snatched felicities, little parties, long talks, with "I'll come to you to-
> morrow," and "No, I'll come to *you*," make-believe renewals of their old life.
> They were fairly at times, the dear things, like children playing at paying visits,
> playing at "Mr. Thompson and Mrs. Fane," each hoping that the other would
> really stay to tea. (I 252)

This view of Maggie and Adam, like all sentimental stories of father-
daughter relations, is an interested one. Charlotte lays its foundation during
her reunion with the Prince, on the occasion of their Bloomsbury "prowl":

> "She's not selfish enough. There's nothing, absolutely, that one *need* do for her.
> She's so modest," she developed—"she doesn't miss things. I mean if you love
> her—or, rather, I should say, if she loves you. She lets it go. . . . She lets every-
> thing go but her own disposition to be kind to you. . . . And nobody . . . is
> decent enough, good enough, to stand it—not without help from religion, or
> something of that kind. Not without prayer and fasting—that is without taking
> great care. Certainly . . . such people as you and I are not. . . . We happen each, I
> think, to be of the kind that are easily spoiled." (I 101–2)

Charlotte and the Prince continue to build upon this foundation, developing a
belief that in their illicit transactions they take nothing from their spouses that
will be missed, and culminating in a jointly created conviction that they have
been driven into one another's arms by the too-trusting Ververs. This "exquisite sense of complicity" (I 335) reaches a crescendo at Matcham ("match
'em"?), where the Prince reads Maggie's trust as provocation:

> the innermost effect of all this perceptive ease was perhaps a strange final irrita-
> tion. He compared the lucid result with the extraordinary substitute for percep-
> tion that presided, in the bosom of his wife, at so contented a view of his conduct
> and course—a state of mind that was positively like a vicarious good con-
> science, cultivated ingeniously on his behalf, a perversity of pressure innocently
> persisted in. . . . it had taken poor Maggie to invent a way so extremely
> unusual—yet to which, none the less, it would be too absurd that he should
> merely lend himself. (I 333–35)

The sentimental reading of Maggie and of her relationship with her father
enables their less innocent spouses to justify their transgression as positively
provoked by the ease with which they are able to pull it off. And the reader,
perhaps, finds it difficult not to share in the Prince's exasperation: so much

passive perfection invites irritation. The Ververs' love for one another lends itself all too easily to a quick gloss as an intense version of a probably normal (and a bit boring) affection. This is how Fanny insists that Charlotte must take it:

> "Your husband doesn't treat you as of less importance to him than some other woman."
> "Ah don't talk to me of other women!" Fanny now overtly panted. "Do you call Mr. Verver's perfectly natural interest in his daughter—?"
> "The greatest affection of which he's capable?"—Charlotte took it up in all readiness. "I do distinctly—and in spite of my having done all I could think of to make him capable of a greater." (I 262)

Charlotte's reply summarizes the judgment generally pronounced upon this father-daughter affection, whether it is seen as innocent but regressive (Charlotte's strategic view), or as rather suspect (the suggestive view that makes Fanny pant). In either case, it is not quite mature, not quite grown-up. It is a lesser thing and certainly something to snap out of. And many readers conclude that Maggie has in fact done so by the end of the novel. Leon Edel's reading persuasively represents just this view: the Prince "wanted a wife," not "an immature, father-attached girl"; "James was writing, in this strange and heavily loaded symbolic drama, a story of the education of a princess, an American Princess."[4] Maggie learns that

> a revolution cannot restore the *status quo ante*. It was exactly this status that had ruined her marriage. By thinking she could live in a fool's paradise of perpetual daughterhood—that is, be a perpetual child—she had lost her husband. By acquiring her maturity, she recovers him. (215)

There are several difficulties raised by this kind of interpretation, which wants to read Maggie's story as that of a girl somehow "growing into" womanhood and her predestined adult role as wife to her husband. Assuming as it does that the novel is "about" achieving a normalized, heterosexual maturity, such a reading implies in the first place that Maggie's marriage is supposed to signal such an arrival. But the maturation model that grounds such a reading rests as well upon a mistaken equivalence. To be a "child" is not the same as to be a daughter. Nor is achieving adulthood a gender-neutral activity, as the myth of Oedipus, Western culture's fundamental growing-up-desiring story, unmistakably dramatizes. The oedipal riddle (both mythic and Freudian) is posed and resolved in the masculine gender. When Adam Verver confronts his own question so successfully (as it at first seems)—"It wasn't only moreover that the word, with a click, so fitted the riddle, but that the riddle, in such perfection, fitted the word" (I 208)—the answer, as we shall see, comes in the feminine. To read daughter as a neuter synonym for "child" is to overlook issues of gender, sexuality, and desire that are absolutely central to this novel.[5]

To read Maggie's story as that of a girl coming, however reluctantly (and reluctantly is the only way our sentimental stories will have her come), to mature womanhood through the son who displaces the father is to read complicitously with the alibis of heterosexual desire. The suggestion that Maggie's job is to relinquish a "fool's paradise of perpetual daughterhood"— leaving aside for the moment the question of whose genitive is being evoked—assumes a freedom of movement, of "growth" past the father, on the part of this daughter and of daughters in general that *The Golden Bowl* puts, precisely, most in question. When Maggie decides to make a difference in the geometry of her life, she works within the constraints of her established character, and she does so primarily for her father's benefit. What Edel calls Maggie's "revolution" is just another turn of the circle and she ends the story as she begins: her father's daughter, the daughter necessary to and implied by both the heterosexual ideology anatomized by Freud and the sentimental innocence encoded in any heroine like Maggie.

Where propriety rather than maturity centers a reading, we again often find innocence invoked. To use Edel as a representative reader once more, we find him approaching and then backing away from the question of literal incest between Maggie and Adam. Unlike the "adulterine" element of the novel,

> the other element in the plot, the "incestuous" element of father and daughter, did not constitute a difficulty. The Victorian daughter was expected to be devoted to the father; she was expected to sacrifice her own interests. . . . Maggie Verver had appeared earlier as Pansy Osmond; and Adam Verver as a whole generation of fathers. . . . There had always been triangles in James's life. . . . Strange fantasies, these, of triangular human relations, and they culminated, in this ultimate work of James's, in two joined triangles. . . . The implication of emotional "incest" is not as relevant in this work as the fact that in the situation everyone begins by having his cake and eating it. (210–12)

Edel is not alone in seeing and then turning away from the father-daughter tangle. It can be mentioned and gently dismissed as "emotional," following Edel, or as otherwise metaphorical. It can also be thematized as pathology, and less gently dismissed.[6]

Affixing such a theoretical label, whether to accept or deny it, functions in much the same way as the sentimental strategy itself. Even such an intendedly protean discourse as the Freudian heresy can become an orthodox label, one which obviates further analysis.[7] But *The Golden Bowl* is a novel about the unspeakable, in which not-naming takes preeminence, and structure means as much as, if not more than, event. That the father-daughter relation somehow engenders the plot is a matter of general agreement; its sustained presence throughout the novel then becomes the residue, the unaccountable, unaccounted-for remainder of the story's symmetrical divisions. The Bowl of Maggie's happiness breaks into three pieces; the omnipresent symmetry of the Verver menage's household might lead us to expect four. To take the father-daughter relation as a dynamic which persists thoughout the novel, which shapes as well as initiates the action, is to ask what happens to the fourth pair: there's Adam and Charlotte, Maggie and the Prince, Charlotte and the Prince, and a missing pair of adulterers. And the answer is neither simple, nor simply carnal.

Pre-Marital Relations

Maggie Verver's first love is the kind women grow up dreaming about. Her partner is good, kind, giving, and able and willing to gratify her wishes. There is no end to the available money; she lives surrounded by beautiful things. Their European travels, their "young adventures," were "wonderful times. . . . The way we've sat together late, ever so late, in foreign restaurants . . . the way that, in every city in Europe, we've stayed on and on, with our elbows on the table and most of the lights put out, to talk over the things he had that day seen or heard of. . . . There were places he took me to—you wouldn't believe!—" (II 343).

Her second love materially changes neither her life nor her father's. But her marrying the Prince has altered "the proportions" (I 167–68) in one sense: Adam is now faced with the unpleasant task of discouraging applicants for the position of wife. So Maggie and Adam convene in the garden, where they discuss the young woman who mothered her during her frightened schoolgirl period; who inspires, after her father and with her husband, the most intense devotion in Maggie's life; who is "so different a figure now from that early playmate of Maggie's as to whom he could almost recall from of old the definite occasions of his having paternally lumped the two children together in the recommendation that they shouldn't make too much noise nor eat too much jam" (I 193). Father and daughter decide, to adjust the proportions, that her father should "call in" his daughter's oldest and dearest friend, Charlotte Stant.

The pre-marital relations of Adam and Charlotte consist first in her demonstrating her ability to perform services Maggie has hitherto seen to. Maggie, before her marriage to Amerigo, kept husband hunters away from her father;

Charlotte clears out the formidable Mrs. Rance and her friends the Miss Lutches in much the same quiet manner as Maggie once had done. Having seen to Adam's security from domestic invasion, Charlotte next displays a (short-lived) facility for domestic entertainment. Maggie and the Prince go abroad leaving Adam and the Principino at Fawns in Charlotte's hands. Adam enjoys his sense of being "quite systematically, eased, and, as they said, 'done for' " by the charming and clever Charlotte who "by becoming for him a domestic resource, had become for him practically a new person." For the first and only time in the novel, Charlotte diminishes in scale, although she does not altogether shrink to Maggie's invariable "little." In Adam's eyes, in their "simplified existence," Charlotte "was directly and immediately real, real on a pleasantly reduced and intimate scale" (I 201).

Charlotte devotes her evenings, as well as her days, to Adam's pleasure; as he reclines on his shaded sofa, smoking "the cigars of his youth, rank with associations," she plays his favorite music "very much as if she might, slim, sinuous and strong, and with practised passion, have been playing lawn-tennis or endlessly and rhythmically waltzing" (I 202). Abetted by his luxurious sense of being tended by one who, like his son-in-law, possesses the secret of palpably placing him "high in the scale of importance" (I 205), this provocative vision opens Adam's question and the final phase of these premarital relations. Charlotte has accepted his invitation to accompany him on his Brighton treasure hunt, and this exchange coming at the close of one of their intimate evenings, Adam takes his accelerating agitation and another cigar out for a midnight stroll on the terrace. A "full word or two dropped into the still-stirring sea of other voices—a word or two that affected our friend even at the moment, and rather oddly, as louder and rounder than any previous sound" (I 203), initiates the unrest which convinces him "that he should never sleep again till something had come to him; some light, some idea, some mere happy word perhaps, that he had begun to want" (I 204).

Looking for the word which will cause "disparities to submit to fusion," Adam finds, persistently, his daughter in his line of vision. At first, this lights only his fear that "a new and intimate tie" will require him to "in a manner abandon, or at the least signally relegate, his daughter." Adam hesitates to "reduce to definite form the idea of his having incurred an injury" in his daughter's marriage. But neither does he want to "chill" her "absolutely unforced compunction" (I 206–7).

The light breaks for Adam when he realizes that he need not replace a daughter in order to restore symmetry, but simply add one. His choosing to marry again need not proclaim a gap; it can generate a surplus. Maggie's preeminence in his life will not be diminished by her father's taking on one who is her equal and contemporary, someone willing and able to supplement her daughterly services. Quite the contrary, Adam will continue to treat his daughter to the kinds of attentions she has come to expect from him. His marriage to Charlotte will keep his paternal affection free from the importunities of those who, as Mrs. Verver, would expect more than he is inclined to give.

The fugitive word Charlotte refers to, the word Adam wants, reveals itself "at a turn of his labyrinth" (I 207). His way out (his way in) is a daughter. The question and the answer come together: "He had seen that Charlotte could contribute—what he hadn't seen was what she could contribute *to*" (I 208). He will marry as a father: "the whole call of his future to him, as a father, would be in his so managing that Maggie would less and less appear to herself to have forsaken him" (I 207–8). He will put his daughter at peace by providing "for his future—that is for hers—by marriage, by a marriage as good, speaking proportionately, as hers had been." Once Adam has "simply settled this service to his daughter well before him as the proper direction of his young friend's leisure" (I 208), his agitation dissipates. To want to marry merely for himself is not possible. "But there was a grand difference in thinking of it for his child" (I 209).

Adam will marry as a father: "But why?"

The Screen Woman

In her germinal exploration of how one might read "in the feminine," Shoshana Felman locates a pivotal narrative use of the feminine in Balzac's "The Girl with the Golden Eyes." Henri de Marsay relies, in his rake's life, on a metonymic substitution of one woman for another:

> "The best kind of discretion . . . , consists of compromising a woman we're not keen on, or one we don't love or don't possess, in order to preserve the honor of the one we love sufficiently to respect her. The former is what I call the *screen-woman*." ("Rereading," 29)

Screens and screening are recurring plot devices in James's fictions (most notably, perhaps, in *The Sacred Fount*); *The Golden Bowl* offers several strata of lesser indiscretions intended to conceal greater ones. Charlotte offers herself as willing to screen Adam's paternal relation from outside incursion, to consent to be no more—even a good deal less—to him than Maggie is because she intends to use Maggie as a screen, invoking the sentimentalized paternal-filial affair to conceal (and justify) her own affair with her son-in-law. And, of course, the basic comic bourgeois plot (cuckolding the husband

of a May-December marriage) screens the tragic substructure invoked by the
father-daughter-son familial relations (the father/husband betrayed by the
daughter/wife—here, times two—with the husband/son). Peering behind yet
another screen we might also see the incestuous constellation that is particularly frightening, so Freud tells us, because it shields the young man's first,
fiercely repressed, desire for his own mother—Charlotte is, at least technically, Amerigo's mother-in-law.[8] Charlotte's prior relation to the Prince
screens the incestuous implications of her relation-by-marriage to him, and
their relationship in turn diverts close scrutiny of the father-daughter
relationship—an even more frightening constellation Freud could deal with
only by declaring it a daughter's fantasy with no basis in *real* fatherly activity:
"almost all my women patients told me that they had been seduced by their
father. I was driven [by what?] to recognize in the end that these reports were
untrue . . ." ("Femininity," 120).[9]

Power, desire, the familial, the heterosexual: throughout *The Golden
Bowl*'s commerce in these cultural artifacts James gives us enough data to
answer the question raised by any complex exchange—cui bono? The young
Italian adventurer? While it is true that he "possesses" both of Adam's
daughter-wives, it is also, and more importantly, true that the Prince usurps
use value only. Exchange value, the cornerstone of capitalist economic power
(and, pace Lévi-Strauss, of both culture and language), remains in Adam's
hands; he retains, after all, not only first refusal rights, but the ultimate loyalty
of both women. A re-vision of the gothic structure of the house that Adam
built points to that inveterate collector as first beneficiary of a policy in which
he figures as silent partner: he acquires a beautiful pliant wife and retains a
devoted dutiful daughter, all in the face of a double challenge from a splendid,
romantic, desirable young rival.

But how?

James's suggestion that *viva-voce* is the way to read the novel (preface xxiii)
amounts to an invitation to *hear* the unspoken story. Two words, and their
suggestive homonyms, reverberate throughout the narrative: gilt and know.
"Gilt" describes the flawed crystal of the golden bowl, as well as at least one
of its original discoverers:

> "As it is, for living with, you're a pure and perfect crystal. I give you my idea—I
> think you ought to have it—just as it has come to me." The Prince had taken the
> idea, in his way, for he was well accustomed by this time to taking; and nothing
> perhaps even could more have confirmed Mr. Verver's account of his surface
> than the manner in which these golden drops evenly flowed over it. They caught
> in no interstice, they gathered in no concavity; the uniform smoothness betrayed
> the dew but by showing for the moment a richer tone. (I 138)

The gilt/guilt pair amounts to a clever, occasionally prophetic, pun. The other pair is more complex.

The "know" which so echoes throughout the second volume (as it does throughout the James corpus) is first suggested by its homonym "no," prominent in the first volume, where the simple act of refusal is invested with an almost melodramatic intensity:

> He feared not only danger—he feared the idea of danger, or in other words feared, hauntedly, himself. It was above all as a symbol that Mrs. Rance actually rose before him—a symbol of the supreme effort that he should have sooner or later, as he felt, to make. This effort would be to say No—he lived in terror of having to. (I 133)

The Ververs, *père* and *fille,* have retained their familial passion through the simple expedient of Adam's refusal to "No." On the circumstantial level, Adam's distress at the prospect of having to say No to the likes of Mrs. Rance is the impetus behind his marriage. But that set of circumstances hardly justifies, by itself, an invocation of haunted fear and terror, particularly as Adam is quite certain he will say No to Mrs. Rance and her successors when he must. Looming behind the disinclination is the more essential one that has sustained the special configurations of the Verver household. Mr. Verver does not say No to the impoverished suitor, as he might have done in another story of a rich daughter falling in love with a charming penniless title, and thus his daughter is not required to choose between lover and father. Like Lear, Adam wants to retain the perquisites of his father's position while relinquishing the dirty work. Unlike Lear, he avoids the question—i.e., do you not love me best?—that would lose him (regardless of her answer) his dutiful daughter.

Adam's evasion of the father's No is largely responsible not only for the "great Palladian church" that is dropped into "their decent little old-time union, Maggie's and his own" (I 135), but also for the "outlandish pagoda" Maggie finds herself circling once she begins looking for the terms standing behind the outward forms of their lives (II 3).

> The pagoda in her blooming garden figured the arrangement—how otherwise was it to be named?—by which, so strikingly, she had been able to marry without breaking, as she liked to put it, with her past. She had surrendered herself to her husband without the shadow of a reserve or a condition and yet hadn't all the while given up her father by the least little inch. . . . What had moreover all the while enriched the whole aspect of success was that the latter's marriage had been no more measurably paid for than her own. . . . That it was remarkable they should have been able at once so to separate and so to keep together had never for a moment, from however far back, been equivocal to her; that it was

remarkable had in fact quite counted, at first and always, and for each of them equally, as part of their inspiration and their support. . . . they liked to think they had given their life this unusual extension and this liberal form, which many families, many couples, and still more many pairs of couples, wouldn't have found workable. (II 5–6)

The pagoda, then, is not simply the adultery; it represents, inclusively and inarticulately, "the arrangement" of these intertwined connections. The outside, the "great decorated surface" (II 4) presented to the world, is baroque, beautiful, inscrutable. Maggie's curiosity as to its inner contents is preceded by a loss of comfort in the sight of it and a reluctance to ask herself why she feels that loss. She has become aware that "the feeling that bound her to her husband" has "begun to vibrate with a violence that had some of the effect of a strain" (II 7). Her initial effort to dismiss the vibration as "the mere working of her own needs" (II 8) fails, and real knowledge comes to her at last. Her subsequent efforts are devoted to her attempts to hide the fact that she knows from her father, and to keep herself from having to know if he does, after all, know.

The word "know" ricochets throughout the second volume of the novel. Maggie finds herself for the first time in her life needing to know. Once she finds out, she lets Fanny know she knows. She lets her husband see that she knows, who in turn does not allow Charlotte to know that Maggie knows. And everyone's prime question is, does Adam know? Thus, with Amerigo:

> "Then does any one else know?"
>   It was as near as he could come to naming her father, and she kept him at that distance. . . .
>   . . . But she had to insist. "Find out for yourself!" (II 202–3)

And with Fanny:

> "So he knows—?"
>   But Maggie hung back. "Amerigo—?" After which, however, she blushed—to her companion's recognition.
>   "Your father. He knows what *you* know? I mean," Fanny faltered—"well, how much does he know? . . . What I should rather say is does he know how much?" . . .
>   Maggie had waited, but only with a question. "Do you think he does?"
>   "Know at least something? . . . He's beyond me," said Fanny Assingham.
>   "Then do you yourself know?" . . .
>   "I've told you before that I know absolutely nothing."
>   "Well—that's what *I* know," said the Princess.

Her friend again hesitated. "Then nobody knows—? I mean," Mrs. Assingham explained, "how much your father does."
Oh Maggie showed she understood. "Nobody." (II 334–35)

Maggie figures her discovery to herself as "the horror of finding evil seated
all at its ease where she had only dreamed of good; the horror of the thing
hideously *behind* . . ." (II 237). She thinks of allowing her father to see her
suspicions as the "hideous card" she can play "only on the forbidden issue of
sacrificing him; the issue so forbidden that it involved even a horror of finding
out if he would really have consented to be sacrificed" (II 107). The preoccupa-
tion of the guilty parties as to Adam's knowing is understandable. But why
should Maggie be so intensely concerned? Once again, the terms of her question seem melodramatic if measured only against an assessment of Maggie's
given "little" character. The "thing hideously behind" Maggie's
maneuvers—one of the things she doesn't know if her father knows—is not
her desire to get her *husband* out of Charlotte's clutches. That is never an
issue; from the moment Maggie knows, the Prince has to be of her party. The
filial sacrifice she needs to avoid is the loss of her place in her father's desire.
Hence her fear that her father might actually know: if he does, then she is the
only one who hasn't known, which would privilege Charlotte's place in her
father's life. If he knows, then it is "only the golden bowl as Maggie herself
knew it that had been broken. The breakage stood not for any wrought dis-
composure among the triumphant three—it stood merely for the dire defor-
mity of her attitude toward them" (II 240).

The confrontation between Adam's wife and his daughter on the veranda at
Fawns points to the hidden source of Maggie's deep distress. Charlotte leads
Maggie to a window and makes her watch the cardplayers inside. As she looks
at her father, wondering to whom he would direct his eyes first were he to
look up, she feels Charlotte's threat:

> Not yet since his marriage had Maggie so sharply and so formidably known her
> old possession of him as a thing divided and contested. She was looking at him
> by Charlotte's leave and under Charlotte's direction; quite in fact as if the par-
> ticular way she should look at him were prescribed to her; quite even as if she
> had been defied to look at him in any other. (II 244)

Charlotte's demonstration is made in her own interest; she is suggesting to
Maggie that she "must remain safe and Maggie must pay . . ." (II 245). But
what Charlotte doesn't know is that Maggie is fighting a different, an unnamed battle. In order that Charlotte may continue to be deceived as to the
stakes, Maggie adopts a policy of apparent submission. Thus, in the final scene

between the two in the garden we see Maggie winning the final battle by appearing to lose it. Charlotte "fairly agree[s] to take her then for the poor little person she was finding it so easy to appear" and simply proclaims victory:

> "I want," Charlotte said, "to have him at last a little to myself; I want, strange as it may seem to you"—and she gave it all its weight—"to keep the man I've married. And to do so I see I must act." (II 315)

Charlotte pretends, then, that her imminent return to the dreaded States is not an imposed banishment, but a planned triumph. Maggie, for her part, pretends that she has been defeated by her stepmother:

> "You want to take my father *from* me?"
> The sharp successful almost primitive wail in it made Charlotte turn, and this movement attested for the Princess the felicity of her deceit. . . . She was ready to lie again if her companion would but give her the opening.
> . . . "I want really to possess him," said Mrs. Verver. . . . Charlotte for another moment only looked at her; then broke into the words—Maggie had known they would come—of which she had pressed the spring. "How I see that you loathed our marriage!" . . . "How I see," [Charlotte] broke out, "that you've worked against me!" . . .
> . . . "You haven't worked against me?"
> Maggie took it and for a moment kept it. . . . "What does it matter—if I've failed?"
> "You recognise then that you've failed?" . . .
> Maggie waited . . . then she made up her mind. "I've failed!" she sounded out. . . . then she sank upon a seat. Yes, she had done all. (II 316–18)

The Golden Bowl's real tragedy *is* oedipal—but in the feminine: Charlotte is only apparently the center of the story of desire, only a screen. And behind the screen Adam makes of Charlotte stands the screen we make of the sentimental. The sentimental gloss enables us to divide and separate the father from his wish—and his "no" and his "*nom*"—so that we can continue to pretend that it all, somehow, just happens to work the way it does. Or to take refuge in the authorized view that it happens just the way the daughter wants it.

> In the period in which the main interest was directed to discovering infantile sexual traumas, almost all my women patients told me that they had been seduced by their father. I was driven [*by what?*] to recognize in the end that these reports were untrue and so came to understand that hysterical symptoms are derived from phantasies [*whose?*] and not from real occurrences. It was only later that I was able to recognize in this phantasy of being seduced by the father the expression of the typical Oedipus complex in women. And now we find the

phantasy of seduction once more in the pre-Oedipus prehistory of girls; but the
seducer is regularly the mother. Here, however, the phantasy touches the
ground of reality, for it was really the mother who by her activities over the
child's bodily hygiene inevitably stimulated, and perhaps even roused for the
first time, pleasurable sensations in her genitals. ("Femininity," 120)

Freud, archeologist of Western desire, can acknowledge a ubiquitous maternal seduction and its ground in reality. But any suggested ground in reality for
a paternal seduction undercuts the asserted daughterly origin of the father-
daughter "phantasy." Father must remain absolutely guiltless of real action;
the "seduction" must be seen as originating with her. And yet, leaving him out
of the account cannot mask his active role:

> The wish with which the girl turns to her father is no doubt originally the wish
> for the penis which her mother has refused her and which she now expects from
> her father. The feminine situation is only established, however, if the wish for a
> penis is replaced by one for a baby, if, that is, a baby takes the place of a penis in
> accordance with an ancient symbolic equivalence. ("Femininity," 128)[10]

Where is the subject occulted by the passive constructions "is . . . established"
and "is replaced"? Who was in charge of those ancient symbolic equivalences
anyway? What would make the girl assume her father would give her what he
had already refused her mother? Where on earth would the girl get all these
ideas to begin with? From the parent who literally touches in baths and dressing? Or from the parent who remains distant, touching her only metaphorically, with ideas and symbols and negations? The pertinent question to put to
the penis-wish/baby-wish progression is whose idea could it be to begin with?
Whom does she aim to please in manifesting such a wish? What is missing
from the account is the activity of the (passive, untouching) father—the activity, that is to say, of the culturally constructed and continously reinforced
place of the father. His place places her, and the figure of the daughter of
sentiment serves to reveal the question begged by the (in)famous "What does
woman want?"—which is, I submit, "Who told her she wants *that*?"

The Unspeaking Eye

Having remained conspicuously present in her life after Maggie's marriage,
Adam in the nursery continues to confirm his place as patriarch:

> It was of course an old story and a familiar idea that a beautiful baby could
> take its place as a new link between a wife and a husband, but Maggie and her

father had, with every ingenuity, converted the precious creature into a link between a mamma and a grandpapa. The Principino, for a chance spectator of this process, might have become, by an untoward stroke, a hapless half-orphan, with the place of immediate male parent swept bare and open to the nearest sympathy. (I 156)

The nearest sympathy being, of course, always and forever Daddy. When Maggie goes to the Principino's nursery at Fawns, "she either frequently found her father already established or was sooner or later joined by him. His visit to his grandson, at some hour or other, held its place, in his day, against all interventions . . ." (I 155).

In the Lacanian rereading of Freud's theory, the Name-of-the-Father (here we are, back to Adam's *nom*) is the notion we use when we are supposed to know the difference between an actual father and the prerogatives of his office:

> Whereas Freud's Oedipal Father might be taken for a real, biological father, Lacan's Name-of-the-Father operates explicitly in the register of language. The Name-of-the-Father: the patronym, patriarchal law, patrilineal identity, language as our inscription into patriarchy. The Name-of-the-Father is the fact of the attribution of paternity by law, by language. (Gallop, *Daughter's Seduction* 47)

But among its many other uncanny revelations, *The Golden Bowl* anticipates a "discovery" of the critical fictions of modernity: as much gets done in the so-called feminine spaces of the unspoken as in the realm of the actually said.[11]

In *This Sex Which Is Not One*, Luce Irigaray quotes Lacan's characteristic remark: " 'Women don't know what they are saying, that's the whole difference between them and me.' " Irigaray's response pervades her discourse: she doesn't say what she knows, and the not-saying is palpable enough to be heard by others who know what they can't say; Irigaray talks *through* the (patriarchal) philosophers *to* women. James also anticipates this method of getting around the limitations of a patriarchal epistemology: *not* saying what you know, allowing thereby an eavesdropper or an onlooker on tiptoe a way into your unspoken discourse, a way of seeing, as he says in the preface to this novel, the "growth of the immense array of terms . . . that . . . in sentence, passage and page, simply [look] over the heads of the standing terms. . . ."[12] But Maggie's story goes farther and sees more: those same feminine spaces are already also colonized by the father's *nom*.

Adam Verver is the father who will not say No, who will not verbally invoke the law. Who does not (will not) know, either in the biblical sense his very name incites us to notice (his marriage to Charlotte has no issue and we're not talking about literal incest between father and daughter), or in the mundane sense of agreeing to recognize his role in the arrangement which serves him so well. His daughter has no name but his: "the Princess—*il n'y avait pas a dire*—might sit where she liked: she would still always in that house be irremediably Maggie Verver" (I 323). Her son has, to an onlooker's eye, no patronymic. The younger and the older married couple pair and re-pair in violation of all received notions of prohibition and proper order. Tech-nically innocent of *any* action, Adam's original choice—to keep his daughter by not saying No—precipitates what comes. Refusal is an act, and in the father-daughter dynamic, the most powerful paternal act of all, as it puts in play what Jane Gallop has called the "veiled seduction" of the father's law (*Daughter's Seduction* 70). But refusal to know—like the refusal to say no— is simply a convenient fiction for the one who is exercising the will power: the cards are stacked so that the father benefits no matter how he plays them. He doesn't have to say a word, he can be as passive (as "feminine") as he chooses, as is necessary to his desire to disclaim any responsibility for his desire and its consequences. His option remains open as long as he can count on the senti-mental daughter, the daughter who has been taught that she wants what he wants—her to want.

Adam Verver benefits from the veiled seduction of the law by his apparent refusal to exert it. The punishment he metes out to his disobliging screen daughter Charlotte is similarly veiled. We see Charlotte suffer the effects of his displeasure; we can't see him inflict it on her. Despite the "long silken halter looped round her beautiful neck" (II 287), despite her anguished contempla-tion of "her doom, the awful place over there" (II 288), her sweet, mild hus-band resembles all the while nothing more vengeful than a shuttlecock "weav-ing his spell" (II 290). How, then, does he reward his acquiescent daughter?

Inconspicuously. Impassively. Silently. From a screened position. He appar-ently does the handsome thing and leaves his daughter, putting the Atlantic Ocean between them. But distance incites: the father who resigns his immedi-ate privilege will gain by that gesture as by all his others. In his 1907 introduc-tion to the Renaissance Edition of *The Tempest* (a play which exhibits some interesting parallels to *The Golden Bowl*), James devotes most of his attention to the immense power over our imaginations exerted by Shakespeare's resign-ing his pen at the height of his powers. While there are moments, he says, when he is willing to simply "let it pass as a mystery. . . . there are others when, speaking for myself, its power to torment us intellectually seems scarcely to be borne. . . . The figured tapestry, the long arras that hides him, is always there, with its immensity of surface and its proportionate underside" (306). The extent to which Shakespeare the man is absolutely untouchable measures the extent to which James the enraptured dreams "of the finer weapon, the sharper point, the stronger arm, the more extended lunge" (310):

> The man himself, in the Plays, we directly touch, to my consciousness, positively nowhere: we are dealing too perpetually with the artist, the monster and magician of a thousand masks, not one of which we feel him drop long enough to gratify with the breath of the interval that strained attention in us which would be yet, so quickened, ready to become deeper still. . . . The man everywhere, in Shakespeare's work, is so efffectually locked up and imprisoned in the artist that we but hover at the base of thick walls for a sense of him. . . ." (300)

Henry James the reader here recalls Maggie the reader circling the base of her family's impenetrable pagoda. James understood the authority and the seduction of silence and withdrawal; his suggestion in the preface that *viva-voce* is the only way to read this story verges on just such a Shakespearean tease, urging his reader toward her own dreams of the finer weapon, the more extended lunge. How can the reader give voice to a story which is about the unsayable?

In the world of *The Golden Bowl*, in spite of its figured tapestry of tropes and *trompes*, much less can be said than can be seen. The Prince's "quintessential wink," for example, the "something unnameable" that comes out for Fanny "in his look" that she will not allow herself to receive (I 271). Or the wordless exchange between Maggie and Adam on the subject of Charlotte's penance (II 292). There are other matters that must be suppressed even more sternly. Maggie puts the Prince on notice that she will not speak of her father (II 346–47), but even not speaking is not sufficient. Wordless communication must also be censored; in their last scene together on the balcony, Maggie understands that as between herself and her father, "reality" can never be an issue: ". . . it would have torn them to pieces, if they had so much as suffered its suppressed relations to peep out of their eyes" (II 362). When her father departs, Maggie returns to the balcony "to follow with her eyes her father's departure," to see only "the great grey space" of his leaving (II 366). Alone at last, her husband declaring, "I see nothing but you" (II 369), Adam's daughter wills herself to stop seeing. Having devoted her eyes to seeing for and seeing after her father, having embodied his no(m) by refusing to have her say, she bequeaths her eyes, the site of desiring, to him. The sentimental daughter's say can only be silent acquiescence and cooperative blindness—a voluntary (so they tell her) surrender of her gaze to her father.

The fourth pair—the other adultery—is thus successfully occulted by the "passive" resistance of the outwardly acquiescent daughter. Maggie's discovery precipitates the breakup by striking the flaw in the familial bowl covered by the gilded abilis of sentimentality: symmetry of desire as between father and daughter is not, never was, must not be spoken; its omnipresent solicitation must remain immanent. Her solution is simple and brilliant: if the fourth relation is to be protected in its place just beyond discourse, another kind of symmetry must screen it. By remaining within her own little character, by maintaining her place—for the eyes of her beholders—as the sentimental daughter, Maggie has worked it so that Adam's family can retain the proprieties of a factitious symmetry: when Charlotte and Adam leave, all parties to the original, doomed arrangement will be deprived of someone they hold dear.

For Maggie Verver, who has penetrated the screens of desire long enough to salvage them, it is time to rest. She is left with her bought (her sold) husband, an absent father about whom she cannot speak, and a need for the expiating blindness she has earned as a modern sister of Oedipus. The conclusion of her drama does not call for the cathartic physical mutilation the hero of the disruptive masculine oedipal myth must undergo; neither does her story's portion include the dignity of tragic closure. For Maggie, as for all daughters, the symbolic mutilation, her figurative and "voluntary" blindness, functions not as the threat which compels proper development, but normatively and simply as the beginning and as the end of desire:

> He tried, too clearly, to please her—to meet her in her own way; but with the result only that, close to her, her face kept before him, his hands holding her shoulders, his whole act enclosing her, he presently echoed: " 'See'? I see nothing but *you*." And the truth of it had with this force after a moment so strangely lighted his eyes that as for pity and dread of them she buried her own in his breast.

In *The Golden Bowl*, Henry James becomes the poet to whom Sigmund Freud commended his (male) audience when he washed his own hands of the riddle of femininity. The familial bowl is unspeakably flawed. James's tale of father and daughter screens the heart of heterosexuality; our sentimental gilt covers up the fault line of the crystalline dream upon which the whole work— of fiction, of theory, of heterosexual desire—is balanced, off-center, and (one can only hope) teetering.[13] The dream of symmetry requires us to be blind to its flaw: the dream of symmetry, the social construction that is heterosexuality, depends upon the continued production of the daughter of sentiment. She becomes the blind spot. She is taught—by her "benevolent" father, by the "neutral" fathers—that she does so willingly. Thus Maggie. Thus: " 'I'm interested in the kind of man who lets me think I'm running the show, but is really in control,' " says a twenty-six-year-old career woman, an Esprit sales representative—and she thinks *she* thought of wanting that.

5

What She Gets for Saying Yes: O

Men and women exchange feelings that are not equivalent.

—Claudine Hermann

Man fucks woman; subject verb object.

—Catharine MacKinnon

From its two beginnings to its two endings, *Story of O* sustains the tone and diction of a fairy tale. The first beginning speaks in the historical present: "Her lover one day takes O for a walk in a section of the city where they never go—the Montsouris Park, the Monceau Park"(3). O and her lover are thus placed in the timeless space of story and myth, and introduced as they enter a territory they have never yet explored. The second beginning is more brusque, occurring at some unspecified but specific time in history: "Another version of the same beginning was simpler and more direct: the young woman, dressed in the same way, was driven by her lover and an unknown friend" (5). In the first beginning, a car which "resembles a taxi" (it features imitation leather seats and window shades) appears "where there are never any taxis" and the two get in, to be driven to an unnamed destination by the silent driver. This quasi-magical transportation becomes more mundane in the second beginning: the "unknown friend" does the driving and the talking (5), the vehicle is just a car. The two beginnings merge upon O's arrival at the chateau, where she stands alone, blindfolded, in a dark room "for half an hour, or an hour, or two hours, I can't be sure, but it seemed forever" (6). This is the last time the storyteller's "I" appears; the other (third-person) narrative voice now takes over.

The highlights of O's first twenty-four hours at the chateau include a costume contrived to make her available to casual sexual use, two prolonged

96

beatings at the hands of strangers, a dozen or so genital violations of one kind and another, and a long speech which concludes with the assertion that the floggings, the violations, the humiliations "are intended less to make you suffer, scream, or shed tears than to make you feel, *through* this suffering, that you are not free but fettered, and to teach you that you are totally dedicated to something outside yourself" (17). O is terrified by the torture, terrified, too, to discover that she can still say "I love you" to her lover when he orders her to do so in the presence of her abusers. She is nonetheless determined that "if torture was the price she had to pay to keep her lover's love, then she only hoped he was pleased that she had endured it." And so, chained to the wall of her cell, the morning after her introduction to Roissy, "soft and silent she waited, waited for them to bring her back to him" (27).

Pornography, fairy tale: two very different kinds of bedtime stories. "Pauline Réage's" text, like her heroine, is provocatively open to a variety of appetites. Common to nearly all attempts to read Réage's text is a suspicion that it is not mere garden-variety pornography. *Story of O* lends itself primarily to readings which position O as an extreme representative of a psychological or mystical position, as an allegory of the Western "soul" (represented as usual by a feminine character, and glossed, equally usually, as "neuter," which is to say "masculine"). An allegorical reading is one which can explain as generic, as Angus Fletcher points out, departures from mimesis in an otherwise representational text:

> Allegory, it might seem, is usually at home with reversals and discoveries, with changes of character from love to hate and hate to love; but these are by no means probable natural changes; they are always imposed changes, like the metamorphosis of thieves in the "Inferno" or the quasi-medical changes of victims in Hawthorne's *Tales*. When an arbitrary conversion occurs at the end of an action, we must ask if that is not the moment when mimesis gives way to allegory. . . . Allegory is structured according to ritualistic necessity, as opposed to probability, and for that reason its basic forms differ from mimetic plots in being less diverse and more simple in contour. (Fletcher 150)

An allegorical reading of a text, then, is a reading which reaches outside of the terms of the text in order to explain textual activity. André Pieyre de Mandiargues, for example, reads O as an allegory of the modern soul turning, through rejection of the body and of the self, to its post-faith consolation and the vocabulary and attitudes of an earlier, punishment-obsessed religion. Against this religious allegorizing, Susan Sontag argues that *Story of O* is indeed an "erotic book," and uses O as an occasion to articulate the relation between the vocabulary of the sacred and the vocabulary of the pornographic. The artist, the erotomane, the left revolutionary, the madman, says Sontag, "have chronically borrowed the prestige of the religious vocabulary" (69). In this reading, that eros is a " 'sacrament' is not the 'truth' behind the literal (erotic) sense of the book" (68), but a "metaphor for it" (69). All of which amounts to a secular allegorizing.

The most compelling version of this stance is Leo Bersani's reading, wherein O's story is seen as an attempt to dismember the coherent, unitary notion of the individual subject that justifies and perpetuates our most conservative, even repressive, political and psychological theories. His discussion of *Story of O* is built upon an analysis of desire which takes as its cornerstone the Lacanian formulation of a nonunitary subject desperately nostalgic for a fictional-linguistic version of the self. Bersani analyzes O's situation as part of a human dynamic centering on attraction toward and revulsion against eros, which produces, or at least mimes, a dangerous and attractive loss of self. People try to have it both ways by placing someone else in the position of self-loser; the one in control participates essentially as voyeur; the one in the object position is helped to lose the self, a project that cannot be attempted individually without disastrous, or at least unsatisfactory, results. Bersani's elegant analysis maps *Story of O* as an allegory of human desire. But Bersani's reading does not take into account the gendered hierarchies of *O*: the one in control is male, and the one whose self is dismembered—presumably to the satisfaction and release of all involved—is female.

A similar analysis is offered by Jessica Benjamin, with the important addition that her discussion centers on the gender assignments such a version of desire inevitably (in our culture, at least) dictates. Benjamin reads *O* as a transcription of what she has astutely called a "fantasy of rational violence." She traces the origin of the fantasy to early infancy, with the "yearning for and denial of mutual recognition" (144) from the mother. The gender difference in erotic roles begins in the characteristic approaches to differentiation taken by each sex: the traditional female roles overemphasizing relinquishing of the self; the traditional male roles overemphasizing "self boundaries" (146). Building upon what she calls Bataille's "discovery of the Hegelian dialectic in eroticism" (153), Benjamin suggests that the traditional male position of making the female an object is based upon the boy's experience of needing to assert his self-boundaries as against the mother, and that the traditional female role of feeling herself a passive object is based upon the girl's tendency to "experience her continuity" by "merging with the mother" (154). Western heterosexual desire is inscribed in and by the nuclear family, and Benjamin's reading attempts to take account of the familial element in desire. Benjamin's project is different from mine: she is attempting to find the psychological data which account for sadomasochism as a "voluntary sexual practice" and for the prevalence of the "fantasy of erotic domination [which] permeates all sexual imagery in our culture" (144). She reads *O* as not so much a text as a valuable piece of clinical data: she applies psychological theories to the novel rather than reading the novel's representations of them. However the heterosexual desire depicted in the novel would be grounded if it were recorded in case histories, that is to say, it seems to me that the reader of *O* must reckon with the fantasy of the father-daughter relation before (instead of) tracing it to O's (unwritten) pre-oedipal history. And to the extent that O enjoys becoming a passive object, she thinks of herself as becoming continuous with the desire of the patriarchal Sir Stephen rather than a maternal, or even a feminine object. Like Bersani's essay, Benjamin's analysis of rational violence is a valuable explication of certain sexual ideologies in our culture, but *Story of O* tells a certain story about the operation of desire which both of these approaches miss in the course of explications which end by reducing *O* to something like a modern psychological allegory of human desire.

In my reading of *Story of O*, I hope to avoid the allegorical temptation; in my view, *O* provides the necessary terms through which to read it. I want to read the relational positions and shifts represented in and by the gendered, familial hierarchies of desire in this text. Throughout this study I have been suggesting that the daughter has been an insufficiently (or inaccurately) theorized nuclear family member, and that a careful reading of the figure of narrative discourse that I have called the daughter of sentiment may begin to account for the daughter as the component of heterosexual desire otherwise left unspoken for. As I pointed out in the Introduction, the daughter of sentiment occupies a unique place in our representations of sexual difference: she is not split into the implicit or explicit polarities with which we otherwise manage the anxiety provoked by difference; she remains whole or she is not a daughter. In the face of the paradoxical requirement that to be desirable she must be both dutiful and unpossessed, our stories of heterosexual desire have produced a version of the desirable daughter who can't say yes but doesn't say no. The result, of course, is that the one who controls the discourse enjoys endless titillation at her expense, which is, I contend, the whole point of the exercise—of stories of fathers and daughters, of stories of heterosexual desire, perhaps even of the novel itself (the reader, like the father, enjoys a seduction for which she need take no responsibility, and also, like the daughter, responds to a desire that is not her own). Although it dispenses with the sexual indirection of its predecessors, it reproduces this dynamic; *Story of O* is, consequently, more legatee than black sheep to its testament. Like the other novels I have discussed, O's story narrates her efforts to please the patriarchal powers of her world. Unlike the other novels, *O* includes the daughter's prepatriarchal history; "Pauline Réage's" text, with its heroine who starts her career by saying no and ends up saying yes (endlessly), reveals what is at stake in sentimental/heterosexual designs on the daughter.

But we have left O hanging.

When her lover finally appears "dressed the way he used to when he had just gotten out of bed and lighted the first cigarette of the day" (28), he is accompanied by another man who "uses" (in the vocabulary of this text) O with René's assistance and then leaves. The next morning René continues O's education by addressing his attentions to another woman in O's presence. After all she has endured, this is the act that drives O to despair.

> O saw. . . . What pleasure was she giving him, yes she, that this girl or any other could not?
> "That hadn't occurred to you?" he added.
> No, that had not occurred to her. She had collapsed against the wall, between the two doors, her arms hanging limp. There was no longer any need to tell her to keep quiet. How could she have spoken? (34–35)

René responds to O's collapse by taking her in his arms and telling her over and over that he loves her. The phrase has the effect of a mantra: "The despair which had overwhelmed her slowly ebbed: he loved her, ah he loved her. . . . He did not leave until he saw that her eyes were clear and her expression calm, contented" (35). Object lessons followed by a moral—the pattern very much resembles the educational process Jo March undergoes in *Little Women*. And both heroines are willing (if not always able) students for the sake of the same reward: when René describes in all its brutal detail what is in store for her both at the chateau and in her life thereafter, "O listened and trembled with happiness, because he loved her, all acquiescent she trembled" (32).

When O's two weeks at Roissy are up, René takes her back to Paris, where the next stage of her training is to take place. O is expected to generalize from the initial training context to her ordinary life; she need not, that is, think she is free just because her surroundings are no longer gothic:

> With one exception, and that was that she was free not to love him any longer, and to leave him immediately. But if she did love him, then she was in no wise free. She listened to him without saying a word, thinking how happy she was that he wanted to prove to himself—it mattered little how—that she belonged to him. . . . (56)

Not long after their return to Paris, René initiates the second major phase of O's erotic conditioning. In the bar of a little Italian restaurant, René introduces her to "a sort of grizzled athlete," the English Sir Stephen H. Sir Stephen

and René are brothers of sorts, related through another loose woman—
René's mother had been married to Sir Stephen's father—and Sir Stephen is
careful to emphasize their respective places in the family hierarchy: " 'If we
are brothers, I am the eldest, ten years older than he' " (73). It doesn't take O
long to recognize the traces of mimetic desire: René "loved Sir Stephen in that
passionate way boys love their elders. . . . Sir Stephen was René's master, without René's being fully aware of it, which is to say that René admired him and
wanted to emulate him, to compete with him, and this was why he was sharing everything with him, and this was why he had given O to him . . ." (90).[1]

Like Paul Dombey, Sir Stephen is aloof, impassive, disdainful. He is unlike
the others at Roissy: O "loathed Sir Stephen for the self control he was display-
ing" (82). He demands obedience of her, but not the kind she's been fobbing
off on the boy René: " 'You're confusing love and obedience. You'll obey me
without loving me, and without my loving you' " (88). At the moment of this
declaration, O has already suffered outrageous physical treatment at Sir Stephen's hands, but it is only in response to this lordly proclamation that O feels
"a strange inexplicable storm of revolt rising within her . . ." (89). O silently
proposes combat:

> she had no intention of being quickly tamed, and by the time she was he might
> have learned to love her a little. For all her inner resistance, and the timid refusal
> she dared to display, had one object and one object alone: she wanted to exist for
> Sir Stephen, in however modest a way, in the same way she existed for René, and
> wanted him to feel something more than desire for her. (89–90)

Clearly, mere physical desire offers O no power at all: she has already had the
physical interchangeability of women graphically demonstrated to her at
Roissy. At first, O tells herself that she is determined to make Sir Stephen love
her in order to guarantee that René's emulation of Sir Stephen will not cause
his love for her to be contaminated by the latter's more contemptuous attitude. Attuned to the triangular nature of masculine desire ("she sensed that he
was ready, if need be, to sacrifice her to any and all of Sir Stephen's whims, in
an effort to satisfy him. She knew with an infallible intuition that René would
follow Sir Stephen's example and emulate his attitude"), O astutely infers that
the younger man "would probably go on loving her insofar as Sir Stephen
deemed that she was worth the trouble and would love her himself" (90). But
by the time O's training by Sir Stephen is virtually complete, René no longer
loves her and O doesn't care:

> But then, what was René compared to Sir Stephen? Ropes of straw, anchors of
> cork, paper chains: these were the real symbols of the bonds with which he had

held her, and which he had been so quick to sever. . . . how peaceful and reassuring the hand of a master who lays you on a bed of rock, the love of a master who knows how to take what he loves ruthlessly, without pity. And O said to herself that, in the final analysis, with René she had been an apprentice to love, she had loved him only to learn how to give herself, enslaved and surfeited, to Sir Stephen. (187)

It is to make him love her that O acquiesces to Sir Stephen's mastery in the first place; this is a battle that O "wins." But in the history of romantic love this particular victory has always been a defeat for the woman.

Compulsory Heterosexuality and Courtly Love

Once upon a time, there was a woman named O, an independent young career woman who worked "in the fashion department of a photography agency" (62). Indifferent and fickle, she enjoys "tempting, by a word or gesture, the boys" who are enamored of her. She knows what their desire is because she too pursues it: her desire for "her girl friends, or for young strangers, girls she encountered by chance" is actually "nothing more than the thirst for conquest." But the stakes change for O when she meets René: "In the space of a week she learned fear, but certainty; anguish, but happiness. René threw himself at her like a pirate at his prisoner, and she reveled in her captivity . . ." (94). As long as it has been a question of desire, or sexual conquest, alone, O (like Sir Stephen) has remained an active subject. But for two years before *Story of O* begins, she is being steadily subordinated to the status of object. The ideology that Adrienne Rich has called "compulsory heterosexuality" ("for women heterosexuality may not be a 'preference' at all but something that has had to be imposed, managed, organized, propagandized, and maintained by force' (156) has intervened in O's story with its most effective stratagem, romantic love:

> This was true to such a degree that when René relaxed his grip upon her—or when she imagined he had—when he seemed distracted, when he left her in a mood which she took to be indifference or let some time go by without seeing her or replying to her letters and she assumed that he no longer cared to see her and was on the verge of ceasing to love her, then everything was choked and smothered within her. (94–95)

The passivity and submission O strives for produce the essential vulnerability which defines the daughter of sentiment. It is illuminating to compare O as an object of desire, as a potential site of transgression, with her literary grandmother, Florence Dombey. Recall Florence's longing for her father's love, her willingness to abase herself over and over again on the chance that he'll accept her offering of herself, her willingness to hide herself in his dark and decaying house, her willingness to assume the victim's posture. As Florence is motivated by an unshakable faith in her culture's fiction of domestic love, so O is motivated by an equally touching faith in the fiction of romantic love. O longs to give her lover what no other woman can, and that desideratum turns out to be identical to that required of the Victorian dutiful daughter: self-abnegation in the service of patriarchal needs and desires. At Roissy, O is told that her suffering is meant to demonstrate "that you are not free but fettered, and to teach you that you are totally dedicated to something outside yourself" (17). Where the twentieth-century text conceives this process as something consciously imposed from without, Florence was conceived with this dedication intact. This same total dedication, rejected by her father, is at last accepted by Florence's soon-to-be-husband, Walter Gay; she tells him, " 'I am nothing any more that is not you. I have no earthly hope any more that is not you. I have nothing dear to me any more that is not you' " (813). But at the novel's close Walter has given her back to her father. In both narratives, a young man, loved by the heroine, gives way to an older, authoritative, forbidding father figure whom she must learn to please and placate—without the benefit of his deigning to offer explicit instruction or encouragement on her path to perfect submission.

O's ordeal, like Florence's, trains her to conform to a prescribed ideal. When we first meet O, she is dressed according to her own taste, in jacket, pleated skirt, formal gloves. As her training progresses, she evolves slowly from an independent career woman to a passive possession, dressing in " '[v]ery little girl-like' " (63) clothes which emphasize her infantilization and vulnerability to violation. Losing herself "in a delirious absence from herself which restored her to love" (39), O constitutes herself Florence Dombey's direct descendant. Like Florence yearning for her father, O longs for love from Sir Stephen: "She wanted him to love her, there, the truth was out . . ." (82). And this truth is out too: the "bliss repressed beneath the stereotype" of each of these emblems of daughterly desirability is the same; the indirection of the Victorian—and possibly much of the sly titillation—has simply been replaced by more modern tastes in transgression. Ultimately both O and Florence succeed in inferring and giving the patriarch what he wants: O's gift is an object of desire (herself as owl) so completely dehumanized that what she finally amounts to is the mere space of desire—or, perhaps more accurately, her gift is a voluntary absenting of herself and a cessation of insistence on sexual relation; in Florence's case, the gift is only nominally less scabrous—a healthy male namesake is finally presented to the father by the daughter he violated.

The curiously mobile narrative voice of "A Girl in Love" (sometimes "I," sometimes "she," sometimes simply nineteenth-century omniscient) tells us that *Story of O* is a love letter, intended for her then-lover, a young man under thirty (this essay appears in *Story of O: Part II*, see p. 105, below). She describes the genesis of one character after another: René is "the vestige of an adolescent love" (13); Jacqueline, a composite of a schoolgirl crush and an actress acquaintance; Anne-Marie, a partial portrait of a good friend's character. As for Sir Stephen, he is both less known and more familiar; he is based upon a fifty-year-old Englishman, pointed out to the narrator in a bar by her lover:

> As for Sir Stephen, I saw him, literally, in the flesh. . . . silent, self-composed, with that air of some gray-eyed prince that fascinates both men and women—he pointed him out to me and said: "I don't understand why women don't prefer men like him to boys under thirty." At the time he was under thirty. I didn't respond. But they do prefer them. . . . this silent unilateral rapport between him and my companion, between him and me, reappeared out of the blue ten years later, in the middle of the night pierced by the light of my table lamp, and the hand on the paper brought him back to life with a new meaning even quicker than reflection. (15)

Like *Clarissa, Dombey and Son, Little Women,* and *The Golden Bowl, Story of O* is a love story—romantic, patriarchal, heterosexual. With its vague period costumes, chateau (complete with dungeon), and secret fraternity of caped men, it recalls the beginnings of Western romantic love. Leslie Fiedler might be describing O's behavior: "the service of love, beginning with an abject surrender of the will to an arbitrary lady, passes readily into an abysmal sort of masochism, and ends with the appearance of certain symptoms which would nowadays be taken to indicate a breakdown . . ." (49–50). But somewhere between Courtly Love and *Story of O*, the daughter takes the place of the gentle, humble, obedient, abject supplicant for love; the father, his place as the unfathomable, capricious, powerful, Mistress (the seeds of this "reversal" were already there, as Fiedler points out, in the custom of referring to the lady as " '*midons*,' not 'my lady' but, literally, 'my lord' " [49]). The abject humility professed by the lover before his mistress was, of course, "pretended" in a world "where, by law and custom, women were disposed of at the will of their fathers and husbands . . ." (Fiedler 48–49). *Story of O* dispenses with the gender-hierarchy fiction of courtly love, but the central pretense of that tradition remains. Courtly love, in Jacques Lacan's words, is

> an altogether refined way of making up for the absence of sexual relation by pretending that it is we who put an obstacle to it. . . . For the man, whose lady

was entirely, in the most servile sense of the term, his female subject, courtly love is the only way of coming off elegantly from the absence of sexual relation. ("*Jouissance,*" 141)

When O names her own desire as wanting "to exist for Sir Stephen," she has found the center of the paradox of heterosexual desire: O's progression from independent subject to object of desire to art object marks the extent to which any possibility of sexual relation is absent. She agrees to become the woman[2] who will consent not to be there, where his desire is:

> And yet nothing had been such a comfort to her as the silence, unless it was the chains. The chains and the silence, which should have bound her deep within herself, which should have smothered her, strangled her, on the contrary freed her from herself. What would have become of her if she had been granted the right to speak and the freedom of her hands, if she had been free to make a choice, when her lover prostituted her before his own eyes? True, she did speak as she was being tortured, but can moans and cries be classed as words? Besides, they often stilled her by gagging. Beneath the gazes, beneath the hands, beneath the sexes that defiled her, the whips that rent her, she lost herself in a delirious absence from herself which restored her to love and, perhaps, brought her to the edge of death. She was anyone, anyone at all, any one of the other girls. . . . (39)

O-10

There is a sequel to *Story of O*, published in France in 1969 and in the States in 1971. It is difficult to know what to call this text. The original French title, *Retour à Roissy*, becomes, on the cover of the Grove Press Black Cat edition, *Story of O: Part II*. The title page's version of a name offers more information about the book's genealogy, with *Return To The Chateau: Story of O: Part II preceded by A Girl In Love*. The "Return to the Chateau" text was included in the manuscript Jean-Jacques Pauvert accepted for publication in 1954. Jean Paulhan asserts that when he wrote "Happiness in Slavery" (appended as a preface to *Story of O*), he had read and responded to the entire manuscript:

> Meanwhile, as promised, I had written the preface to the novel, a preface that emphasized its philosophical and mystical aspects. And here I must say that I was somewhat misled, for Monsieur Pauvert, with the accord of Mme. Réage, had deleted from the book the third part, in which the heroine is confronted with her downfall, without my having been informed. (Deforges 4)

An epilogue to *Story of O* alludes to the missing part:

> In a final chapter, which has been suppressed, O returned to Roissy, where
> she was abandoned by Sir Stephen.
>   There exists a second ending to the story of O, according to which O, seeing
> that Sir Stephen was about to leave her, said she would prefer to die. Sir Stephen
> gave her his consent. (204)

And "Return to the Chateau" is preceded by a note:

> The pages that follow are a sequel to *Story of O*. They deliberately suggest the
> degradation of that work, and cannot under any circumstances be integrated
> into it. —P.R. (19)

If any thing is clear about the genealogy of this text, it is that at least this
portion of it had been the conclusion of the originally conceived story. So
why has this very emphatic note been appended? Paulhan tells us that it was
the publisher who decreed the "suppression." It is probably safe to speculate, given the time lapse between the publication of the two books, that the
"sequel" idea was not the immediate, or at least the sole, motive for deleting
it. The judgment Réage evidently accepted—that the final episodes of her
novel "degraded" the preceding—issues from an interested reading position. "At last a woman who admits it!" gushes Jean Paulhan (xxv); it's all
her idea. René won't flog O, and Sir Stephen doesn't enjoy it; he does it as a
duty: "There is nothing sadistic about them. It all happens as though it were
O alone who, from the outset, demanded to be chastised . . ." (xxviii). As it
happens, Paulhan was able to sustain this interpretation despite the presence
of the "Return to Roissy" section via the simple expedient of punctuating
his use and enjoyment of O by reading the text as a morally uplifting docu-
ment. For the most part, however, reading O as some version of the truth
about what women want is easier to accomplish if the original conclusion is
excluded.[3]
     For David Mickelsen, *Story of O* employs "sex as a metonymy for all hu-
man relationships (since it is *the* fundamental relationship)," and inscribes
those relationships along the following metaphorical axes: lover:beloved;
slave:master; worshipper:God (173). Echoing the Courtly Love alibi, he positions "beloved" on the active side of the dichotomy, and then criticizes O for
her "refusal" of the "responsibility" entailed by her position as the beloved
(analogous to master and to God). Mickelson also adopts the chivalric position when he takes up the cudgels on the text's behalf against its traducers, his
rivals. Jan Gordon, he says, is just wrong in his charge that the novel's voice is

confused and its plot circular and repetitive; John Fraser's reading is "keyed to reflex expectations based on conventional pornography" (172). Gordon's reading is, in fact, relentlessly clever, miming Sir Stephen's appropriation of O's body as a theater for desire. He reads O as a "perverse saint's life" representing the "attempt of a woman to convert 'bad faith' to 'good faith' " (42). To call this novel "a sort of twentieth-century participatory *Everyman*" (43), and to cite its presentation of a "communal [!] titillation" (29), is to miss the intersection of power, love, and desire which *Story of O* dramatizes precisely as problematic and asymmetrical. For his part, Fraser seems to be most interested in the insult to men that the novel, in his reading, embodies. In a particularly witty reverie, Fraser shares one of the fantasies Jean Paulhan's effusions have engendered for him: "It is agreeable to imagine the sort of reception [Paulhan] would get from the extremely busy, competent, lively housewife and mother he eulogizes were he to burst into her kitchen or nursery with the exhilarating tidings about the novel that 'Here we have it at last . . .' " (202–3). Fraser is equally charming on the easy valorization of sadomasochistic fantasies literary types are so prone to: apropos of D. H. Lawrence's "extraordinarily silly" remarks about corporal punishment (in his discussion of Dana in *Studies in Classic American Literature*), Fraser declares that he can well imagine Lawrence's "outraged fury" had anyone "taken a stick to him" (63).

I use these readings as representative. Differ though they may in their conclusions, they share a perception of O as not putting the foundations of its particular heterosexual fantasy under scrutiny; the readers are thus able to take the superior position—whether chivalric, pedagogic, or avuncular—in their intercourse with this problematic text. *Return to the Chateau, etc.* (hereafter called Part II) cannot be "integrated into" *Story of O* not because it is a deliberate degradation of a prior text but because its presence as part of the original story would disrupt any readings of the novel which are predicated upon unquestioning acceptance of the ideologies of heterosexual desire and romantic love. The mythos of romantic love cannot remain unaffected by Part II's dissolution of the dreamlike isolation of O's earlier adventures. The story begins to include family backgrounds, business deals, and the general public; it just begins to look too much like real life to allow for a reading stance of bemused appreciation for a rather literate, very naughty book.

In Part II, Sir Stephen becomes a more specific character: he is a descendant of the earls of Argyll, a member of the Campbell clan, and owns a castle in northwest Scotland. We see more of his acquaintances, some of whom are apparently business associates. In the first text, every glimpse we have of Sir Stephen and his life and connections has strictly to do with his association with the secret fellowship of Roissy and his own sexual appetites; in the sec ond, his life is apparently centered elsewhere, and his sexuality, however perverse, no longer appears to be monomaniacal. He loses none of his patriarchal cachet in this development; quite the contrary, pleasing him is still O's primary function. Doing so is simply (perhaps more "realistically") a more difficult, because less obvious, task for the still-devoted, still-acquiescent O.

Part II opens with O anxiously aware of signs that Sir Stephen's attitude toward her seems to be changed, the most serious of which is his neglecting to punish her after he has turned her over to someone else's use. Having long since decided that Sir Stephen does in fact love her, O now begins to doubt it: "when she asked him in a near whisper whether he loved her he did not say: 'I love you, O,' but only: 'Of course,' and laughed. But did he really?" (27). Sir Stephen is turning her over to other men much more frequently than he had ever done in the early stages of their arrangement. After one such episode, Sir Stephen does have her whipped, cruelly enough to comfort her for a moment.

> But there was no getting around the fact that, once her tears were dry and the searing pain had subsided, she found herself prey once again to the feeling that had terrified her: that some other reason than the pleasure he might derive from it—and did he indeed still derive any?—made him prostitute her, and that she was useful to him as some kind of not-so-legal tender: but to be tendered in exchange for what? (29)

These kinds of suspicions and doubts characterize O's predicament throughout Part II—later, for example, we find O "despondent" at being unable to shake the idea that "if Sir Stephen had prostituted her the other times for no reason, and as it were gratuitously, it was less in order to accustom her to the idea than to sow confusion and make her the instrument, the blind instrument, of something other than his own pleasure" (47). The apparent waning of Sir Stephen's "love" disrupts O's acceptance of her fate:

> she was no longer certain, it was no longer clear in her own mind, whether she was disgusted with herself for being a slave—or because she wasn't slavish enough. But it was neither one nor the other. She held herself in abhorrence because she was no longer loved. (30–31)

The master-slave relation is intact still—"it was apparent that he still wanted her to belong to him" (31)—but it is edging closer to a kind of business proposition. Roissy itself is a slightly different place this time. O's first visit had been limited to the members-only section of the chateau, where men bring their lovers to be shared and trained by the associates of the Club. The other branch of the business is accessible to the more or less general public. Roissy runs a restaurant and bar, a very expensive two-day membership in which is available to anyone with the purchase price. The membership entitles the holder to all the privileges of this discreet brothel. The clientele is largely businessmen. As Anne-Marie, the madam of the establishment, explains, anyone could sleep with O the first time she was there, but the rationale was different:

> ". . . it was for your lover's pleasure, and the only person it concerned was he. Now it's different. Sir Stephen has turned you over to the community. Everyone can still sleep with you, true, but now it's the community's problem. You'll be paid. . . ." (75)

O adapts to her new role well enough to begin keeping a "body count" and to stuff the banknotes she receives as tips into her cleavage (111). But she continues to long for evidence of Sir Stephen's love, and to mourn his absence. She is learning Maggie Verver's lesson—that the absent patriarch is at least as provocative as the present one.

The secret society aspect of Roissy has all but disappeared, together with the blindfolds and the elaborate rules of silence and nonfraternization among the women. Most of the women are free to leave the community and return as they please (O cannot leave as she is still Sir Stephen's property). And they do return, usually when they are out of money (O's first tip is equal to one-third her former monthly income). Roissy, in short, looks much more like a part of the real world than the fairy tale castle it seems in the first volume of O's odyssey. O's suspicions that she is no longer an instrument of pleasure but rather a bargaining tool appear to be confirmed by the last chapter of Part II. Sir Stephen has turned O over to a business associate, Carl. During his final visit to O, Carl presents O with a fortune in diamonds (in the form of a slave collar and bracelets) and informs her that he will soon be her new master. O inwardly rebels:

> And O thought: I'll run away. Oh, not with him, oh, no; I'll run away.
> The jewel case was open on the unmade bed, and the jewels, that O could not wear, sparkled among the disarray of the sheets, a fortune.
> I'll run away, and I'll take the diamonds with me, O thought to herself, and she smiled at him. (151)

This passage suggests that, unlike the diamonds, O is not infinitely transferable. She has succeeded in giving up her self to Sir Stephen, but she has done so for the sake of being loved by him. She has not agreed to be prostituted for the amusement and the flattery involved, as her roommate Noelle has (116); she has done it all in the hope of pleasing Sir Stephen:

She didn't care a damn about Carl, but she did care that Sir Stephen wanted to
use her for his own purpose, in whatever way he desired, and no matter what
that purpose may have been! (132)

When Carl is murdered, O is a material witness, and Sir Stephen, the prime
suspect, is nowhere to be found. O has not seen Sir Stephen in two months.
The price of saying yes is now reckoned: when O has given all she possibly
can, when the last vestige of independent will and resistance to his use of her
has been vanquished, when even his capacious imagination is satisfied, he's
gone, taking the love O hopes to win with him. He has offered O a false choice
all along. When he says to her, " 'if you are mine you have no right to refuse
my commands; but you also know that you are always free to choose *not* to be
mine' " (172–73), he is taking advantage of the power that the difference in
their desires bestows upon him. Sir Stephen can get what he wants in any
number of ways: other women will obey him—through love for him, through
love of some other man, through the connivance of other women, through
economic need or greed. Love is only a very useful tool; his project is satisfaction of desire. All he requires is that his satisfaction be representable (to O, to
himself, to the reader) as *her* desire.

   For O, on the other hand, only obedience, self-abnegation, total devotion
will get her what she wants—if, indeed, anything will. O is transformed from
a rather heartless (so-called), independent woman with a full life and desires
of her own to an object of desire, and from there to an object pure and simple.
Her quest for love is not a spiritual quest, nor is it a search for self-realization
or transcendence. She's just looking for love, the kind of love we are all relentlessly trained (by song, story, and the modern Western family) to look for:
heterosexual, romantic, endless love. That desire once instilled, coercion is
unnecessary, inefficient. Constituted as the one who wants what her father(s)
want, the daughter of sentiment—from Clarissa to O to the perfect 10—is
complicit in a desire she will never know she is absent from.

   Anne-Marie tells her that she is free, free to remove her irons, erase her
brand, take her diamonds, and " 'go home' " (158). She is also free to stay on
at Roissy. There O's story ends. We do not know what she will choose to do.

Snowman's Daughter

O is a desiring daughter, longing for the father's love. *Story of O* includes
another kind of daughter, one apparently impervious to the father's desire.
When O resumes her career after her training session at Roissy, Jacqueline
makes her entrance. Jacqueline is a "blond, green-eyed model with high Slavic

cheekbones and the olive complexion that goes with it" (60). O is immediately infatuated with the aloof and elusive model (qualities O finds fetching in Sir Stephen as well) and takes quantities of pictures of her:

> They were like nothing she had ever taken before. Never, perhaps, had she had such a model. Anyway, never before had she been able to extract such meaning and emotion from a face or body. (63)

The descriptions of the photographs make it clear that O is looking at Jacqueline through eyes modified by the standards of Roissy; it is equally clear that these standards are not so very different from those prevailing in the rest of the world. One photograph emphasizes Jacqueline's slightly parted lips, half-closed eyes, and her pallor (one of O's features, often mentioned as making her more vulnerable, therefore more desirable): "she looked like some blissful girl who had drowned, she was pale, so pale" (64). Another features a gown like a medieval bridal gown, spike-heeled shoes, a choker necklace, and two bracelets:

> And all the time Jacqueline was before O dressed in that gown and sandals, and that veil which was like the premonition of a mask, O, in her mind's eye, was completing, was innerly modifying the model: a trifle here, a trifle there—the waist drawn up a little tighter, the breasts slightly raised—and it was the same dress as at Roissy, the same dress that Jeanne had worn, the same smooth, heavy, cascading silk which one takes by the handful and raises whenever one is told to. (64–65)

The Roissy ideals are compatible with standards of commercial beauty; the seeds of what O will become are perhaps present in every woman.[4] Jacqueline is, in fact, pursued not only by O, but by René as well. Sir Stephen, in his turn, desires her and plots to get her to Roissy through trickery and O's connivance, if necessary. But the story ends and Jacqueline has not yet succumbed, nor is she ensnared in O's fate in Part II. Subjected to much the same temptations and persuasions—she does eventually accept René's advances—why are we allowed to infer that Jacqueline escapes O's fate?

Pornography is generally innocent of individual personalities and family settings. Consequently, that Jacqueline is fixed and contexted by such details is worth some attention.[5] Jacqueline is a daughter. In contrast to O, about whose family we know nothing, Jacqueline has a family present in the novel: mother, grandmother, aunt, half sister. They are Russian refugees, living in crowded genteel poverty on support checks from the father of Jacqueline's half sister, Natalie; this is supplemented by whatever money Jacqueline has left over after buying her clothes and accessories.

Insofar as she is able, Jacqueline has resisted patriarchal control; she has, for example, named herself:

> a name chosen to forget her real name, and with it this sordid but tender gynaeceum, and to set herself up in the French sun, in a solid world where there are men who do marry you and not disappear, as had the father she had never known, into the vast Arctic waste from which he had never returned. She took after him completely, she used to tell herself with a mixture of anger and delight, she had his hair and high cheekbones, his complexion and his slanting eyes. All she was grateful for to her mother was having given her this blond devil as a father, this demon whom the snows had reclaimed as the earth reclaims other men. (132)

Like her missing father, Jacqueline is an opportunist. She will not live with a lover as that amounts to "forsak[ing] one's chances for the future," as her mother has done (133). She accepts O's invitation to live with her, as she later accepts O's caresses and René's pursuit of her—for the sake of the benefits that come with such advances. Jacqueline is attached to material possessions, not to ideas or ideals. She is immune to love; she looks for nothing but legal and material security from men, and dallies, in the meantime, with women and boys (as O had done until René "captured" her). But this time it is René who falls for *her* "head over heels," while the object of his desire remains aloof: Jacqueline "studied him coldly, and when she smiled at him, her eyes remained cold" (186). O is infuriated to discover that Jacqueline cavalierly betrays René, with, for example, the director of the film in which she has a small part:

> He didn't need to open his mouth, it was obvious he was in love with Jacqueline. . . . He used the *tu* form in addressing Jacqueline, who replied with a mere nod or shake of her head. . . . It took no great act of perception to notice that Jacqueline, whose eyes were still lowered, was watching, from beneath the protection of those motionless eyelids, the young man's desire, the way she always did when she thought no one was looking. (187–88)

Jacqueline is susceptible to material and sensual pleasure, but she is, for as long as we know her, immune to love (as are René and Sir Stephen). In that immunity lies her protection. Part II opens with an allusion to Jacqueline (it is the last mention of her) and to René's intention to take her to Roissy, but there is no reason to suppose that this plan will be any more effectual than the other plans he has made for her.

Jacqueline's half sister is another story. Whereas her older sister is shocked by and contemptuous of O's enslaved condition, Natalie longs to follow her example: Natalie "had fallen in love with O" (182), and wants to be like her. She also wants to supplant Jacqueline in O's desires; unlike Jacqueline, she dreams of going to Roissy with O:

> "Teach me, O, please teach me," she started in again, "I want to be like you. I'll do anything you tell me. Promise me you'll take me with you when you go back to that place Jacqueline told me about." (184)

Natalie's devotion to O, far from being a subversive element in the phallocentric structure of desire, feeds directly into the system of domination through love that Roissy epitomizes. As Sir Stephen informs O when Jacqueline's submission is in question, he wants her to seduce Jacqueline in order to lure her to Roissy, where the matter will then be taken out of O's hands—presumably by more masterful ones (123). As for Natalie, her surrender is practically guaranteed in advance: "O's submission was so absolute and so constantly immediate that Natalie was quite incapable of conceiving, so great was her admiration for O, that anyone might ever contradict or disagree with Sir Stephen, since O knelt down before him" (Part II 24). Her mother calls her home before Natalie can be taken to Roissy (but not before she has been "initiated" by Sir Stephen with O's assistance), but it seems unlikely that Natalie will become anything other than another O.

These two half sisters, daughters of the same mother, abandoned by their different fathers, locate themselves on opposite sides. Natalie has accepted her dependence on the patriarchal economy of desire as she has accepted the economic support of the father she has never seen. Jacqueline, more completely abandoned by her father, has found a way to reject the patriarchal economy of desire. O sees her self-sufficiency as a kind of emotional invulnerability: "Since Jacqueline was sure of herself, she had nothing to redeem; she had no need to be reassured, all she needed was a mirror" (102). She is immune to love, indifferent to approval, and desirous only of unproblematic pleasure and economic security.

But then, of course, so was O—once upon a time.

To conclude. All witchcraft comes from carnal lust, which is in women insatiable.
—*Malleus Maleficarum,* Question VI

When it serves his pleasure, Sir Stephen can interrogate O "with a judge-like resolution and the skill of a father-confessor" (113). Once she is well in hand,

> ... O looked like a well-brought-up little girl. ... Everywhere Sir Stephen es-
> corted her she was taken for his daughter, or his niece, and this mistake was
> abetted by the fact that he, in addressing her, employed the *tu* form, whereas she
> employed the *vous*. (168–69)

These are not fortuitous tropes. "Father" and "daughter" are not general
power metaphors; the words name positions in an essentially erotic (not
eroticized) economy, an economy constructed in and by language—as empha-
sized by the insistence on the conversational grammar employed by this pair.

The family novels of earlier chapters assume an innate desire to please in
their daughter-heroines—whether she's failing to do so like Clarissa or learning how to do it like Jo. In *Story of O* the same woman is engaged in pleasing
the same man, but this text imagines its heroine is having a preheterosexual
history (sketchy, to be sure). O's story discloses what is at stake for us in the
smooth operation of our sentimental fictions: these stories cure or neutralize
feminine desires and indifferences that are inimical to the father-daughter
romance. Before she falls in love with René, O is independent, willful, sexually rapacious, bisexual—more accurately, lesbian, since her adolescent
crushes and her later sexual initiatives are all directed at women. These are
precisely the tendencies borne down upon by the whole weight of the
sentimental-heterosexual fictions inscribed in O. O's father-daughter romance addresses itself to all her extraneous (that is, nonpatriarchal) desires:
those it does not eliminate altogether, it simply recycles. Thus, O is required to
confess her own desire for Jacqueline and then to act upon it only under the
hand and eye of Sir Stephen, a maneuver which effectively reclaims O's lesbian activity for patriarchal sexuality.[6]

To take O seriously is to invert Freud's infamous question to ask what the
novel might be able to tell us about what men don't want. Men, according to
Pauline Réage's story, do not want independent career women—or rather,
they do, but only to turn them into something quite other. They don't want to
be wrong about what those women *really* want and have really wanted all
along. And they don't want their female subjects (which is to say, objects) to
talk: no talking while being fucked, no talking while the men talk to each
other while the women are being fucked, and no talking under any circumstances to the other women who are being or have just been or are about to be
fucked. What they want is also instructive: they want to belong to a men-only
club, with rites and secrets and signs; they want to talk to each other over a
woman's body which is available to their common use; they want to demonstrate to one another their prowess in woman training; they want to be
watched by other men when they fuck women; they want the respect and
attention of men with more power than they have; they want their penises

(not "the Phallus") to be the technically forbidden but completely irresistible cynosure of every female eye.

These are the parameters of masculine desire in this putatively literary piece of pornography. They are also the parameters of another highly literate communal masculine fantasy about women and desire: when the Inquisition turned its attention to the detection and prosecution of witches, it did so with the same meticulous attention to detail and order which characterizes the brotherhood at Roissy. When the accused witches were treated harshly enough, they named other women to the men who had control of their bodies, thereby "recruiting" as the women of Roissy do, for the cause. And when they confessed their sacrileges, their confessions were remarkably, impossibly similar. They also struck Sigmund Freud centuries later, as Catherine Clément points out, as oddly familiar:[7]

> But why, he continues, "after having taken possession of these unfortunate women who are his victims, has the devil always fornicated with them, and done so hideously? Why do the confessions extorted by torture have so much similarity to my patients' narratives during psychological treatment?" (*The Newly Born Woman* 12)

One answer is that the Western patriarchal tradition has had a rather limited sexual imagination. Relations between hysterics, doctors, and fathers produced stories like those produced by relations between witches (a category which the *Malleus* consistently conflates with "women," good or bad), priests, and Father(s) because in both historical situations the essential trinity of heterosexuality is reproduced—which in turn enables the doctor/priests to induce (in whatever manner) a desire in the hysterics/witches to tell them stories.[8] This is in essence the story told in "A Girl in Love" about the genesis of *Story of O:*

> One day a girl in love said to the man she loved: "I could also write the kind of stories you like . . ." "Do you really think so?" he answered. (Part II 3)

And so she did.

I maintained at the beginning of this chapter that O can be read through its own fictional terms. What this reading has amounted to, finally, is a distinction drawn between O's terms and O's terms. Shoshana Felman has pointed out that sexuality is not disguised by rhetoric, that sexuality is rhetoric—that is, the coexistence of dynamically antagonistic meanings. What *Story of O* demonstrates is that Felman's remark can also be useful when the metaphor is reduced to its literal terms: in fact, sexuality *is* rhetoric.

But isn't the surest pleasure of all the pleasure of talking about love? What is more, in order to tell the truth? . . .

The pleasure with which psychoanalysts are satisfied? They who know—at least those who are capable of knowing something—that there is no such thing as a sexual relation, that what has stood in its stead for centuries—consider the whole history of philosophy—is love. As this latter is an effect of language, those who know can limit themselves to dealing directly with the cause. A cause thus keeps talking. . . . (Irigaray "Così Fan Tutti," 99)

As Irigaray intimates, it is not only "an effect of language"; it is an organized system of tropes, metaphors, and metonymies taken, and put into operation, quite literally. And like all rhetorical systems it is spoken from an interested position, and produces the grammar, stories, language, and family of Western heterosexual desire.

6

A Child Never Banished from Home: The Daughter's Daughter

To be given up to a strange man; to be ingrafted into a strange family; to give up her very name, as a mark of her becoming his absolute and dependent property; to be obliged to prefer this strange man, to father, mother—to everybody: and his humours to all her own. . . . Surely, sir, a young creature ought not to be obliged to make all these sacrifices but for such a man as she can love.

—*Clarissa*

She had been decided in wishing for a Miss Weston. . . . she was convinced that a daughter would suit both father and mother best. It would be a great comfort to Mr. Weston as he grew older . . . to have his fireside enlivened by the sports and the nonsense, the freaks and the fancies of a child never banished from home; and Mrs. Weston—no one could doubt that a daughter would be most to her. . . .

—*Emma*

Why should a woman have to leave—and "hate"—her own mother, leave her own house, abandon her own family, renounce the name of her own mother and father, in order to take man's genealogical desires on herself?

—Luce Irigaray

The foundation of culture, we are told, is the law of exogamy, enforced by the incest taboo. The story goes that "we" circulate women in order to cement bonds between groups of men; the effect of this circulation is civilization and its stories. But the foundation of desire, it is equally clear, is endogamous: we are produced as desiring subjects in and from a familial position. The daughter of sentiment figures prominently in the bourgeois novel and the increasingly nuclear family,[1] construction sites of heterosexual desire; the sentimental father-daughter romance constructs her as the daughter necessary to this complex system of endogamous desire and exogamous exchange. The sentimental mode implicates (and is implicated in) a familial surplus value consisting in erotic, officially nonillicit (it doesn't damage the merchandise) titillation to be appropriated by the patriarch of the bourgeois, modern, nuclear house.

The such set-ups (mis)represent themselves as natural constructs is the point of Luce Irigaray's interrogation of Freud's analogy between the (asserted) passivity of women in sexual reproduction and the " 'influence of social customs, which *similarly* force women into passive situations.' " Irigaray notes the surplus value produced here by Freud's (and patriarchy's) elision of the issue of ideological priority: "But might one not envisage the possibility that the one might prescribe 'the other,' that is to say by legitimating, even by producing the discourse, the ideology, which determine it as a factor?" (*Speculum* 19). The sentimental daughter figures this interested production of femininity. That the discourse of representation "might have a vested interest in becoming the prop, the accomplice" of the version of femininity multiply constructed in our culture (*Speculum* 19) is one Irigarayan suspicion confirmed by the family plot of heterosexuality as inscribed in and by the novel. The story of heterosexuality and the novel thus far described points to the production of a genre (the modern bourgeois family novel), a story (the middle class father-daughter romance), and a figure (the sentimental daughter) all designed for and invested with the particular purpose of rendering null and void any daughterly desire to deviate from that patriarchal (in)corporation. Thus she is inscribed as the heroine of the oedipal plot, constructed as a quiescent object of (impassive) paternal desire. (Quiescent: being at rest, inactive, causing no trouble *or symptoms*.) Thus, too, I have argued, she is made, in the fictions of culture and the fictions of the novel, an acquiescent medium of exogamous exchange.[2] (To acquiesce: to accept or comply tacitly. Tacit: *without words or speech,* not actually expressed, arising without express contract or agreement, *arising by operation of law.*)

Invented to sentimentalize the ambivalences and aggressions—that is, the sexuality—inherent in family intimacy, this figure also, inevitably, invokes the very structures that she sanitizes. Because she marks the need to prettify, the sentimental daughter provokes the uneasiness she is constructed to allay: Harlowe's rage, Dombey's fear, and strong currents of readerly and critical support for their reactions dramatize the inseparability of the deed and its cover-up. Even the sunniest version of her leaves a shadow of a doubt: the commonsensical Louisa May Alcott, practicing strict generic (gothic vs. sentimental) separation, nevertheless attributes witchy powers to her sentimental daughter—Amy doesn't die, but Jo's anger, in the novel's view of causality, uncannily puts her right next door to it.[3]

I use the term uncannily advisedly. The uncanny has to do with the liminal, with boundaries and thresholds and the presence of that which refuses clear classification. In his essay on the uncanny, Freud underscores the convergence of the word *heimlich* with its opposite *unheimlich* (377), and our concurrent recognition and repression of whatever produces an uncanny effect.[4] The very places, pieties, and fictions—home, familial asexuality, the antiseptic domestic space—we invent to protect us from what "ought to have remained hidden and secret" (376) are most susceptible to the frisson of the uncanny: "we can understand why the usage of speech has extended *das Heimliche* into its opposite *das Unheimliche;* for this uncanny is in reality nothing new or foreign, but something familiar and old-established in the mind that has been estranged only by the process of repression" (394). The sentimental mode covers over illicit desires with pious fictions; both poles of this ambivalence are projected onto the desirable dutiful daughter. Thus though Florence Dombey never does anything even next door to murderous, she too is uncanny: she's just too good to be true, and the reader often enough grants the plausibility of Dombey's dread and ambivalence even without any plot business to anchor it; that she turns out to be as good as she looks may be, from this perspective, the worst of it. Until she is successfully exchanged out of the paternal household, the daughter of sentiment never stops being "daughter"—never leaves the penumbra of the *Heimliche/Unheimliche.*[5] Because she is dutiful, she both acquiesces to her father's desire and exists to deny its very possibility; because she is desirable, she both provokes the very desire sentimental pieties exist to deny and embodies the fiction under cover of which the desire and the pieties alike operate.

What becomes of the sentimental plot when women novelists—at once subject(ed) to their culture's stories and practitioners of a simultaneously resistant and complicit genre—take on the activity of writing novels grounded in the (patriarchal) family romance?[6] It should not suprise us if the daughter's attempt to tell the story of sentimental desire avails itself of a discourse which is able to mime the both/and quality of the uncanny. Juliet Mitchell has argued that the concurrence of the historical phenomenon of an epidemic of hysteria with the rise of the novel was no coincidence. Mitchell contends that the uncanny posture of simultaneous acquiescence and resistance symptomatized by the hysteric is mirrored in that other discourse of representation and memory available to (arguably, invented by) women—the novel.[7] She maps the relations between desire, female subjectivity, and the novel against the notion of hysteria (a useful concept too hastily eschewed by certain feminisms) in this way:

> The woman novelist must be an hysteric. Hysteria is the woman's simultaneous acceptance and refusal of the organisation of sexuality under patriarchal capitalism. It is simultaneously what a woman can do both to be feminine and to refuse femininity, within patriarchal discourse. And I think that is exactly what the novel is; I do not believe there is such a thing as female writing, a "woman's voice." There is the hysteric's voice which is *the woman's masculine language* (one has to speak "masculinely" in a phallocentric world) talking about feminine experience. It's both simultaneously the woman novelist's refusal of the woman's world—she is, after all, a novelist—and her construction from within a masculine world of that woman's world. It touches on both. It touches, therefore, on the importance of bisexuality. (289–90)

Mitchell, then, sees "hysteria" as a particular form taken by ambivalence (a form which has acquired a bad name as have all such manifestations taken up by women at one time or another—compare witchcraft). She suggests that the decision to write a novel grounded in women's experience entails for the woman novelist a simultaneous acceptance of "the woman's world" (she's after all writing about it) and refusal of it (she steps outside it in the very act of writing).[8] This is a useful formulation. Less useful perhaps is Mitchell's notion of a "hysteric's voice." Since it implies an at least temporarily stable speaking position—a speaking position which is firmly, predictably subversive—this in effect fails to distinguish the "woman's masculine language" from the *man's* masculine language, when by "language" we mean "the novel" (the subversion of monologic discourses being the quality for which the novel as a genre tout court is noted).[9] *Huck Finn*, for example, may be read as subversive of its contemporary cultural domestic and racial pieties; to call *Charlotte Temple* subversive is to miss its crucial ideological ambivalence and to mislabel the textual symptoms of that ambivalence as incoherence or inconsistency.

Like her daughter character, the woman novelist, to a greater or lesser degree, has been reared—by her culture, its stories, and her "own" desire—to want what she doesn't want, and that produces effects on the level of desire, of narrative, of the novel. My own reading of that form of ambivalence called hysteria points to the hysterical symptom as less a subversion than an *intrusion:* to subvert is to turn from beneath—to pose a constant resistance to whatever edifice is being undermined; to intrude is to enter without permission, welcome, or fitness—to thrust in (that particularly masculine verb nicely pointing to the bisexuality inherent in hysterical manifestations). The discussion which follows tentatively suggests that certain formal properties of the novel are affected by the woman novelist's own imbrication in her text and in cultural and literary heterosexual sentimentalities, that certain textual symptoms can be located in daughter-produced versions of the sentimental family romance, and that these deviancies are provoked by a simultaneous acquiescence to and refusal of patriarchal heterosexual desire and the novelist's consequent attempt to say something which can't be said within the discourse she has chosen to speak (and which presumes, in a sense, to speak her).

The Hysteric's Father

Yet could it not also be—and at the risk of troubling the concept of an *écriture feminine*—that, suspending her relation to the very fact of sexual identity, the woman equally uses writing to *masquerade?*

To ask George Eliot to be a woman or a man in this context (which has also been described as the question of the hysteric) is impossible. . . .

—Jacqueline Rose

The stories which Freud read to extract the foundational structure of (hetero)sexuality itself, to infer the relation of drive to representation, are father-daughter stories, as Laplanche and Pontalis, for instance, suggest in their discussion of Freud's "A Child Is Being Beaten":[10]

> "A father seduces a daughter" might perhaps be the summarized version of the seduction fantasy. The indication here of the primary process is not the absence of organization, as is sometimes suggested, but the peculiar character of the structure, in that it is a scenario with multiple entries, in which nothing shows whether the subject will be immediately located as *daughter;* it can as well be fixed as *father,* or even in the term *seduces.* ("Fantasy and the Origins of Sexuality" 14)

The individual's identification with subject/object/verb positions in the foundational fantasies of desire, then, is unstable, uncannily liable to slippage and oscillation. The reading positions outlined in the fantasies of Freud's female subjects (the object of the beating, the subject who is beating, the spectator of other subjects and objects, the activity of beating itself) are the reading positions we all—female and male, daughter and father—continually oscillate among in reading and inscribing, whether it be novels, our desire, or our "own" sexuality. And, as Jacqueline Rose points out, Freud's essay

> illustrates at its clearest the relation of drive to *representation.* . . . For what the fantasies of the female patients reveal is the difficulties and structuration of feminine sexuality across contradictions in subject/object positions and areas of

the body—the desire of the woman is indeed "not a clear message" (whoever said it was?). ("The Cinematic Apparatus—Problems in Current Theory," *Sexuality in the Field of Vision* 210; emphasis added)

There can be no satisfying and essentialistically ordered division between active and passive, subject and object: not only are these positions not sex-gender specific, they are not embraced wholly by a single subject at any given point in the circulation of desire.

All of our patriarchal fictions set themselves resolutely against such a sloppy, slippery, untrustworthy state of affairs. The mandate of patriarchal heterosexuality is to make the desire of the woman *look* like a "clear message," thus enabling the fiction that *all* of the positions in the circulation of desire are fixed and stable, even "natural." The production of a daughter with the right (that is, sympathetic to and complicitous with the father) reading perspective is an urgent patriarchal necessity. The one in the daughter's place is asked to agree to incite the very activity and instability she is constructed to disavow and also to repress any knowledge of the contradictions of her position. Essentially, this is the hysterical position—just as hysteria involves "a certain kind of identification" and "certain mechanisms (particularly repression, which is often explicit)" (Laplanche and Pontalis, *Language of Psychoanalysis* 195), so the properly constructed daughter of sentiment is implicitly expected to identify with the father's desire and to repress any consequent glimpse of the infrastructure of his fiction. Identification with the position-which-looks means you don't see anything: which means you must disavow the absence and make something (the fetish, the phallus, the daughter) stand in for what isn't there, or you must both refuse and accept the absence of what you want and don't want (the hysteric's response—I tell and don't tell you that I know and don't know what I can't and can tell).

But the very fictions which are designed to provide this false sense of stability and coherence in desire inscribe an irreducible contradiction. The passive position in the plot of heterosexual desire (occupied by the daughter of sentiment) demands that its occupant engage in ceaseless interpretation (Clarissa, Florence, Jo, Maggie, O—all are constantly "reading" the father); the "active" position (occupied by the father) is that of a sitting duck who may or may not be successful in the patriarchal duty of concealing his desire. (" 'How well you read me, you witch!' interposed Mr. Rochester . . ." [247]) Which means that the queasy suspicion that the father-daughter positions in the circulation of endogamous desire might not be fixed, that the ostensibly fixed father-subject can become the object of the daughter's look, that there might, therefore, be a different (a daughter's) version of the story of father-daughter desire—is constantly agitated even, or especially, by traditionally patriarchal bourgeois novels. Hence, Sir Stephen's excessive drive to annihilate the already acquiescent O's will; hence, the palpitating play of "I see's" of *The Golden Bowl*.

Or, take another play of I/eye/see/sea.

The young Jacques Lacan is on vacation from his arduous labor as an intellectual. He finds himself on a small, frail fishing boat, among men accustomed to struggling with the often dangerous elements for their living. One of them tells Lacan a joke. A sardine can floats in the sun: "And Petit-Jean said to me—*You see that can? Do you see it? Well, it doesn't see you!*" (*The Four Fundamental Concepts of Psycho-Analysis* 95). Lacan takes the story personally and is "not terribly amused at hearing myself addressed in this humorous, ironical way." He attributes his annoyance to his perception that the story bears on his own insignificance "to those fellows who were earning their livings with great difficulty," to whom he himself "looked like nothing on earth," for whom he was "out of place in the picture" (96).

Lacan had been, one surmises, imposing his own sentimental romance of the sea on Petit-Jean and his family; being detected in his desire to be, however fictionally (or fraudulently), a part of that romance seems even years later to be a source of some chagrin. Lacan, perhaps, had been counting on a certain amount of reverence from the simple fisherfolk with and to whom he was unbending. The sardine can joke means that Lacan has been found out in his fiction, caught in his own appropriative net. Lacan looks back on his discomfort as one stemming not from invisibility but from a sudden perception that a representative of the object of his desire (Petit-Jean figuring the manly life of the sea) *does,* unlike the sardine can, look back, and worse, that when the object appropriates the subject position, what is seen does not remain the same. "When, in love, I solicit a look, what is profoundly unsatisfying and always missing is that—*You never look at me from the place from which I see you*" (103).

The uncanny effect of even the most sentimental father's daughter is traceable to the suspicion that when she looks at the father she might be reading something other than the father's fiction.[11] The daughter of the heterosexual family romance is to be seen through and constructed by the father's desire; she is to look back only to see his look. This is Luce Irigaray's masquerade, the experiencing of desire only as it is reflected to the woman from the masculine (to which I add the adjective paternal or paternalized) position. If she can dispense with his look and see some perversion of the father's fiction (and the sardine can is merely the occasion of the story, it is Petit-Jean's look that Lacan is concerned with), he, like Lacan, might be found deserving of a humorous, ironical address; her respect for him and his position may be a charade, may be ironical. (Jane Austen's "pert" heroines, Jane Eyre's disrespectful sparring with Rochester come to mind.) But if, unlike Petit-Jean, she (for reasons of her own) chooses to cling at the same time to the father's fiction, her respect for him and his position may (also) be "hysterical." Which is to say that the allotment of subject and object, masculine and feminine, patriarchal and filial activities and attributes may be less fixed when it's her turn to tell the story.

The Daughter's Father

> I have believed that sex was unspeakable and words so strong and fathers so frail that "aunt" would do my father mysterious harm.
> —Maxine Hong Kingston

How to proceed? Within the scope of this study, I cannot survey every female-written novel which foregrounds a father-daughter relationship, even if I could continue to delimit that category to biological filiality represented as central throughout the entire novel (which delimitation I have, in any case, already forfeited in Chapter 5). But if my analysis is to have anything of what social scientists call "generalizability" it will have to cast a unique slant of light on those women who are central to any consideration of the novel as genre.

What I propose is to present some generalizations about women writers and the father-daughter romance gleaned from the novels of Jane Austen, Emily Brontë, Charlotte Brontë, and George Eliot. While it would be merely fatuous to collapse the work of these writers under a single rubric, they do exhibit what I shall call, borrowing Ludwig Wittgenstein's useful notion, "family resemblances":

> Consider for example the proceedings that we call "games". . . . Don't say: "There *must* be something common, or they would not be called 'games' "—but *look and see* whether there is anything common to all. For if you look at them you will not see something that is common to *all*, but similarities, relation-ships, and a whole series of them at that. . . . And the result of this examination is: we see a complicated network of similarities overlapping and criss-crossing: sometimes overall similarities, sometimes similarities of detail. . . . I can think of no better expression to characterize these similarities than "family resem-blances"; for the various resemblances between members of a family . . . over-lap and criss-cross in the same way. (31e–32e)

The most notable family resemblance in the daughters' interventions as producers of one of the discourses which prop patriarchal femininity is a certain twist given the father figure: he generally exhibits paternal inadequacy to some important aspect of his narrative and cultural authority, thus making room, indeed necessitating, some amount of daughterly authority. The father in the plot is inadequate to the cultural plot of exogamous heterosexual training and trading; the daughter figure consequently steps in, identifies with the father's desire (to have a sentimental daughter, to be a patriarchal father). The daughter novelist writing the story of the daughter reflects on the father's fiction by (tacitly) giving the father exactly what he wants—but that, as we shall see, is more than he ever bargained for. The sentimental daughter—as the daughter with the proper reading perspective—both acquiesces to and resists the position of the passive object; she also—as the daughter with a hysteric reading (which is to say, writing) perspective—both identifies with the father and refuses to pretend that she sees what isn't there. The culturally and narratively (and tacitly) sacrosanct father-daughter contract is not perceptibly abrogated by the daughter's activity; it is preserved by the simple expedient of making the father rather less than the cultural fiction insists that he should be.

George Eliot's *Silas Marner* offers the most blatant example of this stratagem, making the daughter the occasion of the father's paternal education and insertion into cultural exchange. Silas Marner lives his life outside the life of Raveloe, engaging in no unnecessary circulation—whether of conversation, visits, or money. When his hoard of gold goes out of his life and his foster daughter comes into it, Marner begins by wanting to hoard Eppie as well: " 'But I want to do things for it myself, else it may get fond o' somebody else, and not fond o' me' " (180). Eppie first necessitates and then orchestrates the necessary circulation of language, money, and heterosexuality: before Eppie's advent, Silas is not only nonpatriarchal, he is dubiously masculine and doesn't seem at all educable; it is the daughter whose mere presence effects the father's transformation into a thoroughly sentimentalized patriarch.

> Hitherto he had been treated very much as if he had been a useful gnome or brownie—a queer and unaccountable creature, who must necessarily be looked at with wondering curiosity and repulsion. . . . But now Silas met with open smiling faces and cheerful questioning, as a person whose satisfactions and difficulties could be understood. . . . No child was afraid of approaching Silas when Eppie was near him: there was no repulsion around him now, either for young or old; for the little child had come to link him once more with the whole world. There was love between him and the child that blent them into one, and there was love between the child and the world. . . . (189–90)

This heretical assertion of the active role of the daughter in making the father fit, or at least appear to fit, the patriarchal fiction is a recurring feature

in these daughters' novels. For example, in *Pride and Prejudice* and *Emma,*
Jane Austen writes family novels in which a sentimental—but active—
daughter props the patriarchal, familial, erotic authority of the fictional father. Both Mr. Bennet and Mr. Woodhouse love their creature comforts, valu-
ing their easy chairs highly (in the library for the one, by the fire for the other).
Each presents paternal deficiencies which must be made good, and made
good they are by the daughter in the story who most fully occupies a (metaphorically) writerly position. Mr. Bennet is subjected to fathering instruction
by Lizzy on more than one occasion, and she also supplies not one but two
father substitutes (her Uncle Gardner and Mr. Darcy) in the family crisis to
which Mr. Bennet is so eminently insufficient (diplomatically and economi-
cally). At its outset, *Emma* gives us to understand that Mr. Woodhouse has
long since been given up by his daughter as anything other than a figurehead;
Emma has been mistress of his house and of most of the rest of her little world
from a very early age. In fact, in her project of marrying Harriet Smith we see
her presuming to take on the ultimate patriarchal duty of orchestrating
exogamous exchange.

And so with the others. Jane Eyre must take over from her Master the
patriarchal function of enforcing the law in the face of (in the very teeth of) his
raving desire (the adequate patriarch is impassive, does not yield to desire).
The empty paternal place fuels the polymorphous infantile perversities of
Wuthering Heights until a daughter is produced who is capable of teaching
the patrilineal representative of the Earnshaw clan his manners and his letters,
thereby qualifying him for the patriarchal vacancy mere genealogy cannot fill.
Virtually every Eliot heroine faces the necessity of assisting her father or father substitute in some vital patriarchal capacity or prerogative. Eppie
Marner teaches first her foster father and then her biological father appropriate paternal and sentimental values; even Romola, whose intensely filial passion at the beginning of the novel marks her as a sentimental daughter par
excellence, and who, in Savonarola, adopts as authoritative a father figure as
one might find, must find a way to negotiate satisfactorily his deficiencies in
order to get on with her own vocation.[12]

The critical nature of the father's patriarchal inadequacy becomes most
evident when the marriage of the daughter—which, with the exception of the
works of George Eliot, is understood largely as tantamount to the resolution
of the novel—is at issue: the father's patriarchal inadequacy makes her unmar-
ketable, which is to say, unmarriageable (see Chapter 3's discussion of the
first version of Alcott's *Moods* for the most straightforward rendition of this
predicament). Elizabeth Bennet's weak father and consequently improperly
behaving family are acknowledged by her community to be a virtual barrier
to any appropriate marriage for her; Rochester's inadequacy to the patriar-

chal mandate of upholding the orderly exchange of women (the law of monogamous marriage) drives Jane Eyre into the position of nearly accepting a second proposal based upon her unmarketability (St. John: "God and nature intended you for a missionary's wife. It is not personal, but mental endowments they have given you: you are formed for labor, not for love" [354]). Even in the rare instance where marriage is not finally at issue, *Romola* for instance, patriarchal inadequacy nevertheless threatens the daughter's (the novel's) ability to achieve some reasonably happy closure. It is the daughter who must find a way to approximate the culturally correct resolution—she must be married, or at least at rest and settled—while still properly reverencing the father or father figure who couldn't pull it off himself.

The inadequate father does not, however, signal a reversal of familial pieties to afford a patriarchal empowerment of the daughter. Far from any design of arrogating the paternal privilege to herself, the daughter-written daughter props the patriarch up, straightens his collar, reties his cravat, and makes him look like what the heterosexual fiction says he is.[13] She ventriloquizes the father's part, temporarily assuming the patriarchal authority left unclaimed due to a paternal power vacuum in order to ensure that she be appropriately settled—in order to settle herself.[14] Her hysteric strategy—identification with the father and assumption of masculine activity—flouts gender assignments to be sure, but like Portia donning the robes of the law, she does it in the service of the pieties of home, church, state, and the exogamous circulation of daughters.

Presumabbly.

The Disorderly Daughter

Le style c'est l'homme à qui l'on s'addresse.

—Jacques Lacan

Mary Jacobus has written of Brontë's *Villette,* that "text formally fissured by its own repressions" in which the "narrative and representational conventions of Victorian realism are constantly threatened by an incompletely repressed Romanticism" (41), that its alienation from formal constraints mimes Lucy Snowe's alienation from her culture's prescriptions for femininity and feminine desire. She calls upon feminist critics "to theorize" Brontë's "incoherencies and compromises, inconsistencies and dislocations" in relation to her "double quest for literary form and for female emancipation" in order to theorize their own, similar location in the disjunction between "literary response and critical discourse" (60).[15] Because Jacobus accepts rather than admonishes the text's manifestations of disorder, her reading of *Villette* avoids the assignment of generic categories and avoids as well the consignment of Lucy Snowe (as narrator, as character, as authorial stand-in) to any fixed place in the syntaxes of desire and familial positionality. The discourse of this remarkably hysteric (disordered, messy, a-generic) text teaches us how to read its "symptoms" if we are willing to read them against the prescriptive and normalizing drive to closure enshrined in traditional critical discourses.

Villette is, of course, an extreme example of novelistic hysteria—it is a text which palpably intends to refuse and problematize the constraints of categories of gender and genre. But what of more traditional, representational, well-behaved novels, novels which are more available to critical and pedagogical use?

The history of literary criticism of the novel is replete with accusations of what we might call formal hysteria leveled against women's novels. Even the most sympathetic readers have found certain moments in important women's novels to be symptomatic rather than esthetic. Take, for instance, this famous passage from *Jane Eyre:*

> Anybody may blame me who likes when I add further that now and then, when I took a walk by myself in the grounds . . . I longed for a power of vision which might overpass that limit; which might reach the busy world, towns, regions full of life I had heard of but never seen: that then I desired more of practical experience that I possessed; more of intercourse with my kind, of acquaintance with variety of character, than was here within my reach. . . . Who blames me? Many, no doubt; and I shall be called discontented. I could not help it: the restlessness was in my nature; it agitated me to pain sometimes. . . . Women are supposed to be very calm generally: but women feel just as men feel; they need exercise for their faculties and a field for their efforts as much as their brothers do; they suffer from too rigid a restraint, too absolute a stagnation, precisely as men would suffer. . . . When thus alone I not unfrequently heard Grace Poole's laugh. . . . (95–96)

Virginia Woolf takes exception to this passage, finding that Charlotte Brontë speaks through her character so passionately here that the reader cannot fail to be jarred by the sense that one voice has been momentarily lost in (or to) the other:

> the woman who wrote those pages . . . will never get her genius expressed whole and entire. Her books will be deformed and twisted. She will write in a rage where she should write calmly. She will write foolishly where she should write wisely. She will write of herself where she should write of her characters. (*Room* 72–73)[16]

Attributing these disorderly sentiments to the author—"She left her story, to which her entire devotion was due, to attend to some personal grievance" (*Room* 76)—has the auxilliary effect of allowing the reader to take other expressions of desire as utterly consistent with the character. Such a passage as the following, for example:

> "Thank you, Mr. Rochester, for your great kindness. I am strangely glad to get back again to you; and wherever you are is my home—my only home." . . . there is no happiness like that of being loved by your fellow-creatures, and feeling that your presence is an addition to their comfort. (*Jane Eyre* 216)

Reading this desire as consistently Jane's alone grounds such remarks as this rather impatient one of Woolf's: "Always to be a governess and always to be in love is a serious limitation in a world which is full, after all, of people who are neither one nor the other" (Norton 456).[17] The desire Woolf presumably shares is diagnosed as Brontë's, inelegantly (and improprietously) intruding into the text; the desire Woolf presumably does not share (does not wish to share?) is read as fully Jane's and thus cast into the well of formal consistency. Identifying with the "masculine" desire of the author, and repudiating the "feminine" desire of the heroine (a move analogous to hysterical identification), Woolf recovers herself and the novel by recourse to the formal convention of consistent characterization: a representational character must embody some declaration of allegiance to one of the positions of desire; the conventions extracted from the novel by literary criticism suppress any indication in the text of the kind of oscillation in the economy of desire discussed above. In criticism's maxims, the bourgeois novel character is not allowed to be both subject and object—much less the verb too—of the beating, of desire, of the story.[18]

Woolf's implication to the contrary, Charlotte Brontë's novel argues that the cultural discourses of Jane Eyre's time and place do precisely construct women as always governesses (therefore always angry, always marginal daughters to the patriarchal household—note how many households Jane fails to retain her place in) and always in love (therefore also always sentimental, always aspiring good daughters to the patriarchal family—note that Jane never fails to *try* to fit whatever daughterly space she's in proximity to). This both/and-edness of the heroine and her desire, uncanny and hysteric, is mimed by other violations of generic conventions.[19] Laplanche and Pontalis note the salient qualities of conversion hysteria—expressed symbolically by varied somatic symptoms including theatricality, lumps in the throat, and hysterical paralyses—which justify the summary description "a malady through representation."[20] If hysteria is characterized by unruly bodily symptoms crosscutting or impeding (correct) linguistic formulation, we might read traditionally grounded criticism of *Jane Eyre* (taken as a representative case) as diagnosing (sometimes with approval, sometimes not) a textual conversion hysteria, a certain symptomatic malady *in* representation.[21]

Robert B. Heilman praises the resistance to formal expectations which has impelled him to invent a new label ("new Gothic") for Brontë's work: "In her flair for the surreal, in her plunging into feeling that is without status in the ordinary world of the novel, Charlotte discovers a new dimension of Gothic" (Norton 460). Having thus tidily and firmly grounded the author in a gendered category—note the rather condescending use of the term "flair" as well as the feminized and feminizing verbal construction "plunging into feeling"—the critic goes on to classify her heroines. Asserting that "Charlotte's [*sic*] women vibrate with passions," Heilman cites their "almost violent devotedness," "fire of independence," "vivid sexual responsiveness," "self-righteousness," "sense of power, sometimes self-pity and envious competitiveness"—descriptive terms that recall Freud's remarks on "his" hysterics, Breuer's fear of "his," and the usual colloquial use of the epithet "hysterical" then and now.[22] Jane Eyre, as an " 'unheroined' " (Norton 459) Brontë heroine, is nevertheless not unfeminized by these symptoms, and like Freud's (and before him, Charcot's) patients she is subduable by a patriarchal master: "the hypnotic, almost inhuman potency of [Rivers'] influence on Jane" (Norton 461) to which Jane almost yields maps a relationship "which is a structural parallel" to the relationship to which she finally succumbs. Heilman, like Freud, is interested in (pro)claiming his patient (the novel) rehabilitated to/for the genre; he labors to induce the text to accept a new adjective ("new"), thus making generic taxonomy safe from Brontë's (and Jane's) depredations:

> what *really* counts is [old Gothic's] indirect usefulness to her: it released her from the patterns of the novel of society and therefore permitted the flowering [!] of her *real* talent—the talent for finding and giving dramatic form to impulses and feelings which, because of their depth or mysteriousness or intensity or ambiguity, or of their ignoring or transcending everyday norms of propriety and reason, increase wonderfully the sense of reality of the novel" (Norton 458, emphasis added).

The textual hysteria of the novel is recuperated in the act of analysis; the key which will decipher the symptom is found in the generic conventions of the gothic. Just as *Jane Eyre* accomplishes "that discovery of passion, that rehabilitation of the extra-rational, which is the historical office of Gothic" by moving it "deeply into the lesser known realities of human life" (462), Heil-

man rehabilitates the excesses of Brontë's text and her heroine(s) by assimilating them to a set of (only slightly revised) preexisting generic conventions *that
are already there* for the one who listens carefully enough, who is canny
enough to look past the apparently obvious to challenge "the blindness of the
seeing eye" (*Studies in Hysteria* 117 n. 1).[23]

   What Woolf and Heilman have in common is an insistence on definitively
locating the character somewhere, the author somewhere else. And in both
their readings, a note of defensiveness (the other side of condescension) creeps
in—but what could they be defensively reacting to? Perhaps a suspicion that
the complexity of female desire is lost in the patriarchal conventions of the
novel; perhaps a reluctance to wonder if the hysteric's equivocation and ambivalence might be an attempt to transcribe the daughter's ("new"?) filial
romance. In Laplanche and Pontalis' discussion of the origin of fantasy and its
connection to desire, such generic constraints have no place:

> By locating the origin of fantasy in the auto-erotism, we have shown the connec-
> tion between fantasy and desire. Fantasy, however, is not the object of desire,
> but its setting. In fantasy the subject does not pursue the object of its sign: he
> [*sic*] appears caught up himself in the sequence of images. He forms no represen-
> tation of the desired object, but is himself represented as participating in the
> scene although, in the earliest forms of fantasy, he cannot be assigned any fixed
> placc in it (hence the danger, in treatment, of interpretations which claim to do
> so). As a result, the subject, although always present in the fantasy, may be so in
> a desubjectivized form, that is to say, in the very syntax of the sequence in ques-
> tion. (17)

   Perhaps this uncanny mutability of self, desire, and syntax is defended
against by narrative, by the novel, by father-daughter romance. If, then, the
novel is allowed to fail in its task of imposing stable structures on this disorder, if the sentimental father-daughter positions fail to present themselves as
immutable, then heterosexuality as it is culturally constructed and enforced
looks like (may be) a permeable, unstable fiction. The father-daughter story,
which both reinforces and is reinforced by generic rules, has as its object
precisely the fixing of subject/object positions and in turn their distinction
from syntax that Laplanche and Pontalis, reading Freud, expose as cultural
fiction. The originary fantasies inherently lack any such orderliness, any such
grammatical, formal fixity. What both Woolf and Heilman, despite their different starting points, have in common is an attempt to reconfigure Charlotte
Brontë's refusal of formal constraints—perhaps it should be called her deviant use of generic conventions—in order to rescue that refusal or deviance
from its uncanny approximation of the untidy disorder of fantasy and desire

and their relations. A Brontë who is violating the author/character split, a Brontë who is merely furbishing up an already named generic category, is a Brontë recuperable for cultural pieties and alibis about subject and object positions, about suitable subject and object behaviors, about the origins of "human" desire, about the universality of what are culturally and historically grounded notions and constructions of the (gendered, familial, heterosexed) self.

Endogamy's Daughter

Field-workers. . . . are always in danger of confusing the natives' theories about their social organization (and the superficial form given to these institutions to make them consistent with theory) with the actual functioning of the society.

—Lévi-Strauss

Most of the novels written by Austen, the Brontës, George Eliot are distinctly grounded in sentimental family pieties; such a foundation arguably presents the least hope for radical revision of patriarchal structures. Yet, instructively perhaps for feminist criticism (which has its own familial desires and filial pieties to contend with), these women's novels present an effective way to deviantly (re)possess the father's fictions. Simply put: they go them one better. Earlier I appended the word "presumably" to my suggestion that the daughter figures of women novelists underwrite familial pieties. I did so because there is a notable peculiarity in the trajectories of the marriages inscribed by these writers: the theory of exogamous exchange notwithstanding, the daughter's daughter doesn't (won't) "leave her house, abandon her own family, renounce the name of her own mother and father. . . ."[24]

We have seen, in *Dombey and Son* and in *Little Women*, story resolutions which center on daughter marriages which also somehow include the daughter's father in the new family circle: Alcott's final family gathering, with Jo fondly watching her father enjoy the companionship she has given him by presenting him with Professor Bhaer for a son-in-law, is a resentimentalized version of Dickens' final family portrait, presided over by Florence's close observation of the "much-changed" Dombey anxiously lavishing a (grand)father's companionship and attention on his namesake (and on hers). The father who has "lost" a daughter is sentimentally if vestigially included in the happy ending, defusing the aggressive victory embodied by the successful winner of the daughter's hand: notice the faint whisper of continuing endogamous attachment.[25]

Compare the ending of *Pride and Prejudice:* Austen's indolent Mr. Bennet prefers Lizzy's hearth and home so much to his own that this man who hates to exert himself frequently deserts his own house for hers; more intensely, we find Emma Woodhouse and her intended proposing quite literally to expand the father's household. Emily Brontë's subversive plot is resolved by Catherine Linton Heathcliff (about to be Earnshaw) and her prospective husband planning to settle at Thrushcross Grange (*her* father's house), thus restoring to order through daughterly endogamy the libidinal chaos provoked by the preceding exogamous exchanges initiated by her mother's momentous (and culturally correct) decision to marry Edgar Linton. Jane Eyre returns to her "only home" (which is located wherever her Master is domiciled) to marry and to stay. George Eliot's Eppie Marner marries the son of her foster father's parenting partner, Dolly Winthrop, only on stipulation of thereafter forming a Woodhouse-like family:

> "That was what Aaron said—'I could never think o' taking you away from Master Marner, Eppie.' And I said, 'It 'ud be no use if you did, Aaron.' And he wants us all to live together, so as you needn't work a bit, father, only what's for your own pleasure; and he'd be as good as a son to you—that was what he said." (*Silas Marner* 209)

The family resemblances among the works of these novelists, then, include two kinds of pressure on the sentimental father-daughter paradigm: a patriarchally inadequate father and a metaphorically endogamous marriage. The father fails to meet the sentimental standard in some way; his daughter must therefore exert a version of paternal authority in order to inscribe *herself* as sentimental daughter and so as marriageable. The daughter's marriage is an *italicized* sentimental one, which is to say an endogamous one, and it is, paradoxically, the inadequacy of the father which makes it possible for him to exchange his daughter and have her too. To put it another way: in writing the family novel—which mimes the story of the origin of the self and is transversed by the plot of desire—these nineteenth-century bourgeois women novelists imagine a daughter "never banished from home." At first glance, this may strike us as a plot resolution fairly complicit with the prescriptions of patriarchal heterosexuality. But if the daughter's *leaving* home is precisely the foundation of all kinds of patriarchal economies, and if her presence in the paternal space destabilizes that structure even as it accomplishes its covert task of continuously provoking heterosexual (father-daughter) desire, keeping the daughter home may prove symptomatic of an interesting "both/and-edness" in the *daughter's* inscription of heterosexual desire.

The Daughter's Sentiment

Put them all together, they spell Mother / A word that means the world
to me.

—H. Johnson

What am I going to make of these family resemblances, these deviations from
the generic oedipalized pronouncements and prescriptions of literary criticism and the novel? I find myself in a position analogous to Tania Modleski's
in her discussion of the female oedipal trajectory in *The Women Who Knew
Too Much*:[26]

> . . . I am taking exception to the notion of the influential French film theorist
> Raymond Bellour that all Hollywood narratives are dramatizations of the male
> oedipal story, of man's entry into the social and Symbolic order. In rejecting
> Bellour's thesis and arguing that there is at least one film dealing with woman's
> "incorporation" into the social order . . . I do not mean to suggest that *Rebecca*
> is thereby a "progressive" film for women; the social order is, after all, a patriar-
> chal order. I do, however, maintain that all kinds of interesting differences arise
> when a film features a woman's trajectory and directly solicits the interest of a
> female audience. Besides, as I have said, I do not believe the assimilation of
> femininity by patriarchy can ever be complete. My own analysis is dedicated to
> tracing the resistances that disturb the text. (45)

Literary criticism, when it is concerned with assessing a given novel in
terms of what Teresa de Lauretis calls the "mechanisms of coherence," is
inevitably complicit with the fiction that male oedipality[27] accounts for the
novel's version of the story of heterosexual desire. What I have argued
throughout this study is that when textual elements traditionally considered
excrescent—the sentimental, textual hysteria, endogamized endings—are at-
tended to, we begin to see the fault lines in the smooth surface fictions which
freeze the narrative messiness of desire into coherent, stable, predetermined
forms.

Like Modleski, I don't think we are hopelessly forever oppressed by the
patriarchy. Not only is the heterosexual story not as automatic or monolithic
as it wants to look, but it is inherently a plot which needs assistance from its
objects (pupils, victims, products—put them all together, they spell "daughter"). And not only their willing cooperation, but—when a daughter writes
it—their active intervention. The deviations, excesses, refusals of certain
nineteenth-century women's family novels point to the innumerable assists
and nudgings into place our orderly fictions require in order to stay viable.
From this point of view, even such an apparently innocently conservative

running gag as Mrs. Bennet's utter incomprehension of the entail on the family estate may function as a remark upon the precariousness of the father's fiction:

> "I do think it is the hardest thing in the world, that your estate should be entailed away from your own children; and I am sure that if I had been you, I should have tried long ago to do something or other about it."
>
> Jane and Elizabeth attempted to explain to her the nature of an entail. They had often attempted it before, but it was a subject on which Mrs. Bennet was beyond the reach of reason; and she continued to rail bitterly against the cruelty of settling an estate away from a family of five daughters, in favor of a man whom nobody cared anything about. (61–62)

In fact, "the nature of an entail" *is* precisely to settle an estate away from a family of five daughters. An entailed estate is an instance of the law intervening in the unpredictable messiness of reproduction which, perversely, does not always cooperate with the patriarchal construction of families and estates. ("When first Mr. Bennet had married, economy was held to be perfectly useless; for, of course, they were to have a son" [308].) The silliness of Mrs. Bennet (and the unpleasantness of Lady Catherine de Bourgh, who *has* inherited her estate) effectively draws our attention from the silliness and unpleasantness of this patrilineal security device. The entail *is* "cruel," as Mrs. Bennet hysterically insists; it is not Mrs. Bennet's matrimonial ambition for her daughters which is responsible for the very material necessity of marriage for the Bennet girls; nor is Mrs. Bennet's silliness and vulgarity (Darcy's fastidious objection notwithstanding) the primary obstacle to their marrying without loss of class status. The entail means the Bennet daughters must leave home, and it significantly affects the size of their dowries.

> "How any one could have the conscience to entail away an estate from one's own daughters I cannot understand; and all for the sake of Mr. Collins too!— Why should *he* have it more than anybody else?"
>
> "I leave it to yourself to determine," said Mr. Bennet. (130)

The cui bono question, however risibly couched in Austen's text, remains unanswered, because it is unanswerable: Mr. Collins, who is at least as silly as Mrs. Bennet, *is* a man about whom nobody cares. That he, rather than the Bennet daughters, should inherit Mr. Bennet's estate is a circumstance just as far "beyond the reach of reason" as Mrs. Bennet ever could be: he inherits because the legal fiction of patrilineality is thus, paradoxically (Collins is only remotely "kin" to Mr. Bennet), best defended. When a conflict arises between fictions of descent and fictions of gender, the former prevails, tacitly. From the oscillation of the daughter between subject (the father's heir) and object (the father's property) the law of primogeniture defends the bourgeois family: it inserts a designated "son," asserts the fiction of his superior relatedness to the father, and thereby aligns daughters legally with their mothers as irrelevant to patrilineality. Daughters thus become stabilized, fixed as objects, by operation of law; their filial connection to the mother is disqualified as descent, and thereby made to be legally unarticulable, even legally disarticulated.

Thus the legal system provides strenuous backup for the fictions of bourgeois family ideology. Why does Austen represent the law of entail as still, on the very threshold of the era of modern capitalism, taking such pains to ensure that the daughter will never usurp the father's privilege and that she will be separated not only from her father but from her mother as well? Julia Kristeva points to such excessive control as evidence of fear: "the masculine, apparently victorious, confesses through its very relentlessness against the other, the feminine, that it is threatened by an asymmetrical, irrational, wily, uncontrollable power" (*Powers of Horror* 70).

Jane Austen's Emma Woodhouse perhaps best testifies to the empowerment granted to the daughter who is not banished, whether by entail or romantic love or exogamous exchange, from the familial home:

> "Fortune I do not want; employment I do not want; consequence I do not want: I believe few married women are half as much mistress of their husband's house, as I am of Hartfield; and never, never could I expect to be so truly beloved and important; so always first and always right in any man's eyes as I am in my father's." (84)

In addition to occupying her dead mother's place as mistress of her father's house, Emma Woodhouse also identifies with the father's place in her attempts to orchestrate the exchange of women—she counts Miss Taylor's marriage as produced by her arrangement, and she spends much of the novel scheming to marry Harriet Smith, this last greatly to the disgust of the paternalistic Mr. Knightley.[28]

> "Your time has been *properly* and *delicately* spent, if you have been endeavouring for the last four years to bring about this marriage. A worthy employment for a young lady's mind!"

> "You are more likely to have done *harm to yourself,* than good to them, by interference." (12, 13)

That there is something unclean, improper, contaminant in the daughter's impinging/infringing upon the father's prerogative (forfeited by his inadequacy—in "Mr. Smith's" case, figured by his refusal to act as Harriet's father in any but the biological and economic sense) is testified to by Mr. Knightley's oddly adamant reaction to Emma's usurpation of it, even in the relatively harmless game of matchmaking. What are we to make of his exclamations? As we have seen, even the most patriarchal version of the daughter's desire evokes the background theme music of the uncanny. What makes the daughter of sentiment uncanny are the lurking questions always haunting femininity (and female subjectivity) as construct and social artifact: what if she just *acts* as if she's consented? What if she has her *own* reasons? Her own desire?

Emma's attempt to arrange Harriet Smith's matrimonial fate figures her successful arrangement of her own marriage *faute de père*, as it were. The daughter who props her father's patriarchal position in order to provide herself with sentimental credentials uncannily disorders the father's fiction; the daughter who arranges a figuratively endogamous marriage and thus refuses to leave the father's house confuses the orderly syntax of genealogy and patrilineality, introducing the ambiguity which is, Mary Douglas tells us, so much cultural dirt, so much "matter out of place" (35). For what is she doing if not bringing the son (in-law) into her father's house, thus occupying simultaneously two inappropriate familial positions: her father's in heterosexual exchange, her mother's in heterosexual desire. For if it is true that

> "Separation is our chance to become subjects of representation." But becoming a subject of representation means casting out or 'abjecting' the mother. (Mary Jacobus discussing one of her theoretical mothers, Julia Kristeva, *Reading Woman* 178)

then figurations of endogamy as closure for the bourgeois family romance may indeed signal/trace a (hysterical?) desire to go home (back to the future, back up the genealogical divide) to mother.

These daughters' daughters, then, come as close to returning to the mother (the mother's place) as is possible without directly and explicitly disrupting the father's fiction, which is always ultimately based on separation from the mother: "If language, like culture, sets up a separation and, starting with discrete elements, concatenates an order, it does so precisely by repressing maternal authority . . ." (Kristeva, *Powers of Horror* 72). The inadequate father and the endogamous resolution are narrative elements which evoke the masquerade of the *father*, which look at his power, his law, and his name— and see what there is not to see. The daughter who props the father's fiction and directs it to an ending which underscores the father's inadequacy to his culture's desire and his own is hysteric in that she identifies with the father's desire in a resistant, coded, symptomatized way; she's uncanny in that her refusal to leave the paternal home can be read as also a refiliation with the (never completely absent) mother. Julia Kristeva, for instance, speaks of "the institutionalizing of bisexuality through endogamic marriage" (82) as one of the important effects of such marriage practices.

> The endogamic principle inherent in caste system amounts, as everywhere else, to having the individual marry within his group, or rather to his being prohibited from marrying outside of it. Endogamy, in Indian castes, implies in addition a specific filiation: the passing on of membership in the group by *both* parents at the same time. The result of such a regulation is in fact a balancing, symbolic and real, of the role of both sexes within that socio-symbolic unit constituted by caste. The highly hierarchical nature of Indian society does not come into play between the sexes, at least not where filiation is concerned—a major criterion of power in those societies. One could say that caste is a hierarchic device that, in addition to professional specializations, insures, in the passing on of group membership, an *equal* share to the father and to the mother. (79)

If the daughter both tells and is the story, she's disordering an important subject/object family position separation—affecting not only gender, but parent position: she takes on herself both father and mother, both masculine and feminine, which is also what hysterics do. Hysteria and endogamy make an uncanny mess of generational and patrilineal articulations and taxonomies, the generic and genderic (and fictional) stabilities of story and desire.

> Let me note only that . . . without classic exogamy, social order is not elaborated on the basis of clear-cut oppositions represented by *men* and *women* as tokens of "one's own" and the "foreign," the "same" and the "different" (sex, group, clan, etc.). . . . one avoids the binarism of the exogamic system, that is, the father/mother, man/woman strangeness at the level of the *matrimonial* institution. . . . (79–80)[29]

If the novel is centered on the production and formation of identity in the generic sense, the issue of female identity—how to inscribe it, how to describe it in language—has been one of the novel's most problematic issues since the birth or rise of the form. If desire is a motivating factor in fiction—the force behind the plot—then the daughter's articulation of female desire is thus made doubly difficult, lacking as she does both a conventional syntax by which her desire can be ordered and a narrative structure "of one's own" in which to represent that desire's workings. Formal deviance intrudes: lacking syntax and story, the daughter speaks anyway, across the body (of the text, of the law, of the father).

Female hysteria and the sentimental family romance, modes of simultaneous representation and repression of heterosexual desire invented (not coin-
cidentally) at about the same moment, conspire together to produce novels
which take us to the brink of a conceivable (and uncanny) daughter's desire.
Culturally, the sentimental family romance necessitated the productive mode
of hysteria to express whatever remained of (possibly mythical) nonoe-
dipal(ized) female heterosexual desire. Similarly, assertions by traditional literary criticism of generic constraints have attempted to confine a mode of
writing arguably invented by women to a set of formal conventions which
necessitates a (metaphoric) hysteria on the part of the woman who would use
it to tell the story of an already subsumed daughter's desire. The daughter's
family romance novels display deviant points of pressure, exaggerations of
emphasis, peculiar textual insufficiencies—differences from the patriarchal
father-daughter sentimental paradigm[30] which lean on a certain necessary
uncanny quality in the daughter of sentiment, the heroine of the family romance. These are the family resemblances traceable in the texts of Austen, the
Brontës, and Eliot.

The hysteria and uncanniness shadowing these texts and their heroines
may turn out to trace an erased, even a forgotten desire—a perhaps nonexis-
tent, but necessary to postulate, daughter's desire. But much more must be
done before a "feminine" heterosexual desire can even be hypothesized. The
story of heterosexual (i.e., sentimental father-daughter) desire as written by
canonical nineteenth-century women writers needs a book in which to test
and use a whole body of theoretical speculations to query the degree and
kind of female investment in and investiture with heterosexuality. One of the
lines of that investigation must be the place of the mother in heterosexual
(father-daughter) desire. Such a reading would involve, at the outset, careful
selection of feminist rereadings of psychoanalytic theories together with cultural analyses of institutional ideologies of motherhood, enabling a reading
of female heterosexual investment in the mother. The investigation should
also incoporate work on the lesbian version of desire for and struggle with
the mother (and father);[31] the possibilities of nonbourgeois paradigms in the
writing of women of color and nonbourgeois class origins must certainly be
explored.
      That there can be no "feminine" without the additional vector of familial
position and a specific designation of the prescriptive discourse (here, the
novel) and mode (here, the sentimental) of representation one is dealing in is
certainly clear; that the next step is to query daughterly desire as written by
important women novelists equally so. A note of caution must be sounded
however: heterosexual ideologies depend on and from assumptions of symme-

try and complementarity; it may be that *any* logical symmetry inevitably re-inscribes the very constructs feminisms exist to challenge and analyze.[32] As a finale to this book, this chapter on the daughter-written romance represents a vision of closure, that formal convention invented precisely to cover up the unsightly, asymmetrical body of heterosexuality's fictions. The desire it inscribes therefore, whether I will or no, is necessarily the desire for symmetry which, as I argued in Chapter 4, turns out to be a particularly effective policing device for heterosexual ideology.

In the very project of producing this book, then, I, like Anzia Yezierska's struggling daughter of sentiment, Sara Smolinsky, feel "the shadow still there, over me. It wasn't just my father, but the generations who made my father whose weight is still upon me" (297). Yet in its impulse to both accept and refuse the formal conventions of the conclusory chapter, its simultaneous articulation of the fathers' critical weaknesses and retention (largely) of academic discourse, its climactic attempt to end up in the place occupied by the feminist theorists I have chosen to genealogically align myself with while refusing to leave the house of literary criticism, I have hoped to display a prepossessing family resemblance to the textual mother lode of the (fictional, critical, theoretical) daughters of sentiment.

Notes

Works Cited

Index

Notes

Introduction

1 See R. S. Crane, "Suggestions toward a Genealogy of the 'Man of Feeling,' " for the seminal essay on the historical origins of sentimentalism.

2 For a history of these words, see Erik Erametsa.

3 Barbara Welter, in "The Cult of True Womanhood, 1820–1860," discusses the cultural phenomenon of the True Woman ideal.

4 In *Deceit, Desire, and the Novel.* For a brilliant reading of Girard's notion of triangular desire, see Toril Moi, "The Missing Mother: The Oedipal Rivalries of René Girard," wherein she argues that Girard's theory of mimetic desire cannot account for feminine desire.

Chapter 1. "My father has, you know, a terrible voice"

1 John Allen Stevenson, building on the work of Lawrence Stone, discusses the extent to which Richardson's novel reflects the reigning ideology of his time and place, particularly the contemporary elevation of the "new marital ideal, the so-called companionate marriage, which elevated compatibility and affection (if not passion) over economic considerations as the basis for choosing a mate" (758). Interest in family configurations and related issues remains lively; see, for example, Lieb.

2 Freud's first announcement of his abandonment of the seduction theory can be found in his September 21, 1897, letter to his friend Wilhelm Fliess: "I no longer believe in my *neurotica* . . . in every case the father, not excluding my own, had to be blamed as a pervert" (*SE* 1:259).

3 Even a quick perusal of Freud's "Femininity" reveals this impulse; compare this passage, for example, ". . . almost all my women patients told me that they had been seduced by their father. I was driven to recognize in the end that these reports were untrue . . ." (120), with this passage: "And now we find the phantasy of seduction once more in the pre-Oedipal prehistory of girls; but the seducer is regularly the mother. Here, however, the phantasy touches the ground of reality, for it was really the mother who by her activities over the child's bodily hygiene inevitably stimulated, and perhaps even roused for the first time, pleasurable sensations in her genitals" (120).

4 Questions of power and the text are addressed in several strains of *Clarissa* criticism. For feminist criticism concerned with the dimension of power, see, among others, Katharine M. Rogers, who sees Richardson as a radical feminist; Judith Wilt, who sees Richardson as an antifeminist; and Terry Castle, who offers us a

Clarissa who lacks power insofar as she is a naive reader of naturalized signs. Problems of power, reading, gender, and class in the production and reading of *Clarissa* are considered by William Beatty Warner, Terry Eagleton, Sue Warrick Doederlein, and Terry Castle.

5 For a generic analysis of sentimental drama that examines the material reward system it covertly invokes, see Parnell.

6 For a discussion of the covert and overt relationships between sentimentalized religion and material rewards, see Parnell.

7 For an analysis of *Clarissa* focusing on tropes of self, will, and penetration, see Braudy.

8 Leslie Fiedler also, albeit from a perspective different from my own, reads Clarissa as founding a long genealogy. He terms *Clarissa* a "sacred book" which manages to be a "treasure house of symbols dear to the rising bourgeoisie" without sacrificing, at the same time, "verisimilitude, without ceasing to be a scrupulous portrayal of contemporary manners and modes of consciousness" (72–73). Samuel Richardson's influence on the American novel is seminal: "For better or for worse, the values of the Sentimental Love Religion, inextricably bound up with the example of Richardson, entered into the American novel at the moment of its creation" (75). This influence, Fiedler notes, is by and large exhibited as a diminishment of Richardson's accomplishment.

9 In Felman's unparalleled analysis of James's "The Turn of the Screw," she has occasion to note: "That the letter of *Nothing* can in fact signify a *love letter* is reminiscent of Cordelia's uncanny reply to King Lear: by virtue of his imposing paternal and royal authority, King Lear, although soliciting his daughter's expression of love, can symbolically be seen as its censor. In saying precisely 'nothing,' Cordelia addresses her father with the only 'authentic' love letter . . ." (147 n. 29).

Chapter 2. The Fear of the Father

1 Dombey's difference from other Dickens fathers has earned him a good deal of critical approval, not to mention readerly sympathy. See especially Julian Moynahan, who urbanely traces Dombey's passage from "hardness through debility to a maundering, guilt-ridden submission to feminine softness" (130); A. E. Dyson, who speaks disapprovingly of Florence's "possessive obsession, which is fulfilled only when Mr. Dombey's manhood is broken in the game of life" (131); and Nina Auerbach, whose analysis of the sexual sadness caused by the separation of the spheres of the sexes is informative, subtle, and closely argued ("Dickens and Dombey").

2 The generic application of Little Dorrit's sobriquet is suggested by Alexander Welsh, *The City of Dickens* 210.

3 Auerbach points out that in this gesture Dombey accomplishes a "masculinization of the too flowing Polly Toodle" ("Dickens and Dombey," 99).

4 I owe this insight into the nature of Polly Toodle to Amy A. Doerr.

5 Dr. Blimber has a daughter and no son—like Dombey after Paul's death. Dr.

Blimber simply marries his daughter off to his assistant, thus ensuring the survival of the family business. Dombey arrives at a similar resolution by the end of the novel, but his journey to it is not so graceful.

6   The phrase is Dickens' epitaph for his beloved sister-in-law, Mary Hogarth, who died at the age of seventeen, and seems to have haunted him for the rest of his life.

7   The phrase is Roland Barthes's, and note too that Barthes considers that the preparation for the erotic scene is what makes a text a book of "desire" rather than of mere "pleasure," which make *Dombey* one of the former (*The Pleasure of the Text*).

8   Quoted in Tillotson 171–72 n. 3.

9   Moynahan notes the "sybilline" quality and general haziness of reference of the preface.

10 Monod also quotes the writer of a letter to the editor of *The Dickensian* (October 1925) who was so annoyed with Florence that he actually counted the number of times she cries in the novel—eighty-four (249).

11 For an extended analysis of the social construction of desire in our "social order that eroticizes potency (as male) and victimization (as female)," see Catharine A. MacKinnon, "Feminism, Marxism, Method, and the State: An Agenda for Theory." Her analysis of the dynamic of desire and power differs importantly in its basic assumptions—which are not only feminist and Marxist but also more Foucauldian than either of those persuasions taken alone tend to be—from another kind of analysis which on a superficial level bears some resemblance to my own. Robert Clark, in "Riddling the Family Firm: The Sexual Economy in *Dombey and Son*," presents a reading which proposes to acknowledge the "text's libidinous desire" (82). He correctly and astutely identifies Florence's relation to her father as the central riddle of the novel, and traces Lévi-Strauss's suggestion that women as objects of exchange cement the social relations necessary to the continuation of our economic system. Like Lévi-Strauss, however, Clark can only bow to the woman's double, and paradoxical, status as both object *and* (presumptive) subject. Dombey becomes, in Clark's reading, a sort of allegorical British businessman and Florence becomes merely the poetic causality of his downfall. Like previous *Dombey* readers, Clark sees Florence at the novel's end as living a life of "sexless felicity" (70) with Walter; Dombey "ends the novel impotent, emasculated, superseded by this very child" (73). Clark cites Foucault's *History of Sexuality*, but retains a very non-Foucauldian notion of a monolithic political power which is prior to the social structure: ". . . the phrase "Dombey and Daughter" confronts us with the fact that social structure is constructed by political power" (72). Clark's reading is informative on the historical-contextual level, and the blind spots he reproduces in that reading are by no means traceable to any critical incapacity. Like his predecessors, and like those of us who would follow other paths, he is inevitably enmeshed in the discourses which produce his text as well as the texts he reads, an important element of which is a reluctance to analyze the details of the father-daughter dynamic. In Clark's case, this reluctance results in a turning away from the particularity of this father's and this daughter's dance of

denial, delay, and desire, and, consequently, the analysis has much more in common with the traditional patriarchal attitudes it purports to criticize than with, for
example, the kind of reading Nina Auerbach, whose work Clark mentions with
approval, presents in "Dickens and Dombey," and in a broader historical context
in her superb *Woman and the Demon* (the epigraph of which is from Maxine
Hong Kingston's *The Woman Warrior:* "Perhaps women were once so dangerous
that they had to have their feet bound").

12 These are the words of the model of Deportment, Mr. Turveydrop (*Bleak House*
175). Mr. Turveydrop is fond of dropping just such pieces of "very disagreeable
gallantry," as Esther Summerson puts it, in honor of "the sex."

13 Edith has, of course, failed not only her daughter Florence, but also her son by her
first marriage, who dies as a result of his nurse's neglect.

14 In *The History of Sexuality* Foucault discusses the ubiquity of the confession in the
West since the Middle Ages as a ritual of discourse unfolding within a power
relationship, hence implicated in the maintenance of power even as it purports to
be productive of Truth (see pp. 60ff.).

Chapter 3. *Little Women*

1 The female escapee from Aunt Sally seems to escape more often to death (Little
Eva, Edna Pontellier, Lily Bart) than to the Territory.

2 Discussion of the connections between *The Tempest* and the New World has a
long history. Leo Marx's classic "Shakespeare's American Fable" reads the play
in terms of an essentially American dialectic between technology and the pastoral ideal; Annette Kolodny's *The Lay of the Land* continues this exploration
with a brilliant analysis of the American version of the pastoral as an essentially
linguistic and gendered fantasy. My interest in the play here draws upon both
these discussions: what I want to suggest is that while the European pastoral was
inevitably altered in its new, American sociohistorico-economic context, the
father-daughter romance seems essentially to transcend such marked historical
differences.

3 "Know," it seems scarcely necessary to point out, has its biblical resonances of
the end of innocence and the beginning of carnal knowledge, and "farther" echoes father—and may well have done so much more strongly in Shakespeare's
English.

4 This is Leslie Fiedler's label for the novel. Susanna Rowson was born in England,
but her career was largely transatlantic, and Charlotte Temple's betrayal and demise are played out in the New World (by a British redcoat, I might add). In any
case, the division between "American" and "English," still often an equivocal
one, is problematic in the eighteenth century. (So, for that matter, is the term
"American" used as I do here for United States literature.) For another view of the
place of Rowson's novel in American literature and in feminist criticism, see
Jehlen.

5 I am drawing here from the particularly cogent analysis of the collision of cultur-

ally inscribed reading expectations and fictions written by women presented in Nancy K. Miller's remarkable essay "Emphasis Added."

6 It seems to me that the extent to which feminist disputes over the theoretical and practical implications of the female body, women's historical experience, and "*écriture feminine*" have become inappropriately polarized can be gaged by the spectacle of the irrefragably empirical Jo/Alcott living out her own rhythms in writing, experiencing what looks suspiciously like the excess that is feminine jouissance.

7 This is, for my purposes and despite important differences among them, the distinguishing characteristic of the readings of Auerbach, Bedell, Douglas, Janeway, and Spacks. The biographical material used in this chapter has been gathered primarily from the fine standard critical work written by Madeleine B. Stern, the psychoanalytically inflected (and occasionally too-indignant) biography written by Martha Saxton, and the compendious and uniquely wide-angled family portrait written by Madelon Bedell. Information particular to any given work will be so noted in the text. Other variously useful and illuminating recent biographically oriented works include Macdonald, Marsella, Meigs, Strickland (whose social history orientation is particularly interesting for those interested in sentimentality as a cultural artifact).

The epigraph is taken from Bronson Alcott's journals (Saxton 148). (For an amusing view of Bronson's stylistic peculiarities, see T. Beer.) The Alcott family's journals were not exactly personal diaries; they were always open to the scrutiny, and even unsolicited editorializing, of the rest of the family. This ambiguously public status makes this kind of remark (or the one about dark-skinned people [like Louisa] being demonic and blue-eyed blonds [like sister Anna] being closest to God) a particularly poignant reminder of the difficulties of life in the nuclear family.

8 For a useful accompaniment to Welter's reading of the cult of True Womanhood, as well as a graceful acknowledgment of Douglas' pioneering albeit antisentimentalist work on the sentimental writers, see Tompkins' analysis of the literary and gender politics of *Uncle Tom's Cabin*.

9 Luce Irigaray, among others, has demonstrated the power of this figure for feminist analysis, most notably in the title essay of *This Sex Which Is Not One*.

10 The patriarchal construction of motherhood has been noted by many feminist thinkers: Colette Guillaumin in 1979 declared that "women's claiming as virtues qualities that men have always found convenient" is not "liberatory" (paraphrased in Jones's important review, 371). Jane Gallop, in a *Critical Inquiry* essay which appeared after this chapter was completed, makes a similar observation: "The masculine is inscribed in motherhood; patriarchal discourse structures the institution and the experience of motherhood as we know it" (328). It is not, I think, possible to produce a version of the mother completely untouched by the discourse we speak and which speaks us; what is possible is to examine rigorously the particular structures which call for and benefit by any given version—see, for example, Julia Kristeva's brilliant "Stabat Mater."

11 Baym's confrontational rhetoric, and the dangerous (for feminist studies) reification of "marginality" in some current Anglo-American feminisms, have been thoroughly and thoughtfully explored in Laurie Finke's very insightful response to the "Feminist Issues" number of *Tulsa Studies in Women's Literature*.

12 "Reversal" is finally, of course, a conservative stratagem which maintains rather than subverts a given dichotomy. The readings of DeLamotte, Fetterly, Kaledin, and Saxton, while making important and insightful contributions to the analysis of the ambiguities and ambivalences of Alcott's work and life, leave the implications of the thriller (or early) fiction/family (or juvenile) fiction dichotomy unexamined. With one exception (*A Modern Mephistopheles*), Alcott stopped writing sensation fiction after *Little Women* was published: it is my contention that this is a turning point only in fictional rhetoric; Alcott continued to work essentially the same fictional material after 1868 as she had before that date. Alcott's good girls and her bad girls learn to act (more or less consciously) in identical ways in order to enact an essential identity of desire.

13 For an enlightening discussion of such abilities, see DeLamotte.

14 *Moods* is the novel generally agreed to be represented by Jo March's first serious literary attempt. After Alcott had become a famous writer, her publisher decided without consulting her to reprint *Moods*. Alcott objected, but Roberts had the right to republish it; she was allowed, however, to make substantial changes. Alcott deleted passages, rewrote portions, included some material that had been cut from the original version. The differences between the two versions have been remarked upon generally—both Stern and Saxton discuss the republishing, Bedell considers the 1864 version superior ("Introduction"), and Macdonald notes several salient plot differences—but the marked changes Alcott made in the father-daughter relationship are not included in these discussions.

15 Toots and Blimber appear in *Dombey and Son*. The Dickens-Alcott connection is noted by nearly all Alcott scholars. Stern notes similarities between the death scenes of little Paul Dombey and Beth March; the Pickwick Club in *Little Women* is discussed by Ann Douglas and Nina Auerbach, among others; Sarah Elbert discusses points of convergence between *Bleak House* and *Little Women*. Alcott was an inveterate literary borrower, and echoes of the plots of Hawthorne, Wilkie Collins, Mrs. Gaskell, and many others abound in her fiction. But the Dickens allusions are of a different order. The stories of Little Dorrit's devotion to an impecunious, financially shameless father and of Alcott's lifelong indenture to what she jauntily called the "Alcott sinking fund" necessitated by her father's Skimpole-like inability to make a living are, for example, startling similar. So too are the stories of Florence Dombey's and Louisa May's filial courtship/training. It may be that these convergences facilitated Alcott's fine sensitivity to the dark Dickens, dark not as the casual flip side of the comic-sentimental, but dark as integrally, inevitably, structurally inextricable from it. After all, even the light-hearted *Pickwick Papers* is about debt, matrimony, and wife beating as an amiable weakness.

16 I mean, of course, the Name-of-the-Father, Lacan's term for the cultural, linguis-

tic, always preexisting law which produces the relations of self, other, and desire: "Even when in fact it is represented by a single person, the paternal function concentrates in itself both imaginary and real relations, always more or less adequate to the symbolic relation that essentially constitutes it. It is in the *name of the father* that we must recognize the support of the symbolic function which, from the dawn of history, has identified his person with the figure of the law" ("The function and field of speech and language in psychoanalysis," *Ecrits* 67).

17 The material cited here can now be found, in expanded form, in Radway's book.

18 Other simultaneities in the lives of the father and daughter include a birthday in common, and the peculiar refractions of their careers: Bronson's *Tablets* and his daughter's *Little Women* were both published in 1868 (in time for Abba's birthday on October 8); it was her portrait of Father March (presumptively representing Bronson's philosophy) rather than Bronson's own philosophical work which produced his (short-lived, as usual) success on the lecture circuit (where he billed himself, against Louisa's wishes, as "the Father of *Little Women*").

Chapter 4. "She couldn't say yes, but she didn't say no"

1 Fathers and daughters in general are generating a good deal of provocative and fascinating feminist criticism. My attention in this essay is restricted to the fictional presentation of filial relations between a professedly neutral father and a sentimentalized—that is to say, an acquiescent, domestic, loving, self-abnegating—daughter. Fathers and daughters lend themselves to other kinds of analyses as well. In a recent essay, Sandra M. Gilbert attempts, for example, a much more panoramic view of fictions of fathers and daughters, with particular attention to daughter-written texts. The daughter she reads is rather more monolithic than the one I read, and her version of patriarchal demand more blunt-edged ("you must give yourself to your father" [364]) than the allusive, silent, and unavowed solicitation the daughter of sentiment receives from her father.

2 Accounting for the missing story is a major project of feminist literary criticism. See, for a small sampling of the insightful and brilliant work done from this perspective, Kamuf, Kolodny, and Miller.

3 See Herman and Hirschman for important feminist analysis of actual incestuous abuse of women and children.

4 Leon Edel's position is important because his interest in James is biographical and psychoanalytical, enabling him to consider the familial structures in *The Golden Bowl*, and because his masterful biography of James's life and mind is the starting point for every student of the Master.

5 As Leo Bersani points out, James does not present the self as prior to language, but rather "insists on the fact that fictional invention is neither evasive nor tautological; instead, it *constitutes the self*" (132). It is not, however, altogether useful to talk about "the" self: "selves" exist in and are constructed by culture; they are always gendered, and gendered with respect to some familial positioning. It is through the web of silent fictions that Maggie retains her daughter's place even

upon the separation necessitated by her taking Cordelia's position—refusing to
pay for her father with her husband. Bersani's discussion of James and Stendhal
starts with the idea that "[b]oth James and Stendhal are consistently ironic about
the independent value of an idea—that is, about an idea presented apart from the
desire which it both expresses and disguises. They are, we might say, willing to
desublimate social life—to decipher the intellectual abstractions of an official
social code in order to indicate the individual needs which the code's rhetoric
obscures" (128–29). In *The Golden Bowl,* James submits the official social codes
of filial and marital relations to such a desublimation. Maggie and Adam are not
oddities, but representatives of the official social code constraining the specific
father-daughter relation, and *The Golden Bowl* is about the "individual needs"
(*not* identical for father and daughter) which the "code's rhetoric obscures." They
are, in short, all too *normal.*

6 See, for example, Mildred E. Hartsock: "The idea that the relationship of Adam
and Maggie is Oedipal or in any way pathological cannot be sustained by the
events of the novel . . ." (285). R. B. J. Wilson dismisses the suggestion of "incest," instead seeing Adam as perpetrating a forgiving deception on Maggie, for
whom he marries Charlotte: "Maggie still idolizes her father, not really knowing
him, and he continues to the end to try to bluff her into accepting as real his
simulated appreciation of his wife" (254). Nicola Bradbury is willing to use the
word "incestuous," but only in the context of Maggie's invincible "innocence":
"For Maggie, wistful for a childlike innocence, the incestuous relation is not
thinkable; for 'other persons' it is not speakable" (182). Ruth Yeazell refers to
"the innocent Electra bond" (120), and Philip Sicker, in a study which refresh-
ingly takes account of love and sex in Henry James's canon, concludes his arguments in gender-neutral vocabularies and issues: "[Maggie] escapes both the
constrictive prison of the ego and the dissolution of self in another by recogniz-
ing two distinct centers of consciousness through two equal loves" (164). Similarly, Virginia C. Fowler argues that it is by "disentangling herself from the
'family' she shares with Adam" that Maggie "achieve[s] selfhood" (137).
Bersani also denies "that Maggie and her father have an 'unhealthy' attachment
to each other . . ." (131).

7 The extent to which even such an intendedly protean discourse as psychoanalysis
can become fixed, in its own interest, behind heresies-turned-orthodoxy was am-
ply demonstrated in the recent Jeffrey Masson controversy. Nina Baym is charac-
teristically succinct on this issue: "The real Freudian scandal, of course . . . is the
substitution of the Oedipus complex for the *seduction theory* on the grounds that
it would be impossible for all those women (and men) to be telling the truth when
they testified to childhood sexual abuse. What we learn every day, these days,
exposes this uncharacteristic eruption of 'common sense' into the Freudian discourse as a dreadful hypocrisy" (59 n. 16). Elsewhere in the same essay, speaking
of the concept of penis-wish as the "legitimizing basis of every sexist stereotype
and proscription," Baym points out that the notion is "too patently useful, too
crassly interested, and too culturally sophisticated, to qualify as an emanation

from the Unconscious" (54). (It is interesting to note that here Baym takes a position identical to that of Luce Irigaray—whom Baym has grouped, as we saw in the
previous chapter, with the wrong-headed feminist theory party. See note 13, below.) Apropos of the personal interest Freud might have had in the subtitution of
the Oedipus complex for the seduction theory, see Gilbert (374) for a suggestive
biographical connection.

8 For his speculations on the mother-in-law problem, see Sigmund Freud, *Totem
and Taboo* 16.

9 This lecture (Sigmund Freud, "Femininity") was written in 1932, but never delivered, as Freud had undergone surgery for cancer of the mouth. See Felman's "Rereading Femininity," 19–21, on the relevance of this work for feminist criticism.

10 The reader familiar with Luce Irigaray's work will notice my indebtedness to her
in the passage which follows this quotation. Most feminist or proto-feminist
readers have decorated the margins of their books with what Jane Gallop has
called "impertinent questions"; what is new is the permission to ask them publicly and in print that a decade and a half of feminist criticism and theory has
generated.

11 In *Gynesis*, Alice A. Jardine brilliantly interrogates those spaces and their relationships to theoretical and fictional discourses, the constitution of ideologies, the
possibility of specific differences between texts written by men and by women,
and current American and French literary practice.

12 Lacan's remark appears in *Encore, Le Seminaire XX*, quoted in *This Sex* (86).
Annette Kolodny's germinal reading of Susan Glaspell's "A Jury of Her Peers"
analyzes the story as a drama of just this kind of feminine discourse ("Map for
Rereading").

13 "All this is certainly very 'obscure' and will remain so as long as 'femininity' and
the roles ascribed to it are not perceived to be both 'secondary' formations and
prescriptions that are 'useful' to masculinity. Any other explanation that attempts to relate 'femininity' to 'woman'—constitution, biological destiny, castra-
tion, and even Oedipus complexes, frigidity, envy of the penis, and all the rest,
vanity, shame, and weaving . . . —amounts to a set of statements so contradictory as to be surprising in a *masculine* argument." *Speculum* 120; Irigaray's
ellipses.

Chapter 5. What She Gets for Saying Yes

1 This situation is reflected in the work of René Girard on the triangular structure of
desire. Toril Moi presents an extraordinary and persuasive account of the inability
of Girard's theory of mimetic desire to account for feminine desire.

2 Cf. Jacques Lacan's often-misused remark: "There is no such thing as *The*
woman, where the definite article stands for the universal" ("God and the
Jouissance of *The*Woman," 144), made in the course of discussing real women's
absence in Western fantasies and theories of love and sexual relation.

3 When O was first published, many readers refused to believe that Réage was a

real woman and/or that O was meant to be a straight work of pornography. Pearl Chang suggests, for example, the O is a bit "off center as a pornographic novel," in that "tumescence seems not to be the central issue, and may not be the issue at all" (16). She goes on to speculate that the "atmosphere of prestidigitation, of double and triple meanings" suggests "an elaborate literary joke or riddle which extends even to the question of O's authorship," noting that Paulhan's style (in the preface, the tone of which is reminiscent of Charles Kinbote's ramblings, and which tells another, "historical" story of voluntary enslavement, revolving around a character with the unlikely name of Glenelg) is "not unlike that of the novel itself" (16). Chang focuses her discussion on the issue raised by the novel of the role of self-annihilation in female sexuality. The question of a writer's gender is an important one for feminist criticism. The Kamuf-Miller debate, conducted in the pages of the Summer 1982 issue of *Diacritics*, designates the question of the signature as a central concern in feminist criticism: Kamuf arguing that locating the feminine is the most crucial task; Miller maintaining that, assertions that anyone may occupy either "masculine" or "feminine" positions notwithstanding, it is important to her to know whether a book like O was written by a biological female. I suspect that if we take Catharine MacKinnon's contention seriously—that consciousness-raising is feminism's unique methodology—we will find that there are some truths, some perceptual stances, that are possible only for biological women. That some aspects of the "feminine" may be written, and even "signed," by males, is also accurate—particularly if we are investigating those aspects of the feminine position that our stories return to again and again and that our philosophies and sanctioned critical schools find particularly worthy of comment. It is crucial that feminist criticism continue to be informed by both perspectives.

4 For an analysis of the omnipresence and determining power of the male-centered sexualization of the entire class "woman," see Catharine A. MacKinnon. See also Carol Cosman's sensitive reading of O which focuses lucidly and effectively on the opportunity the novel affords us "to reflect on the degree to which myths about feminine identity have been internalized in the fantasies of women themselves" (27). Cosman discusses the role of the father in the internalization process, rather apologetically introducing Freud's (1919) "A Child is Beaten: A Contribution to the Origin of Perversion" (31); Cosman's article appeared at a time when feminist critics were markedly more reluctant than they are now to use anything of Father Freud's, and so her caution may well be historically determined.

5 See Ann Barr Snitow for useful discussion of this aspect of character in pornographic works.

6 One might recall here the pornographic cliché of the lesbian scene climaxing with the welcome (needless to say) intrusion of the male bearing the real instrument of pleasure.

7 Freud also spoke of the connections between these witches and his patients in an 1897 letter to Fliess, another instance of men talking over women's bodies.

8 For a definitive historical and theoretical analysis of this episode in Western hetero-

sexual history, see Mary Daly. (Mary Daly herself might be taken as an instance of the current impossibility of disengaging from the sex-gender-economic power network: as a radical lesbian feminist theorist advocating separatism, she nevertheless must speak from a forum provided by a Jesuit-founded, originally Catholic college.)

Chapter 6. A Child Never Banished from Home

I want to thank Professor Tenney Nathanson for suggesting that I use Wittgenstein's notion of family resemblances, and Professors Patrick O'Donnell and Nathanson for invaluable readings of the early stages of this chapter.

1 Very useful, indeed crucial, sociohistorical discussions of these and related issues can be found in Stone and Laslett; Dianne Sadoff and Nancy Armstrong are two of the many literary critics of the novel who put these discussions to very good use, albeit from different critical perspectives.

2 For an invaluable discussion of what she calls "the operations by which narrative and cinema solicit women's consent and by a surplus of pleasure hope to seduce women into femininity" (10), see Teresa de Lauretis' *Alice Doesn't*. What I am focusing on here is the value placed upon sentimental virtues in the exchange: at the historical juncture where these attributes were added to money, family, social position, the family novel is born. My point throughout has been that the novel is an active political and cultural force in inculcating the marketable daughterly virtues.

3 As the discussion of this episode in Chapter 3 points out, it is simultaneously her resemblance to her mother (her anger) and her difference from her mother—the absence of the suppression figured by Marmee's folded lips—that lays the responsibility for Amy's accident at Jo's door. This simultaneous sameness and difference from the mother has been in one way or the other a crucial issue in all the texts I have discussed; it is also quite possibly the ultimate source of the uncanniness of the daughter figure. I cannot develop this line of investigation here; my work in progress, *Blood Relations: Mothers and Daughters in the Novel* begins where this study must leave off.

4 And it is certainly no coincidence that Freud's essay is laden with examples and analyses drawn from the universe of sexual, gender, familial relations—especially relations with and to the mother (see note 3).

5 This point is made slightly differently in the Introduction.

6 That the novel is both resistant to and complicit with the dominant culture is by now a venerable argument, one important version of which follows the analyses of Roland Barthes's *S/Z* and *The Pleasure of the Text*. See Coward and Ellis for an extremely cogent and useful analysis of realist bourgeois fiction. I would also like to note here that rather than confine myself to Freud's definition of "family romance," I use the term throughout this chapter in its more colloquial sense and with the additional coordinates I have been tracing in the previous chapters of this study.

7 That the novel was invented by women at least as much as by men is the argument
   of Dale Spender's invaluable study, *Mothers of the Novel*. That the novel is itself a
   metaphorically hysterical discourse, or at least peculiarly receptive to ambivalence
   and cross-gender identification, is supported, for just one example, by the recur-
   rent controversies over the sex of anonymous authors. What I want to argue is that
   over and above these generic characteristics, we may be able to locate a more
   specific hysteric strategy, one which can be provoked only by the task of
   anatomizing the daughter's desire from the daughter's point of view.

8 Feminist criticism has frequently and fruitfully focused on the central contradictions involved in women's writing. *The Madwoman in the Attic* argues that
   women writers simultaneously subvert and conform to patriarchal standards.
   Mary Jacobus' subtle and compelling *Reading Woman* argues that reading femininity is itself a contradictory and endlessly displacing activity. To these two
   important investigations, from which I have learned and profited, I add this
   question: in what way do these ambivalences and oscillations particularly
   manifest/represent/resist the story (the sentimental father-daughter romance) I
   contend is most centrally and specifically productive of modern heterosexual
   ideologies?

9 I want to emphasize that I am not pointing here to the subversion of cultural
   discourses. I am proposing a technique I believe to be common to novels which
   attempt to write the story of the daughter's desire from within the patriarchal
   heterosexual plot and from the daughter's point of view (in other words, the story
   of the patriarchalized sentimental daughter *looking* at the father). The intrusions
   on this plot which I am discussing can be found in both avowedly culturally subversive texts and in traditional, conservative texts as well. The generic techniques of
   the novel which undermine monologic discourses—of power, political institutions, gender hierarchies—have often been noted, and have been discussed in a
   wide variety of vocabularies and from a wide variety of perspectives. See, for
   example, Dale Bauer for a recent, important, and brilliant argument for a feminist
   use of Bakhtinian dialogics.

10 As far as I know, the first literary critical analysis of the nineteenth-century novel
   to make use of Laplanche and Pontalis' reading of Freud's essay is Dianne F.
   Sadoff's *Monsters of Affection*, which focuses on the various versions and varia-
   tions of the primal fantasies discussed by these essays. Sadoff's study is a valuable
   and insightful deployment of Freud's primal fantasies to engage the texts of
   Charles Dickens, Charlotte Brontë, and George Eliot in *their* engagement with
   origins, retroactivity, and the figure of the father—a figure who, Sadoff argues, is
   made to stand by these authors for a variety of abstractions. My own project,
   while it shares many of the same concerns and approaches, is a very different one.
   The Laplanche and Pontalis essay has also been put to extremely good use by any
   number of feminist film critics, some of whom I in turn use in this chapter.

11 In this little reading, I have effected some hysterical intrusions: Petit-Jean is the
   daughter who reads the father; he is using the sardine can to ventriloquize and so
   defuse his refusal of Lacan's fiction. The sardine can fiction is itself a form of

masquerade, of hysterical intrusion, which enables and occults the worker's simultaneous rebellion (the story tells against Lacan) and acquiescence (the story retains the outward signs of respect) vis-à-vis the bourgeois.

12 Jacqueline Rose's essay (from which I take my epigraph for section 1), "George Eliot and the Spectacle of Woman," (*Sexuality in the Field of Vision*) includes both a powerful analysis of writing as undermining "even as it rehearses at its most glaring, the very model of sexual difference itself" (121) and a crucial reading of Gwendolen Harleth's hysteria as halting and at the same time exposing "the ceaseless dispersion of the text" (119). Noting the often-remarked breakdown of narrative coherence from *Middlemarch* to *Daniel Deronda,* as do Gillian Beer and Mary Jacobus among others, Rose persuasively proposes that Eliot's writing increasingly acknowledges that the mastery inscribed by narrative structures unleashes the hysteria intrinsic to representations of female identity and emblematized by Gwendolen.

13 The family resemblances which I am treating are not, of course, confined to women novelists: Maggie Verver can be described as doing so, Florence Dombey does it in her "confession," and Bella and R. Wilfer in *Our Mutual Friend* are a comic example. The crucial issue here is the end to which this particular kind of pseudoreversal of gender and familial hierarchy is put.

14 For an illuminating and absorbing discussion of ventriloquy and voice, see Patrick O'Donnell's exemplary and insightful essay.

15 My only quarrel with this position is its assumption that Brontë was in pursuit of "form," which seems to me a normalizing assumption which works against the radicality of Jacobus' brilliant reading and conclusion.

16 As it happens, I disagree with this reading: seen as Jane's speech, the passage is consistent with Jane's habit of substituting any handy strong emotion for a recognition of her own sexual longing.

17 The following quotations from the Norton Critical Edition's "Criticism" section will be cited as "Norton." It may be unnecessary to note the pedagogical importance attained by the texts thus elevated to the literary critical canon.

18 I am aware that a counterargument could be constructed on the basis of a reading of *Orlando.* For my purpose, it is important to note that the title character oscillates not only between genders, but "literally" between sexes as well. In any case, Virginia Woolf's criticism has a stature in feminist studies which warrants analysis specifically directed to it, even where Woolf's own fiction may undermine it.

19 One recalls that Freud's "The Uncanny" is marked by its concern with the simultaneity of opposite reactions to Home and its accoutrements.

20 I have profited greatly from the abundant (one might say burgeoning) and very useful literature which discusses and uses hysteria—in its avatars of disease, cultural phenomenon, subject of patriarchal discourse, and feminist tool of analysis—to read and analyze narrative. My use of this material is directed to a historically, politically, sexually specific narrative site: the bourgeois, nineteenth-century, family novel as written by the now-canonical women novelists of the era. The reader is directed to the Bernheimer and Kahane (especially the editors'

invaluable introductions) and Garner, Kahane, and Sprengnether collections for particularly enlightening essays.

21 A resistance to formal expectations has often been noted of novels that feminist literary critics and theorists now take to be the germinal monuments of *our* tradition. This resistance may be located by the feminist reader at those textual sites denominated in other traditions as incoherent or excessive or sentimental—that is, in some way or other as narrative (or technical) failures. Emma Woodhouse, for example, is often seen as (unaccountably) unpleasant for an Austen heroine.

22 "Anna O." (Bertha Pappenheim), who actually invented and named "the talking cure" (Bernheimer, "Introduction: Part One," Bernheimer and Kahane 8), for example, certainly exhibited a violent devotedness to Breuer (who, unlike Freud, was thereby frightened away from the analysis of hysteria and from psychoanalysis entirely). See Dianne Hunter's brilliant essay.

23 Heilman argues that Brontë recuperates the Gothic's original goals by simply furbishing up its basic tools (which is not a very radical change in any event). I disagree with his assessment of Brontë's *difference*, an assessment which can be asserted only by devaluing and condescending to the "old" Gothic. In any event, Heilman's point is that by assimilating Gothic to the feminine psyche Brontë succeeds in taming both of these spooky topographies. Heilman thus accomplishes a recuperation of his own; the uncanniness of the gothic mode and of female sexuality are canceled out, "increas[ing] wonderfully the sense of reality in the novel" (Norton 458); both the gothic mode and female sexuality are thus redomesticated.

24 Arguably, when marriage isn't at issue they don't either; the quotation is from the Irigaray epigraph (*This Sex* 65).

25 We might note that James must have had such sugary luridities in mind in his extended inscription of what might happen if the familial fantasy were continued *after* "Reader I married him." And, as I argued in Chapter 4, the final rejection of the literal Verver arrangement as *The Golden Bowl* inscribes it amounts to an intensification of that fantasy. Which might make Henry James an honorary daughter, and it certainly suggests his skill in gender bilinguality—or narrative cross-dressing—since we might read him as responding to the daughter's response to the patriarchal sentimental father-daughter romance. For an important analysis of James's roots in the popular (which is to say, largely female-written) fiction of his day, see William Veeder.

26 The quotation is taken from Modleski's compelling discussion of Hitchcock's discovery, in making *Rebecca*, of the terrors of identification with the mother who is an insistent absence in the film (as she is in most of the novels I discuss).

27 Ground-breaking theoretical work on oedipality (male and female, positive and negative) has recently been initiated by Kaja Silverman, whose *The Acoustic Mirror* is absolutely crucial to any literary analysis which seeks to make heuristic use of psychoanalysis.

28 This doesn't, of course, prevent Mr. Knightley from acting as young Martin's metaphoric father in judiciously sanctioning the latter's marital intentions.

29 Kristeva goes on to discuss the way in which such systems multiply abjections at

the ritual level. The sentimental trajectory stops short of literal endogamy; implications for literary analysis of the balance of Kristeva's discussion are best seen in conjunction with texts trading in the gothic mode, an intersection I pursue in *Blood Relations*.

30 A story which, like the fiction of the phallus, masquerades as universal—whenever it is allowed to.

31 For a brilliant, groundbreaking analysis of lesbian sexuality and theory, see Roof.

32 To analyze and challenge the cultural and psychic coercions of symmetry itself is the vast project of Luce Irigaray's *Speculum*.

Works Cited

Alcott, A. Bronson. *Tablets*. Boston: Roberts, 1868.

Alcott, Louisa May. "Behind a Mask, *or*, A Woman's Power." *Behind a Mask: The Unknown Thrillers of Louisa May Alcott,* ed. Madeleine Stern, 1–104. New York: William Morrow-Quill, 1975.

Alcott, Louisa May. *Hospital Sketches*. 1869. Ed. Bessie Z. Jones. Cambridge: Harvard UP, 1960.

Alcott, Louisa May. "Literary, Artistic and Personal." *Commonwealth* [Boston], 21 Sept. 1867, 1.

Alcott, Louisa May. *Little Women, or Meg, Jo, Beth and Amy. Parts I and II*. New York: Collier Books, 1962.

Alcott, Louisa May. "A Marble Woman: or, The Mysterious Model." *Plots and Counterplots: More Unknown Thrillers of Louisa May Alcott,* ed. Madeleine Stern, 131–237. New York: Popular Library, 1978.

Alcott, Louisa May. *A Modern Mephistopheles*. No Name Series. 1877. Boston: Roberts, 1889.

Alcott, Louisa May. *Moods*. Boston: Loring, 1864.

Alcott, Louisa May. *Moods*. Boston: Roberts, 1882.

Alcott, Louisa May. *Work*. Ed. Sarah Elbert. 1873. New York: Schocken Books, 1977.

Alcott, Louisa May. *Transcendental Wild Oats and Excerpts from the Fruitlands Diary*. 1873. Introd. William Henry Harrison. Harvard, MA: The Harvard Common P, 1975.

Armstrong, Nancy. *Desire and Domestic Fiction: A Political History of the Novel*. New York: Oxford UP, 1987.

Auerbach, Nina. "Austen and Alcott on Matriarchy." *Novel* 10 (1976): 6–26.

Auerbach, Nina. "Dickens and Dombey: A Daughter after All." *Dickens Studies Annual* 5 (1980): 95–114.

Auerbach, Nina. *Woman and the Demon: The Life of a Victorian Myth*. Cambridge: Harvard UP, 1982.

Austen, Jane. *Emma*. 1816. Ed. R. W. Chapman. Oxford: Oxford UP, 1926.

Austen, Jane. *Pride and Prejudice*. 1813. Ed. R. W. Chapman. Oxford: Oxford UP, 1926.

Barthes, Roland. *The Pleasure of the Text*. Trans. Richard Miller. New York: Hill and Wang, 1975.

Barthes, Roland. *S/Z*. Trans. Richard Miller. New York: Hill and Wang, 1974.

Bauer, Dale. *Feminist Dialogics: A Theory of Failed Community*. Albany: State U of New York P, 1988.

Baym, Nina. "The Madwoman and Her Languages: Why I Don't Do Feminist Theory." *Tulsa Studies in Women's Literature* 3.1–2 (1984): 45–59.

Bedell, Madelon. *The Alcotts: Biography of a Family.* New York: Clarkson N. Potter, 1980.

Bedell, Madelon. Introduction. *Little Women,* by Louisa May Alcott, ix–xlix. New York: Modern Library, 1983.

Beer, Gillian. *George Eliot.* Bloomington: Indiana UP, 1986.

Beer, Thomas. "An Irritating Archangel." *Bookman,* Dec. 1927, 357–66.

Benjamin, Jessica. "The Bonds of Love: Rational Violence and Erotic Domination." *Feminist Studies* 6:1 (Spring 1980): 144–174.

Bernheimer, Charles, and Claire Kahane, eds. *In Dora's Case: Freud—Hysteria—Feminism.* New York: Columbia UP, 1985.

Bersani, Leo. *A Future for Astyanax: Character and Desire in Literature.* 1969. New York: Columbia UP, 1984.

Bradbury, Nicola. *Henry James: The Later Novels.* Oxford: Clarendon Press, 1979.

Braudy, Leo. "Penetration and Impenetrability in *Clarissa.*" In *New Aspects of the Eighteenth Century,* ed. Phillip Harth, 177–206. New York: Columbia UP, 1974.

Breuer, Joseph, and Sigmund Freud. *Studies on Hysteria.* 1895. SE 2.

Brissenden, F. *Virtue in Distress: Studies in the Novel of Sentiment from Richardson to Sade.* New York: Harper & Row, 1974.

Brontë, Charlotte. *Jane Eyre: An Autobiography.* 1847. Ed. Richard J. Dunn. Norton Critical Edition. 2d ed. New York: Norton, 1971.

Butt, John. Introduction. *Clarissa,* by Samuel Richardson. New York: Everyman's Library, 1967.

Castle, Terry. *Clarissa's Ciphers: Meaning and Disruption in Richardson's "Clarissa."* Ithaca: Cornell UP, 1982.

Chang, Pearl. "O Dear." Rev. of *Story of O,* by Pauline Réage. *New York Review of Books,* 16 Apr. 1966, 16–18.

Cixous, Hélène, and Catherine Clément. *The Newly Born Woman.* Trans. Betsy Wing. Theory and History of Literature Series 24. Minneapolis: U of Minnesota P, 1986.

Clark, Robert. "Riddling the Family Firm: The Sexual Economy in *Dombey and Son.*" *ELH* 51 (Spring 1984): 69–84.

Cosman, Carol. "*Story of O.*" *Women's Studies* 2 (1974): 25–36.

Coward, Rosalind, and John Ellis. *Language and Materialism: Developments in Semiology and the Theory of the Subject.* London: Routledge & Kegan Paul, 1977.

Crane, R. S. "Suggestions toward a Genealogy of the 'Man of Feeling.' " *ELH* 1 (1934): 205–30.

Daly, Mary. *Gyn/Ecology: The Meta-Ethics of Radical Feminism.* Boston: Beacon Press, 1978.

Deforges, Régine. *Confessions of O: Conversations with Pauline Réage.* Trans. Sabine d'Estrée. New York: Seaver-Viking, 1970.

DeLamotte, Eugenia. "The Power of Pretense: Images of Women as Actresses and Masqueraders in Nineteenth-Century American Fiction." *Studies in American Fiction* 11 (1983): 217–31.

de Lauretis, Teresa. *Alice Doesn't: Feminism, Semiotics, Cinema.* Bloomington: Indiana UP, 1984.

Dickens, Charles. *Bleak House.* 1853. New York: Norton, 1977.

Dickens, Charles. *Little Dorrit.* 1857. Ed. John Holloway. London: Penguin, 1967.

Dickens, Charles. *Dealings with the Firm of Dombey and Son: Wholesale, Retail, and for Exportation.* 1848. New York: New American Library-Signet, 1964.

Dickens, Mamie. *My Father as I Recall Him.* New York: E. P. Dutton, n.d.

Doederlein, Sue Warrick. "Clarissa in the Hands of the Critics." *Eighteenth-Century Studies* 16 (1982): 401–14.

Douglas, Ann. *The Feminization of American Culture.* New York: Knopf, 1977.

Douglas, Ann. Introduction. *Little Women,* by Louisa May Alcott, vii–xxvii. New York: New American Library-Signet, 1983.

Douglas, Mary. *Purity and Danger: An Analysis of Concepts of Pollution and Taboo.* London: Routledge & Kegan Paul, 1966.

Dworkin, Andrea. "Woman as Victim: Story of O." *Feminist Studies* 2 (1974): 107–11.

Dyson, A. E. "The Case for Dombey Senior." *Novel* (Winter 1969): 123–34.

Eagleton, Terry. *The Rape of Clarissa: Writing, Sexuality and Class Struggle in Samuel Richardson.* Oxford: Basil Blackwell, 1982.

Eaves, T. C. Duncan, and Ben O. Kimpel. *Samuel Richardson: A Biography.* Oxford: Oxford UP, 1971.

Edel, Leon. *Henry James, the Master: 1902–1916.* Philadelphia: J. B. Lippincott, 1972.

Elbert, Sarah. *A Hunger for Home: Louisa May Alcott and "Little Women."* Philadelphia: Temple UP, 1984.

Eliot, George. *Silas Marner: The Weaver of Raveloe.* 1861. New York: Penguin, 1967.

Erametsa, Erik. *A Study of the Word "Sentimental" and of Other Linguistic Characteristics of Eighteenth Century Sentimentalism in England.* Annales Academiae Scientiarium Fennicae. Ser. B. Vol. 74(1). Helsinki, 1951.

Esprit de Corp. Fall 1985 mail order catalog.

Felman, Shoshana. "Rereading Femininity." *Yale French Studies* 62 (1981): 19–44.

Felman, Shoshana. "Turning the Screw of Interpretation." *Yale French Studies* 55/56 (1977): 94–207. Rpt. in *Literature and Psychoanalysis: The Question of Reading: Otherwise,* ed. Shoshana Felman. 1977. Baltimore: Johns Hopkins UP, 1982. 94–207.

Fetterly, Judith. "Impersonating 'Little Women': The Radicalism of Alcott's *Behind a Mask.*" *Women's Studies* 10 (1983): 1–14.

Fiedler, Leslie A. *Love and Death in the American Novel.* New York: Stein and Day, 1966.

Finke, Laurie. "The Rhetoric of Marginality: Why I Do Feminist Theory." *Tulsa Studies in Women's Literature* 5 (1986): 251–72.

Fletcher, Angus. *Allegory: The Theory of a Symbolic Mode.* 1964. Ithaca, NY: Cornell UP, 1970.

Foucault, Michel. *The History of Sexuality, I: An Introduction.* Trans. Robert Hurley. New York: Vintage Books-Random House, 1980.

Foucault, Michel. *Power/Knowledge: Selected Interviews and Other Writings.* Ed. Colin Gordon. New York: Pantheon, 1972.

Fraser, John. "A Dangerous Book?—*The Story of O.*" *Western Humanities Review* 20 (1966): 51–65.

Freud, Sigmund. *The Standard Edition of the Complete Psychological Works of Sigmund Freud.* 24 vols. Ed. James Strachey. London: Hogarth Press, 1953–74.

Freud, Sigmund. "Femininity." Lecture XXXIII in *New Introductory Lectures on Psychoanalysis,* trans. James Strachey, 112–35. New York: Norton, 1965.

Freud, Sigmund. *Totem and Taboo: Some Points of Agreement between the Mental Lives of Savages and Neurotics.* Trans. James Strachey. New York: Norton, 1950.

Freud, Sigmund. "The Uncanny." 1919. *SE* 17.

Gallop, Jane. *The Daughter's Seduction: Feminism and Psychoanalysis.* Ithaca, NY: Cornell UP, 1982.

Gallop, Jane. "Reading the Mother Tongue: Psychoanalytic Feminist Criticism." *Critical Inquiry* 13.2 (Winter 1987): 314–29.

Garner, Shirley; Claire Kahane; and Madelon Sprengnether, eds. *The (M)other Tongue: Essays in Feminist Psychoanalytic Interpretation.* Ithaca, NY: Cornell UP, 1985.

Gilbert, Sandra M. "Life's Empty Pack: Notes toward a Literary Daughteronomy." *Critical Inquiry* 11 (1985): 355–84.

Gilbert, Sandra, and Susan Gubar. *The Madwoman in the Attic: The Woman Writer and the Nineteenth-Century Literary Imagination.* New Haven: Yale UP, 1979.

Girard, René. *Deceit, Desire, and the Novel: Self and Other in Literary Structure.* Trans. Yvonne Freccero. Baltimore: Johns Hopkins UP, 1965.

Girard, René. *Violence and the Sacred.* Trans. Patrick Gregory. Baltimore: Johns Hopkins UP, 1977.

Gordon, Jan B. "*The Story of O* and the Strategy of Pornography." *Western Humanities Review* 25 (1971): 27–43.

Hagstrum, Jean H. *Sex and Sensibility: Ideal and Erotic Love from Milton to Mozart.* Chicago: U of Chicago P, 1980.

Hartsock, Mildred E. "Unintentional Fallacy: Critics and *The Golden Bowl.*" *Modern Language Quarterly* 35 (1974): 272–88.

Harrison, Jane Ellen. *Themis: A Study of the Social Origins of Greek Religion.* 1927. Gloucester, MA: Peter Smith, 1974.

Heilman, Robert B. "Charlotte Brontë's 'New' Gothic." In *Jane Eyre,* Norton Critical Edition 458–62.

Herman, Judith Lewis, and Lisa Hirschman. *Father-Daughter Incest.* Cambridge: Harvard UP, 1981.

Hunter, Dianne. "Hysteria, Psychoanalysis, and Feminism: The Case of Anna O." In Garner et al.

Irigaray, Luce. "The Blind Spot of an Old Dream of Symmetry." *Speculum of the Other Woman*, trans. Gillian C. Gill, 13–129. Ithaca: Cornell UP, 1985.

Irigaray, Luce. "Così Fan Tutti." *This Sex Which Is Not One* 86–105.

Irigaray, Luce. "The Power of Discourse and the Subordination of the Feminine." *This Sex Which Is Not One* 68–85.

Irigaray, Luce. *Speculum of the Other Woman*. Trans. Gillian C. Gill. Ithaca, NY: Cornell UP, 1985.

Irigaray, Luce. *This Sex Which Is Not One*. Trans. Catherine Porter with Carolyn Burke. Ithaca: Cornell UP, 1985.

Jacobus, Mary. *Reading Woman: Essays in Feminist Criticism*. New York: Columbia UP, 1986.

James, Henry. Preface to "The Altar of the Dead." *The Art of the Novel*, ed. R. P. Blackmur. 1934. New York: Scribner's, 1962. 241–66.

James, Henry. *The Golden Bowl*. Vols. 23 (I) and 24 (II). New York: Scribner's, 1909.

James, Henry. "The Tempest." *Selected Literary Criticism*, ed. Morris Shapira, 297–310. London: Heinemann, 1963.

Janeway, Elizabeth. "Meg, Jo, Beth, Amy and Louisa." *Between Myth and Morning: Women Awakening*. New York: William Morrow, 1974.

Jardine, Alice A. *Gynesis: Configurations of Woman and Modernity*. Ithaca: Cornell UP, 1985.

Jehlen, Myra. "Archimedes and the Paradox of Literary Criticism." In *The Signs Reader: Women, Gender and Scholarship*, ed. Elizabeth Abel and Emily K. Abel, 69–95. Chicago: U of Chicago P, 1983.

Johnson, Edgar. *Charles Dickens: His Tragedy and Triumph*. 2 vols. New York: Simon and Schuster, 1952.

Jones, Ann Rosalind. "Writing the Body: Toward an Understanding of *l'écriture feminine*." In *The New Feminist Criticism: Essays on Women, Literature, and Theory*, ed. & introd. Elaine Showalter, 361–77. New York: Pantheon Books-Random House, 1985.

Kahane, Claire. "Introduction: Part Two." *In Dora's Case: Freud—Hysteria—Feminism*, ed. Charles Bernheimer and Claire Kahane. New York: Columbia UP, 1985.

Kaledin, Eugenia. "Louisa May Alcott: Success and the Sorrow of Self-Denial." *Women's Studies* 5 (1978): 251–63.

Kamuf, Peggy. *Fictions of Feminine Desire*. Lincoln: U of Nebraska P, 1982.

Kamuf, Peggy. "Replacing Feminist Criticism." *Diacritics* 12 (1972): 42–47.

Kolodny, Annette. *The Lay of the Land: Metaphor as Experience and History in American Life and Letters*. Chapel Hill: U of North Carolina P, 1975.

Kolodny, Annette. "A Map for Rereading: or, Gender and the Interpretation of Literary Texts." *New Literary History* 9 (1980): 451–67.

Kolodny, Annette. "Turning the Lens on 'The Panther Captivity': A Feminist Exercise in Practical Criticism." *Critical Inquiry* (Winter 1981): 329–45.

Kramer, Heinrich, and James Sprenger. *The Malleus Maleficarum of Heinrich Kramer and James Sprenger.* Trans. Rev. Montague Summers. 1928. NY: Dover Publications, 1971.

Kristeva, Julia. *Powers of Horror: An Essay on Abjection.* Trans. Leon S. Roudiez. New York: Columbia UP, 1982.

Kristeva, Julia. "Stabat Mater." *Poetics Today* 6 (1985): 133–52.

Lacan, Jacques. *Ecrits: A Selection.* Trans. Alan Sheridan. New York: Norton, 1977.

Lacan, Jacques. "God and the *Jouissance* of The Woman. A Love Letter." In *Feminine Sexuality: Jacques Lacan and the "école freudienne,"* ed. Juliet Mitchell and Jacqueline Rose, trans. Jacqueline Rose, 137–48. London: Macmillan, 1982.

Lacan, Jacques. *The Four Fundamental Concepts of Psycho-Analysis.* Ed. Jacques-Alain Miller. Trans. Alan Sheridan. New York: Norton, 1981.

Laplanche, Jean, and J.-B. Pontalis. "Fantasy and the Origins of Sexuality." *International Journal of Psycho-Analysis* 49 (1968): 1–18.

Laplanche, Jean, and J.-B. Pontalis. *The Language of Psycho-Analysis.* Trans. Donald Nicholson-Smith. New York: Norton, 1973.

Laslett, Peter. *The World We Have Lost: England before the Industrial Age.* 2d ed. New York: Charles Scribner's, 1971.

Lévi-Strauss, Claude. *Structural Anthropology.* Trans. Claire Jacobson and Brooke Grundfest Schoepf. New York: Basic Books, 1963.

Lieb, Laurie. " 'An Increase of Kindred,' Or Definitions of Family in Richardson's Novels." Diss., Pennsylvania State University, 1981.

Macdonald, Ruth K. *Louisa May Alcott.* Boston: Twayne, 1983.

MacKinnon, Catharine A. "Feminism, Marxism, Method, and the State: An Agenda for Theory." *Signs* 7.3 (1982): 515–44.

Mandiargues, André Pierre de. "A Note on Story of O." In *Story of O*, Pauline Réage, xv–xx.

Marcus, Jane. "Still Practice, A/Wrested Alphabet: Toward a Feminist Aesthetic." *Tulsa Studies in Women's Literature* 3.1–2 (1984): 79–97.

Marsella, Joy A. *The Promise of Destiny: Children and Women in the Short Stories of Louisa May Alcott.* Westport, CT: Greenwood, 1983.

Marx, Leo. *The Machine in the Garden: Technology and the Pastoral Ideal in America.* New York: Oxford UP, 1964.

Meigs, Cornelia. *Invincible Louisa: The Story of the Author of "Little Women."* Boston: Little, Brown, 1933.

Mickelsen, David. "X-Rated O." *Western Humanities Review* 31 (1977): 165–73.

Miller, Nancy K. "Emphasis Added: Plots and Plausibilities in Women's Fiction." *PMLA* 96 (1981): 36–48.

Miller, Nancy K. "The Text's Heroine: A Feminist Critic and Her Fictions." *Diacritics* 12 (1972): 48–53.

Mitchell, Juliet. *Women: The Longest Revolution.* London: Virago, 1984.

Modleski, Tania. *The Women Who Knew Too Much: Hitchcock and Feminist Theory.* New York: Methuen, 1988.

Moi, Toril. "The Missing Mother: The Oedipal Rivalries of René Girard." *Diacritics* 12 (1982): 21–31.

Monod, Sylvère. *Dickens the Novelist.* Norman: U of Oklahoma P, 1967.

Moynahan, Julian. "Dealings with the Firm of Dombey and Son: Firmness *versus* Wetness." In *Dickens and the Twentieth Century,* ed. John Gross and Gabriel Pearson, 121–31. Toronto: U of Toronto P, 1962.

O'Donnell, Patrick. " 'A Speeches of Chaff': Ventriloquy and Expression in *Our Mutual Friend.*" *Dickens Studies Annual* 19 (1990): 375–410.

Orwell, George. *Critical Essays.* London: Secker and Warburg, 1946.

Parnell, Paul E. "The Sentimental Mask." *PMLA* 78 (1963): 529–35.

Radway, Janice. *Reading the Romance: Women, Patriarchy, and Popular Literature.* Chapel Hill: U of North Carolina P, 1984.

Radway, Janice. "Women Read the Romance: The Interaction of Text and Context." *Feminist Studies* 9 (1983): 53–78.

Réage, Pauline. *Return to the Chateau: Story of O, Part II.* Trans. Sabine d'Estrée. New York: Grove Press, 1971.

Réage, Pauline. *Story of O.* Trans. Sabine d'Estrée. Pref. Jean Paulhan. New York: Grove Press, 1965.

Rich, Adrienne. "Compulsory Heterosexuality and Lesbian Existence." In *The Signs Reader: Women, Gender and Scholarship,* ed. Elizabeth Abel and Emily K. Abel, 139–68. Chicago: U of Chicago P, 1983.

Richards, I. A. *Practical Criticism.* London, 1929.

Richardson, Samuel. *Clarissa. Or, The History of a Young Lady.* 4 vols. New York: Everyman's Library, 1967.

Rogers, Katharine M. "Sensitive Feminism vs. Conventional Sympathy: Richardson and Fielding on Women." *Novel* 9 (1975): 256–70.

Roof, Judith. *A Lure of Knowledge: Lesbian Sexuality and Theory.* New York: Columbia UP, 1991.

Rose, Jacqueline. *Sexuality in the Field of Vision.* London: Verso, 1986.

Rowson, Susanna. *Charlotte Temple: A Tale of Truth.* New Haven: New College and University P, 1964.

Sadoff, Dianne F. *Monsters of Affection.* Baltimore, MD: Johns Hopkins UP, 1982.

Saxton, Martha. *Louisa May: A Modern Biography of Louisa May Alcott.* Boston: Houghton Mifflin, 1977.

Shakespeare, William. *The Tempest.* Ed. Robert Langbaum. Signet Classic Shakespeare. Gen. ed. Sylvan Barnet. New York: New American Library-Signet, 1964.

Sicker, Philip. *Love and the Quest for Identity in the Fiction of Henry James.* Princeton: Princeton UP, 1980.

Silverman, Kaja. *The Acoustic Mirror: The Female Voice in Psychoanalysis and Cinema.* Bloomington: Indiana UP, 1988.

Snitow, Ann Barr. "Mass Market Romance: Pornography for Women Is Different." In *Powers of Desire: The Politics of Sexuality,* ed. Ann Snitow, Christine

Stansell, and Sharon Thompson, 245–63. New York: Monthly Review Press, 1983.

Sontag, Susan. "The Pornographic Imagination." *Styles of Radical Will*. 1966. New York: Delta-Dell, 1978. 35–73.

Spacks, Patricia Meyer. *The Female Imagination*. New York: Avon Books, 1972.

Spender, Dale. *Mothers of the Novel: 100 Good Women Writers before Jane Austen*. London: Pandora, 1986.

Stern, Madeleine B. *Louisa May Alcott*. Norman: U of Oklahoma P, 1950.

Stevenson, John Allen. "The Courtship of the Family: Clarissa and the Harlowes Once More." *ELH* 48 (1981): 757–77.

Strickland, Charles. *Victorian Domesticity: Families in the Life and Art of Louisa May Alcott*. University: U of Alabama P, 1985.

Stone, Lawrence. *Family, Sex, and Marriage in England, 1500–1800*. New York: Harper and Row, 1977.

Tillotson, Kathleen. *Novels of the Eighteen-Forties*. London: Oxford UP, 1956.

Tompkins, Jane P. "Sentimental Power: *Uncle Tom's Cabin* and the Politics of Literary History." In *The New Feminist Criticism: Essays on Women, Literature, and Theory*, ed. & introd. Elaine Showalter, 81–104. New York: Pantheon Books-Random House, 1985.

Veeder, William. *Henry James—The Lessons of the Master: Popular Fiction and Personal Style in the Nineteenth Century*. Chicago: U of Chicago P, 1975.

Warner, William Beatty. *Reading Clarissa: The Struggles of Interpretation*. New Haven: Yale UP, 1979.

Watt, Ian. *The Rise of the Novel*. Berkeley: U of California P, 1957.

Welsh, Alexander. *The City of Dickens*. London: Oxford UP, 1956.

Welter, Barbara. "The Cult of True Womanhood, 1820–1860." *American Quarterly* 18 (1966): 151–74.

Wilson, R. B. J. *Henry James's Ultimate Narrative*. St. Lucia, Queensland: U of Queensland P, 1981.

Wilt, Judith. "He Could Go No Farther: A Modest Proposal about Lovelace and Clarissa." *PMLA* 92 (1977): 19–32.

Wittgenstein, Ludwig. *Philosophical Investigations*. Trans. G. E. M. Anscombe. New York: Macmillan, 1953.

Woolf, Virginia. "The Continuing Appeal of *Jane Eyre*." In *Jane Eyre*, Norton Critical Edition 455–57.

Woolf, Virginia. *A Room of One's Own*. New York: Harcourt, Brace & World, 1929.

Yeazell, Ruth Bernard. *Language and Knowledge in the Late Novels of Henry James*. Chicago: U of Chicago P, 1976.

Yezierska, Anzia. *Bread Givers*. New York: George Braziller, 1925.

Index

Domestic tale, 56
Douglas, Ann, 147*n8*, 148*n15*
Douglas, Mary, 137, 147*n7*
Dowry, 135
Drama, sentimental, 144*n5*
Drive, 121
Duke of Exeter's daughter, 36
Dyson, A. E., 39–40, 44, 144*n1*

Eagleton, Terry, 144*n4*
Eaves, T. C. Duncan, 10
Economy of desire, 113, 114
Ecrits, 149*n16*
Écriture feminine, 121, 147*n6*
Edel, Leon, 81, 82, 149*n4*
Elbert, Sarah, 148*n15*
Electra, 150*n6*
Eliot, George, 125–26 *passim,* 139
Ellis, John, 153*n6*
Elsewhere, 108
Emma, 30, 117, 133, 136–37
"Emphasis Added," 147*n5*
Encore, Le Seminaire XX, 151*n12*
Endogamy: 12, 132–33, 157*n29;* as closure,
    137; daughterly, 133; as foundation of de-
    sire, 117; and marriage, 68, 133, 138; as
    uncanny mess, 138
Entail: in *Pride and Prejudice,* 135–36
Equivocation, hysterical, 131
Erametsa, Erik, 143*n2*
Erotic economy, 114
Esprit, 95
Estate, 135
Euphrasia, 75
Exchange, heterosexual: of daughter, 9, 119;
    daughter taking father's place in, 125,
    137; disrupted by flawed father, 68;
    exogamous, 118, 125, 126, 132, 133, 136;
    law of exogamous, 117
Exchange value, 86
Exchange of women, 127, 136–37
Eyre, Jane, 126, 133

Fairy tale, 74, 96, 97, 109
Fallen woman, 45
Family: business, 37; configurations, 143*n1;*
    desire, 32; and gender, 13; fictions, 11–
    12, 13; intimacy, 118; middle class, 11;

nuclear, 118; patriarchal, 15; position,
    139; relations, 76
Family resemblances, 124, 133, 134, 139,
    140, 155*n13*
Family romance: 6, 119, 121, 137, 139,
    153*n6;* daughter's new, 131
Fantasy: and desire, 131, 132–33; mascu-
    line, 115; originary, 131; primal, 154*n10;*
    seduction, 121
"Fantasy and the Origins of Sexuality," 121
Father: benefit of, 93; curse of, 25; discourse
    of, 49; fear of, 6, 32, 37, 42; fiction of,
    123, 124, 132, 135, 137; figure, 103; hos-
    tility of, 34; impassive, 79; nonpatriarchal,
    125; professedly neutral, 149*n1;*
    ventriloquized, 6; will of, 24, 25
Felman, Shoshana, 78, 85, 115, 144*n9,*
    151*n9*
Female development: immaturity, 78, 81, 82;
    normative fictions of, 81–82, 95, 150*n5;*
    preheterosexual, 114; pre-oedipal, 99
"Feminism, Marxism, Method, and the
    State: An Agenda for Theory," 145*n11*
Feminist criticism, 132, 146*n4,* 149*n1,*
    149*n2,* 151*n9,* 151*n10,* 152*n3,* 154*n8,*
    154*n9;* Anglo-American, 148*n11;*
    antitheoretical, 62–65; critics, 127; film,
    154*n10;* familial fictions in, 62; reading,
    61, 151*n10;* readings of mother, 62;
    theory, 140, 151*n7,* 151*n10*
Feminine, 4, 8
Femininity, 95, 118, 127, 137, 154*n8*
"Femininity," 143*n3,* 151*n9*
Fetish, 122
Fetterly, Judith, 148*n12*
Fictions: of culture, 118; of descent, 135; of
    gender, 135; of the novel, 118
Fiedler, Leslie, 25, 27, 104, 144*n8,* 146*n4*
Finke, Laurie, 148*n11*
Fletcher, Angus, 97
Fliess, Wilhelm, 143*n2,* 152*n7*
Form: alienation from, 127, 131, 138,
    155*n12;* conventions of, 139, 140,
    155*n15;* consistency of, 129; fixity of,
    131; and propriety, 120
Foucault, Michel, 9, 13, 145*n11,* 146*n14*
*The Four Fundamental Concepts of Psycho-
    Analysis,* 123
Fraser, John, 107

156n21; interested, 79; as seduction, 99; positions, 121, 125; sentimental, 80
Reading Woman, 137, 154n8
"Réage, Pauline," 151–52n3
Realist fiction, 153n6
Rebecca, 156n26
Recuperation, 131
Representation: of desire, 139; malady in/through, 129; mode of, 139; distinguished from psychology, 99; relation to drive, 121
Repression, 122, 139
Reproduction, 135
Retour à Roissy, 105
Return to the Chateau: Story of O: Part II, preceded by A Girl in Love, 105
"Reversal," 148n12
Re-vision, 68, 69, 86. *See also* Life-text
Rhetoric, 105, 116
Rich, Adrienne, 102
Richards, I. A., 41
Richardson, Samuel, 10–29 *passim*
Rogers, Katharine M., 143n4
Roissy, standards of beauty, 111
Romance: contemporary, 71; as defense, 131
Romola, 126
Roof, Judith, 157n31
A Room of One's Own, 128–129
Rose, Jacqueline, 121, 155n12
Rowson, Susanna, 50, 146n4

Sacred, 97–98
The Sacred Fount, 85
Sadoff, Dianne, 153n1, 154n10
Sadomasochism, 98–99, 107
Sardine can, Lacan and, 123–24, 154n11
Satisfaction, of desire, 110
Saxton, Martha, 63, 68, 70, 72, 75, 147n7, 148n12, 148n14
Scavenger's daughter, 36
Screen, 85–95
Seduction, 9, 20, 23, 86, 91, 143n2, 150n7
Self: abnegation, 54, 103; boundaries, 98; inscription, 67, 120, 133; origin of, 133
Sensation stories, Alcott's, 65–69, 148n12
Separate spheres, 144n1
Separation, 119, 136, 138
Sex-gender, 152n3, 154n7
Sexuality: discourse of, 13; female, 156n23;

patriarchal, 114; sexual difference, 4, 99, 155n12; sexual relation, 105
Sexuality in the Field of Vision, 155n12
Shakespeare, 22, 47–50, 93, 146n3
"Shakespeare's American Fable," 146n2
Sicker, Philip, 150n6
Silas Marner, 125, 133
Silence, 58–59, 61, 78, 94, 114–15
Silverman, Kaja, 156n27
Skimpole, Harold, 148n15
Smolinsky, Sara, 140
Snitow, Ann Barr, 152n5
Snowe, Lucy, 127
Son, 8, 57
Sontag, Susan, 97
Spacks, Patricia Meyer, 57, 147n7
Speculum, 118, 151n13, 157n32
Spender, Dale, 154n7
Sprengnether, Madelon, 156n20
"Stabat Mater," 147n10
Stern, Madeleine, 63, 74, 147n7, 148n14, 148n15
Stevenson, John Allen, 13, 143n1
Stone, Lawrence, 143n1, 153n1
Story, 3, 77, 138, 149n2
Story of O, 96–116
Story of O, Part II, 105
Stowe, Harriet Beecher, 59
Strickland, Charles, 147n7
Studies in Classic American Literature, 107
Studies in Hysteria, 131
Subject: desiring, 118; female, 119–20, 137; nonunitary, 122
Subversion, 120, 154n9
Summerson, Esther, 146n12
Surplus value, 84, 118
Symmetry, 83, 84, 95, 139–40, 157n32
Symptom, 118, 119–20, 121, 128, 129–30, 138
Syntax. *See* Desire, syntax of
S/Z, 153n6

Tablets, 149n18
"Talking cure," 156n22
Teacher, father as 50, 55, 61, 70–71, 72
The Tempest, 47–50, 75, 93, 146n2
This Sex Which Is Not One, 92, 147n9
Thrillers, Alcott's. *See* Sensation stories
Tillotson, Kathleen, 147n8